THE SUNDAY TIMES

GUIDE TO PERSONAL FINANCE

2001

EDITED BY

DIANA WRIGHT

HarperCollins*Publishers*

HarperCollins Publishers
77–85 Fulham Palace Road
Hammersmith
London W6 8JB

The HarperCollins website address is www.**fire**and**water**.com

First published in 2000 by HarperCollins Publishers
New edition 2001
Copyright © Times Newspapers Ltd 2000, 2001

ISBN 0-00-711023-5

The Sunday Times is a registered trademark of Times Newspapers Ltd

British Library Cataloguing in Publication Data
A catalogue record for this book is available from the British Library.

Typesetting and artwork by
Morgan Studios, Linlithgow EH49

Printed and bound in Great Britain by
Omnia Books Ltd, Glasgow G64

Contents

About the Authors

CHRISTOPHER GILCHRIST has been involved in the financial world since leaving university in 1970. He has written for *The Sunday Times*, *Financial Times*, *Daily Telegraph* and *Daily Mail*. He is the author of five books on personal finance including *The Sunday Times Personal Finance Guide to Tax-Free Savings*. He has contributed extensively to radio and TV on personal finance and also lectures on the art of sound investment. He edits a newsletter on the subject, *The IRS Report*, and is a non-executive director of a firm of investment advisers. He is the author of Chapters 1, 2, 10 and 11.

KEVIN PRATT has been writing on insurance and personal finance issues for over 16 years. After editing publications for insurance brokers and independent financial advisers, he became a full-time freelance journalist in 1992. He has since contributed regularly to *The Sunday Times*, *The Times*, *Financial Times*, *Daily Telegraph*, *The Scotsman*, *Yorkshire Post* and *Manchester Evening News*. He is the author of *The Sunday Times Guide to the Protection Game*. He wrote Chapters 4 and 5.

HELEN PRIDHAM became a journalist specialising in personal finance after gaining a degree in economics. She has more than 20 years' experience in the field and has written for *The Sunday Times*, *The Times*, *Money Observer* and *The Herald* in Glasgow. She has also won a number of awards and commendations for her work, including the 1999 Scottish Life Best Freelance Pensions Journalist of the Year Award. She is the author of Chapters 3, 8, 9 and 15.

DIANA WRIGHT has been writing on personal finance issues since 1982. She was editor of *The Sunday Times* Money section for ten years to 1995, and since then has been a regular contributor to the paper as well as writing a number of books, including *The Sunday Times Guide to Your Retirement*. She has won numerous awards for writing on pensions, unit trusts and insurance, including the Association of British Insurers Lifetime Award for insurance journalism in 1998. She is the author of Chapters 6, 7, 12, 13 and 14.

Introduction

This book is all about money: how to borrow it, save it, invest it – and how to protect what you already have. If you're interested in the subject of money, this book should be an invaluable guide. And if you count yourself as someone who is not particularly interested in it, then congratulations for getting this far: this book should be equally, if not more, relevant to you. We all need money, because we need a place to live, we need to look after our dependants, we need or want to live interesting lives and we need an income after we stop work. I suspect that most of us would also welcome the chance to make sure we don't end up paying more tax on our money than we have to.

Every week, *The Sunday Times* Money section receives a big pile of letters from readers, asking for advice, information and help – in all, we receive several thousand such letters over the course of a year. We simply cannot help everyone individually, but we know that there is an immense appetite for straightforward information on all the various aspects of personal finance.

Thanks to labyrinthine tax laws and the explosion in the numbers of financial products and services on the market, it's more than a full-time job keeping up with what is happening, and many people, understandably, don't know where to start. Although there is plenty of information and advice on offer (if you're prepared to spend time looking for it) it's not so easy to judge the quality.

This book aims to start you off on the right foot, to help you reach sensible decisions based on what you want and need, now and in the future, and to recognise good products and appropriate strategies for your particular circumstances.

What you won't find here is a simple recipe for everyone to follow, to get rich quick. If only it were so easy! Of course, it's not. But armed with the right information, and whether you are interested enough in the subject to pursue your own researches or prefer to leave it all to someone else while you get on with the rest of your life, this book should help to make you more comfortable with money, better protected and – yes – richer than you would otherwise have been.

The four contributors to the book, Christopher Gilchrist, Kevin Pratt, Helen Pridham and Diana Wright, are all personal finance writers whose articles have appeared in *The Sunday Times* and who, between them, have amassed more than 80 years' experience of the subject.

Diana Wright, April 2001

1

Financial Planning

Most people deal with money issues as one-off events. When they decide to move house, they go looking for a mortgage. When they have a good pay rise, they look for a savings plan. When retirement approaches, they start thinking about their pension. Each of these issues has its own rules, its own legislative and regulatory complexities, its own pitfalls and its own set of factors determining what is and is not a 'good deal'. These issues are all covered in these pages and you can, if you wish, use this book simply to help you deal with your personal finances in this way.

Such information is vital to help you make the most of your money, but you need to be aware that over-compartmentalisation can cause problems. Particularly in relation to the longer-term issues concerning saving, investment and passing on your wealth, using a purely one-off approach can result in missed opportunities, higher tax bills and, most important of all, higher risks: risks to your capital, your income and the standard of living of your dependants.

Personal financial planning, which some practitioners nowadays style holistic financial planning, is intended to minimise such risks and to provide you with a framework for meeting your own objectives in life. Its starting point is not finance at all but you: who are you and what do you want? Where do you want to go in life? What are your ambitions, your fears, your dreams?

You may ask what relevance these have for choosing a mortgage, but the great truth about money is that in itself it is nothing. Any flavours, colours or qualities money has are ones that we impose. Money reflects all the qualities of human nature and if we see it as predominantly one colour, that is likely to be more to do with our eyes than the colour of money itself. If you want money to serve you rather

1

than being the servant of money, you have to set your own agenda and this means starting with yourself. Allow yourself to dream...

Imagine your future

Let go of any notions of money. Focus your attention on what you really want. Sit back and dream. What would you like to be doing in five years' time? Try and see as much of your life as you can. What job are you doing? Where are you living? What is the family situation? What are your leisure activities?

Now try it for ten years ahead.

Now write down your aims.

This is where financial planning really starts. For you to achieve those aims, what has to happen? What has to happen now and what has to happen later? You have to quantify what you need in terms of income and capital, and you will have to make assumptions about the rate at which they will grow. You will also have to estimate the risks involved. These key variables – growth and risk – are covered later in this chapter.

Objectives and goals

Personal financial planning starts from your 'big picture' objectives and translates these into money terms. It does so by creating a set of long-term aims, each of which has its own set of shorter-term goals. These will cover every aspect of your personal finances, from life and health insurance to savings and investment. The aims can be quite vague, but the goals need to be reasonably precise. Your long-term aims are unlikely to change much, but changes in circumstances may require you to alter your goals.

Realistic aims

When you have imagined your future, you test it by asking what has to happen for you to achieve your aims. For example, you may have imagined being financially independent – capable of living comfortably without working – at the age of 55. If you are now aged 40, have a net income of £30,000 a year and want an income at that level (in real, spending power terms) by age 55, then you will need capital resources of about £600,000.

Imagine you have pension rights worth £100,000 today. They may grow by, say, 5% a year in real terms (in terms of spending power) so that they would be worth (in terms of today's money) some £208,000 in 15 years' time when you are 55. Say you have another £25,000 in invested capital and assume that it grows at a slightly faster rate of 7.5% to produce £74,000 in 15 years. And you have savings plans to which you are contributing £100 a month which could also grow at around 7.5%, producing another £35,000. That reduces the shortfall to just over £280,000 in 15 years.

Perhaps you expect an inheritance of about £50,000 in the next ten years – that could bring your capital up to £400,000 and reduce the shortfall to £200,000 after allowing for growth. At a 7.5% growth rate, you would need to save a constant £600 a month over the next 15 years to accumulate the extra £200,000. But maybe you could get a better real rate of return on your savings, say 10% a year: that would cut the monthly saving required to accumulate the same sum to £500.

Such a high savings rate may well be unrealistic. You may only be able to afford an extra £100 per month today. So you may face the choice of adjusting your required income at age 55 downwards, or of deferring your retirement.

'What if?' projections like these not only enable you to test the attainability of your aims but will help you define shorter-term goals and take appropriate action.

Your aims will change as you progress through life, as shown in a simplified way in the chart. These are only a few examples and everyone will have their own aims and associated goals.

	Aims	Goals
Age 20-40	Improve skills, qualifications, earnings	Build up emergency fund to £X
		Get adequate insurance cover
	Get good education for children	Start savings scheme for £X per month, independent of mortgage
	Move to bigger, better house	
Age 40-60	Build up capital for retirement	Increase monthly savings by £X
		Top up pension funds by £X
	Help children through college and to establish themselves	Draft will to protect inheritance
Age 60+	Generate good returns on capital to support lifestyle	Revise will to protect inheritance
		Avoid risking loss of capital
	Help grandchildren	

Critical assumptions

All financial planning is based on assumptions. The longer the period over which you are planning, the bigger the difference that will result from changing the assumptions. This is why it is important to be as realistic as possible in the assumptions you use.

In the example above, the reason it was said you need a sum of £600,000 to produce a net income of £30,000 a year is that this represents an annual return of 5% on the capital. This is a higher income than you would currently get from shares and a lower income than is available from fixed-rate investments, so a combination of these different types of investment would produce the requisite income.

You could get the same income from a smaller capital sum, but only by consuming some of the capital as income, a tactic that you may have to use but is best to avoid if you can.

As we will see, it is possible to use historical evidence to define a reasonable range of rates of return for such projections. Still, reality will diverge from those projections, for better and worse, over short periods of time. And you will need to review your plans and take those deviations into account when doing so.

Nominal and real returns

When you are undertaking long-range planning, it is no use just using nominal returns – the returns without adjusting for inflation. Some planners do project returns in nominal pounds and then adjust for assumed rates of inflation, but it is actually much simpler to work in terms of pounds of today's spending power.

You do this by deducting the expected average rate of inflation from the expected average rate of return from savings and investments. This gives you the 'real' or inflation adjusted rate of return and tells you what your future capital would buy you in terms of today's money values.

To see how this simplifies things, imagine you are trying to estimate what your current £10,000 of investments will be worth in ten years' time. You could say: "Well, my investments are in the stock market so they could grow at 10% a year over the next ten years, which would mean my £10,000 would grow to £26,000... but inflation will probably average 2.5% a year, so that in ten years' time I would need £1.28 to buy what £1 buys me today... which means my £26,000 would really be worth £20,000."

Or you could say: "I expect to get an actual return of about 10% a year, but if I deduct inflation at, say, 2.5% I can expect a real return of 7.5% to give me £20,000 in today's money after ten years."

The second approach is far simpler, because you already know about today's money values and the purchasing power of money. And provided you remember to adjust everything into 'real' terms this method gives you a much better grasp of what you are doing.

Unfortunately, the projections you get from unit trusts, life insurers and pension providers will not do this. They will all be in nominal terms with tables attached showing you what the effects of inflation would be at various rates. They leave it to you to use the tables to adjust the nominal figures into real terms. But this only takes a few minutes. If you need figures other than the tables they provide, you only require a calculator that has a constant or 'k' function so that you can do compound interest calculations.

As the example above shows, even a 'low' rate of inflation such as 2.5% does erode the real value of money over longer periods. So you cannot afford to ignore it. The table gives you some examples.

What you will need to buy what £1 buys today if the annual rate of inflation averages

	2%	3%	4%	5%
After 5 years	£1.10	£1.16	£1.22	£1.28
After 10 years	£1.22	£1.34	£1.48	£1.63
After 15 years	£1.35	£1.56	£1.80	£2.08

The power of compound interest

It was Albert Einstein who once described compound interest as the second most astounding feature of the world (after relativity, of course). It is well worth studying its effects for yourself; some examples are included in the tables on the next page.

In fact, the term compound interest may be slightly misleading since it is normally applied to assets which grow in value. It measures the rate at which a sum of capital, or a regular monthly saving, grows in value. That growth may derive from payments of interest, from capital growth or from a combination of the two.

The 'real rate of return' is the compound interest rate adjusted for inflation. Compound interest rates and the real rate of return are always calculated on an annualised basis, though this may not always be explicitly stated.

Returns on savings and investments

£100 per month accumulating at an annual rate of

	5%	7.5%	10%
At the end of			
5 years	£6,900	£7,400	£8,000
10 years	£15,700	£18,100	£20,900
15 years	£27,000	£33,600	£42,200
20 years	£41,500	£56,100	£77,300
25 years	£60,100	£89,000	£135,000

£10,000 lump sum accumulating at

	5%	7.5%	10%
At the end of			
5 years	£12,800	£14,400	£16,100
10 years	£16,300	£20,600	£25,900
15 years	£20,800	£29,600	£41,800
20 years	£26,500	£42,500	£67,000
25 years	£33,900	£61,000	£108,000

The power of compound interest only becomes evident with time. Over five years, on a monthly saving of £100, you would get £8,000 instead of £6,900 by achieving a return of 10% instead of 5%. The difference is £1,100, which means that doubling the rate of return has produced a final value 15% higher. But over 25 years of saving £100 a month at 10%, you would get £135,000, which is an extra £74,900, or 125%, more than the £60,100 you would accumulate at 5%. With a lump sum of £10,000, you would have £108,000 after 25 years at 10% – more than three times as much money as you would have with a return of 5%.

There is one simple conclusion you can draw from these tables: longer-term saving pays off in a very big way. Start saving as much as you can as soon as you can, increase your savings whenever you can, and choose savings schemes with the potential for high returns. This alone will add many thousands or tens of thousands of pounds to your wealth. You can also see how increasing the rate of return you obtain on your money dramatically boosts the final values.

Accumulation and protection

Most of us have both an acquisitive and a defensive side to our natures. We want to increase our wealth, but we also want to protect what we have. The more we try to increase our wealth, the greater the risk we must run of losing some of it. The more defensive we are about protecting what we have, the less likely we are to increase it. Each of us has to find a balance between these acquisitive and defensive motivations that we are comfortable with.

We also need to recognise that changing priorities in our lives will require changes of emphasis. For example, however ambitious you are to accumulate wealth, if you have responsibilities towards young children, your first priority must be to safeguard their future by arranging adequate insurance against your death or ill health – even though this will be at the expense of your own accumulation of capital.

In general, insurance is concerned with the defensive motivation; it is to do with protecting ourselves against all kinds of risks. Saving and investment, in contrast, reflect the acquisitive motivation.

The polarity and the tension between these motivations is present in each of us. This is reflected in the financial markets and contributes to the alternation between greed-driven and fear-driven phases. Shares rise on waves of optimism – when the majority of people believe that businesses will prosper – and fall in waves of pessimism – when people believe that businesses will struggle and fail.

As will be emphasised in Chapter 11, anyone who succumbs totally to the mood of the moment – which is the mood of the crowd – when taking financial decisions is asking for trouble.

Greed and fear are contagious emotions which erode our ability to think straight. Markets may grow quickly for some time but they do not grow indefinitely. On the other hand, the biggest financial crashes have not reduced free-market economies to rubble. At the high points and low points of markets, the majority of people will tend to be far too optimistic or far too pessimistic in relation to what actually happens in the future.

If you act on the basis of these unrealistic expectations, you are certain to suffer financially: the only question is by how much. Having the framework of your own financial plan to refer to can help you avoid being infected by these pernicious financial diseases.

Protecting what you have

The desire to secure and protect what we have is one of the strongest human motivations. Generally, we achieve this by purchasing insurance against specific risks. Those risks affect your property and possessions, your health, your life, and your capital. Your aim should be to buy as much insurance as you need to prevent you or your family being in a worse position as a result of misfortune.

This is fairly straightforward in the case of property and possessions. You know pretty well what they are worth and would cost to replace, and that is the amount of insurance you need.

In the case of your health it is not so obvious. Some people will have limited cover providing an income if they are unable to work because of ill health through schemes run by their employers, while others including the self-employed will have none at all. If you are fit, cover is cheap and it may be easy to afford. If you are in poor health, it may be so expensive that to buy adequate cover you would have to skimp on something else. So you may have to compromise.

The same applies to life insurance. Most of us vastly undervalue ourselves and have tiny amounts of life insurance compared with what our families would need to keep going in the same way. This may be partly because we prefer to save in schemes that produce lump sums at some future date and dislike paying for cheap life insurance cover, such as term insurance, that pays out nothing if we survive. Still, providing adequately for dependants should be a higher priority than saving for the future.

Insuring against losing capital is rather different because we can do it simply by holding much of our capital in forms subject to minimal risk. We can also make sensible arrangements to transfer wealth so that it suffers as little tax as possible.

In each of these areas what we ideally want may be more than we can afford. So a major part of financial planning is concerned with prioritising different needs. For example, if you are married at age 35, have two young children and no long-term savings, buying adequate insurance against death or ill health is a high priority. But if you are aged 45 with children in their late teens and have built up substantial capital, while such insurance may be useful it is no longer so necessary.

Risk and reward

Our wish to acquire more and earn high returns on our money is tempered by the fear of loss. A number of academic studies have shown pretty conclusively that the vast majority of people fear loss more than they value profit, and that we will seek to avoid the pain of loss more eagerly than we pursue the pleasure of profit.

However, if we all have this aversion to risk, how is it that we have runaway stock market booms? The answer is that at times of excessive optimism we simply wave a magic wand and abolish the risk; we claim that it does not exist and use all kinds of specious reasoning to justify a belief that investing is no longer as risky as it used to be.

So far, every such fairytale pretence that has led stock markets into periods of exceptionally rapid rises has been shattered by the realisation that the golden coach and horses were still, in fact, only pumpkins and mice. Time and again speculative exuberance has been transformed into panic and crash.

Quite why we go on speculative and progressively more irrational binges of this kind, with their inevitably painful hangovers, is still unclear, but the character of speculative boom today remains much as it has been for the last 300 years.

Managing and controlling risk is what the evolution of more complex financial instruments and personal financial planning is all about. But in order to manage and control it we need to understand its nature.

What is risk?

The dictionary definition of risk is 'the chance of loss or injury'. As outlined above, we insure against risks to our property and ourselves, but when it comes to investing our money, we have no choice but to incur some level of risk if we want our capital or investment income to grow.

The dictionary definition does not correspond with how risk is perceived by financial analysts or by the regulators who determine what may and may not be said to individual investors. To the analysts and regulators, risk means volatility. The greater an investment's variations in price, the riskier it is.

Such volatility can be measured and analysed by all sorts of sophisticated mathematical techniques – which will mean next to nothing to you unless you have an 'A' level or better in maths.

For our purposes, a simple example will show why volatility is not the same as risk. Investment B rises and falls in price much more than investment A. Does this mean that B is riskier than A? Not necessarily. Suppose we are quite sure we want to hold an investment for at least five years. Let's assume that at no point from the end of the fifth year on does the value of B fall below the value of A. So at all the points that interest us, B delivers a better return. Relative to A, then, B does not (from the fifth year on) produce a greater risk of our losing money: it is no riskier, though it is more volatile.

If we now alter our viewpoint to that of someone who is likely to need their capital back in two to three years, the picture is different: within that period, B's price falls not only below that of A but below its own starting point. For someone with this shorter timescale, B is indeed more risky than A.

The essential point is that the common-sense definition of risk is subjective. My chance of losing money depends on me, my circumstances and how I behave; your chance of losing money depends on you, your circumstances and how you behave. Volatility, on the other hand, is objectively quantifiable.

Most important among the subjective factors or variables involved in risk are:

◆ **Timescale** The longer your money is invested, the less influence volatility has on the rate of return that you get. The table gives an example of variations in price and their effect on returns. After a long period even apparently large variations have little effect.

Effect on an initial investment of £1,000 of growth followed by a sharp decline

Term	Capital value assuming a 10% pa return	Effect of 25% fall in value at end of term		An annual return of
5 years	£1,610	£1,200	=	3.7%
10 years	£2,600	£1,900	=	6.6%
15 years	£4,200	£3,100	=	7.8%
20 years	£6,700	£5,000	=	8.4%
25 years	£11,000	£8,100	=	8.7%

The longer the term of an investment, the less the effect on the annual rate of return of a given percentage fall in value. After 25 years, the apparently huge loss of £2,900 from £11,000 still leaves an annual return of 8.7%.

◆ **Resources** The pattern of behaviour of investments differs. If you hold a number of different investments each of which behaves differently, the ups and downs to some extent balance each other out. The more capital you have, the more you can diversify your investments and damp down the effects of volatility. The less capital you have, the less able you are to do this.

◆ **Character** If you are the kind of person who gets a sick feeling in your stomach when you lose money, or lies awake at night worrying about it, you had better avoid volatile investments. Even if you buy them 'for the long term', if they crash in price you may feel so bad that you sell, incurring a big loss. Someone with a calmer temperament may find it easier to sit out panics and slumps.

The effect of gearing

Most of us do quite substantially increase the risks we run with our biggest investment. When we buy our home, we put down as little as 10% of the purchase price and borrow the rest. If the price falls by 20% and we have put down 10%, we are in trouble – exactly this happened to up to a million homeowners who bought using large mortgages in 1987-89 and saw the value of their homes plummet by 30% or more in the following five years or so. They had 'negative equity' – they owed more than their property was worth.

Using borrowed money to acquire an asset is called gearing (the American term is leverage). When it works in your favour, it dramatically increases the return on your money. If you buy a house for £100,000 using £80,000 you have borrowed from a bank and the price rises to £120,000, you have not actually made a profit of 20%. You only invested £20,000 of your own money, and on this 'equity stake' you have made a return of 100%.

Gearing is the simplest way of increasing the potential return from an investment – but also of increasing the potential loss, something you should never forget, especially when people start making pronouncements that the price of property 'can never go down'. It has, and it can again.

Many people talk about the huge gains they have made over a period of 20 or 30 years from owning houses, without ever appreciating that this was mainly the result of using mortgages to achieve a high level of gearing. The use of borrowed money meant that an average increase in house prices of, say, 10% a year was translated into a return on their own equity of 30% or 40% a year.

If they had invested in the stock market using borrowed money in the same way over the same period, they would have made even bigger profits – but most people would have regarded this as far too risky.

The perception of risk is highly subjective. Despite the experience of 1989-95, most of us still believe that owning a house with a large mortgage is less risky than investing on the stock market. Whatever you feel about this, the important thing in planning terms is to know what you are doing and understand the risk involved. If you feel it is too high, you can look for ways of reducing it.

For example, if you own a £100,000 house with a £50,000 mortgage and inherit £100,000, you may think about buying a second property. This may seem 'safer' than the stock market. But one essential principle of investment is that diversification, owning different types of asset, reduces risk. If you end up with all your capital in property, you are far more vulnerable than if you have some money in other types of investment as well.

Diversification

The principle of 'not putting all your eggs in one basket' is probably the most important in lowering risk. If all the shares you own are in internet companies, you may make a fortune, but you may lose most of your money, as recent events have shown. If you own shares in internet companies, oil companies, supermarkets, banks and utilities, you are far less likely to lose a high proportion of your money.

The same principle applies to every type of investment. The fact that £18,000 is the maximum amount of compensation you will get under UK legislation if your bank goes bust may not cause you to limit your deposit to that level if you deal with the largest banks, but it may make you think harder about depositing £50,000 with a smaller or newer bank. The maximum compensation will increase to 100% of the first £2,000 and 90% of the next £33,000 in late 2001, but this could still leave you out of pocket.

Knowing that life insurance companies have produced widely varying payouts from the same monthly savings in the same types of personal pension plan may encourage you to think in terms of having policies with more than one company. And knowing that the past performance of unit trusts is of virtually no use in predicting their future performance may make you wary about committing a high proportion of your capital to any one fund manager.

In each case, diversification may reduce your returns, because you invest less money in what turns out to be the best performer. But this is something you will only know after the event, while what you know certainly at the point when you invest is that spreading your money reduces risk.

The three types of investment

The world of savings and investment may appear very complicated but is in essence quite simple. There are only three major types of investment – deposits, fixed-rate investments and equities – though these can be packaged and combined in different ways. Each has different characteristics and uses, and the art of successful saving and investment is matching them to your needs.

Deposits

Deposits give you capital security and a variable rate of interest. You can get your capital back at whatever period of notice is agreed. With 'instant access' accounts you can have the money on the day you ask for it, but other accounts may require a week or a month's notice or even more.

The security of your capital is effectively guaranteed by the institution you deposit it with, so the actual security depends on its financial status. We think of banks as secure, and indeed the large UK and European banks have huge amounts of capital and are well regulated. Smaller or newer banks, even in the EU, may comply with banking regulations while being considerably less secure, while banks located outside the EU may be subject to far less stringent regulation and have far lower capital resources.

In each currency there is a going, short-term rate of interest, which is usually determined by the central bank. Thus the interest rates payable on US dollar deposits are essentially determined by the Federal Reserve in New York regardless of whether the account is in New York, London or Tokyo. Likewise, the interest rates payable on sterling deposits are determined by the Bank of England.

These central banks are the lenders of last resort to the financial system, and by setting the interest rates at which they lend to the banks, they also set the minimum rate at which any bank will lend money. This in turn determines how much they will pay to borrow money from you, which is what they do when you open a deposit account.

While the central banks thus define a 'going rate', the rates offered on deposits will be in a range around this figure. Central banks review interest rates monthly, and any change they make in their minimum lending rates will quickly be reflected in the rates payable on all types of deposit.

Fixed rate

Fixed-rate investments offer a fixed rate of return for a specified period, which may range from six months to 30 years. At the end of the period, you get your original capital back. In the meantime, you get a fixed rate of interest, which may be paid as income or accumulated with the original sum. With most fixed-rate investments, the only capital guarantee is at the end of the term. If you want your money back earlier, you may suffer a penalty, or have to take your chances selling in the marketplace, where prices may be below what you paid.

Though central banks can fix short-term interest rates, they cannot fix longer-term rates, which are essentially determined by supply and demand. Since governments usually borrow a lot of money, they do have significant effects on longer-term rates, but many other factors also come into play.

The most important is 'inflationary expectations'. Before you lend money to someone for ten years you will want to have thought hard about what you expect the average inflation rate to be and to feel confident you are getting a decent return on top of whatever your estimate of inflation is. The average inflation expectation, therefore, plays a large part in determining long-term interest rates.

Equity

Equity investments are those where both the income and the capital value can fall as well as rise. This category includes property but is usually used to refer to shares and collective investment funds which invest in shares, such as unit trusts and investment trusts. Deposits give you security of capital, fixed-rate investments give you security of income, and equity investments give you no security. But, unlike deposits or fixed-rate investments, they do offer prospects of growth in both income and capital.

The valuation of shares in general is largely determined by expectations of growth in companies' profits and dividends, and these depend on a wide range of economic factors – including inflation and interest rates – as well as on specific factors affecting each industry.

A shareholder is a part-owner of a business. Business owners are last in line for any payout from the business. The government, in the form of the tax authorities, has first claim on the revenues (and, if it comes to it, the assets) of the company; then come employees, suppliers and banks, followed by any other lenders. Only when the claims of all these have been satisfied are the owners entitled to take anything. Since shareholders are entitled to everything that is left after meeting these prior claims, they do extremely well when companies prosper and can lose all their money if companies fail.

Average returns

Given the quite different characteristics of the three types of investment, you would expect that the returns from each of them over a period of time would also be quite distinct. And so they are, as the figures in the table show. One of the most important features of all financial plans is the allocation of capital and savings to these three types of asset.

How the three types of asset have performed

The real average annual return over

	10 years	20 years	50 years	101 years
Deposit	4.2%	4.7%	1.4%	0.9%
Fixed rate	9.4%	7.7%	1.2%	1.1%
Equity	11.8%	11.8%	7.7%	5.5%

Average annual return on top of inflation and before tax. All periods to December 2000.
Source: Barclays Capital Equity-Gilt Study 2001

Most people need to have some of their money in each of the three types of investment. How you do this effectively is covered in detail in Chapter 10.

Advice

Once you understand the principle it is not particularly difficult to create your own financial plan. But, like many people, you may find it hard to maintain the discipline of reviewing it and adjusting it. There are now software packages that enable you to log and manage most of your financial affairs, which may make this aspect easier. And there are an increasing number of advisers who can help you create your own financial plan. Chapter 15 deals in detail with the subject of financial advice.

2

Savings

In the UK, there is a state safety net in the form of financial provision for widows, those in ill heath and pensioners. But state support is at subsistence level and anyone wanting more will have to pay for it for themselves. Provision against ill health or death are covered in Chapter 4, and providing for retirement is covered in Chapters 8, 9 and 12. Here we consider building up savings to cover emergencies and their use to meet other longer-term needs.

The key point about saving is that you have to feel strongly motivated to do it. For most people, it is always easier to spend money than save it. So why should you make the effort to save? The answer will be in the form of personal goals. Defining those goals more clearly will help you to sustain the motivation to save. Those goals will be concerned either with very short-term needs, such as having the money to mend the roof or go on holiday, or longer-term ones such as paying your child's university fees in 15 years' time.

Short-term needs

Everyone needs a sum of money available at short notice to meet emergencies or unexpected requirements. The amount depends on your personal situation and your responsibilities. For example, as a single person in your first job and living in a rented flat, an emergency fund equal to three months' expenditure will probably cover any cash needs you may have. But a couple in their late 20s with two children and owning their own home and car will require more, both to cover the children's needs and the things that may go wrong with the boiler, the roof or the gearbox.

Financial planners generally consider that a sum equal to between three and six months' expenditure is an adequate emergency fund. If you are self-employed, you could need more because you will not receive sick pay as you would if you were an employee. Retired people will usually need less because their pension income is more secure than income from employment.

Your emergency fund should be placed in a form that is easily accessible, preferably in an instant access account which means that you can withdraw it at any time without notice. If you live with a partner, your common emergency fund should be in a joint account that either of you can access. This means, for example, that Individual Savings Accounts (Isas) are unsuitable for emergency funds. Isas have to be in the name of one individual and cannot be opened as joint accounts. If you were ill and could not access your account, neither could your partner, or anyone else.

Until recently, most people used a building society instant access account as their emergency fund. The big societies have many branches and most offer accounts where cash can be withdrawn from thousands of cash machines. Today, most societies operate a 'tiered' interest rate structure where the more you invest, the more you get. Your fund may be below the size where it gets a good rate, but with a little shopping around you should be able to find an account that pays reasonably.

New types of account

New arrivals on the scene will certainly offer higher rates of interest, in particular the telephone-only, internet-only or telephone-and-internet-only accounts offered by newly established banks. Some of these provide you with cash cards so you can easily withdraw money. For an emergency fund, both partners need cards to access the account.

Some of the new accounts do not provide cards. Instead you transfer the money to your current account by making a phone call or sending an e-mail. It will usually be one to three days before the money reaches your account. This delay may be acceptable, but watch out for the security controls. Most of these accounts cannot be operated without knowing the security keywords you have set up. If you use an account like this as an emergency fund, make sure you both have a record of the keywords. Do not rely on memory – in a real emergency you are quite likely to forget.

Some of these new banks are run by substantial companies such as Sainsbury's, Tesco and Standard Life, and it is reasonable to regard these as equal in security to familiar high street banking names. But some internet accounts are run by brand-new companies with far less capital. Remember that your emergency fund is intended to meet emergencies. There is no point in risking it not being there when you need it for 0.5% more interest a year.

Cash returns

Many people like to have more cash on deposit than they genuinely need for emergencies. And many use deposit accounts to accumulate the cash they need for purposes such as buying a house or a car. You can, of course, have just one account that includes both your emergency fund and other money. But if you know you would be tempted to dip into the emergency pot, you may be better off keeping this separate.

If you do not need access to the money for emergencies, you can consider placing it in an account where you have to give notice before you can withdraw. Such notice accounts sometimes offer better rates of interest than instant access accounts. Typical notice periods are 30, 60 and 90 days. If you do not get a reasonable addition to the interest rate for having to give the extra notice, it is not worth bothering.

Postal accounts also used to offer premium rates of interest. With these you can only make deposits and withdrawals by post, and can only get a withdrawal in the form of a cheque that you pay into your bank account. Telephone accounts have not entirely superseded postal accounts, so you may still find one that offers a good deal, but check the terms.

Usually, you only get interest from the date when a cheque paid into your postal account is cleared, which can take up to four days. And you may cease to get interest from the date when you pay a withdrawal cheque into your bank account – though it may be several days more before you have the cleared funds in your account. Postal accounts are designed for people who do not make many transfers in or out.

Telephone and internet banks also offer notice accounts and their rates of interest tend to be higher than for branch-based accounts.

Comparing interest rates

In the UK, the rates for deposits are usually quoted gross of tax. But rates may be quoted on two different bases. The nominal rate is the rate of interest applied to the account, while the annual effective rate (AER) is the rate taking into account the frequency of interest payments.

The nominal rate is not affected by whether you draw your interest or leave it in the account. But if interest is paid more than once a year and you leave it there, you will earn interest on interest and end the year with more in your account. The table on the next page shows the difference between the nominal and effective rates depending on how often interest is credited to the account.

If you plan to spend all your interest, you can compare different accounts on the basis of their nominal interest rates. But if you plan to leave the interest to accumulate, as the table shows, an account with a lower nominal interest rate could give you a better deal if it is credited more frequently. In this case, you should use the annual effective rate as a comparison.

Annual effective rate if interest is credited

Nominal rate	Yearly	Half-yearly	Quarterly	Monthly	Daily
5.0%	5.0%	5.06%	5.09%	5.12%	5.13%
8.0%	8.0%	8.16%	8.24%	8.30%	8.33%

Tax on interest

Legislation in the UK requires banks and others offering deposit accounts to deduct tax from the interest before paying this to the account holder. The rate of tax deducted is 20%, and this is regarded as eliminating the account holder's liability to the basic rate of income tax, even though at the time of writing this is higher than 20%. If you pay tax at only 10% and have interest paid to you net, you can reclaim the tax you have 'overpaid'.

To have interest paid without deduction of tax, the account holder must sign a form (R85) declaring he or she is a non-taxpayer. Parents may sign this on behalf of their children. Note that if the interest a child gets from money given by parents is over £100 per year gross, it will be taxed as if it were the parents' income.

Banks based outside the UK are not subject to UK tax legislation and may offer accounts where no tax is deducted from interest. In particular, many UK banks and building societies have subsidiaries in the Channel Islands or Isle of Man that offer such gross interest paying accounts to UK residents.

Whether you receive interest gross or net, you are still bound by law to declare it on your tax return. And if you receive gross interest and do not receive a tax return, it is your legal responsibility to ask the Inland Revenue to send you one and to declare the income. If you have not had tax deducted at source, you will be assessed for the amount due. In the case of higher rate taxpayers, the total liability will be the higher rate of tax less any tax paid by deduction at source.

Some National Savings accounts pay interest without deduction of tax at source. The interest is still taxable, however.

Choosing an account

UK banks and building societies offer a wide variety of accounts with different features. Most pay a variable rate of interest but some offer rates fixed for a specific period.

Children's accounts

These sometimes offer better variable interest rates than can be secured on a small deposit in a normal instant access account. They may also offer other features, such as magazines, stickers, moneyboxes and savings clubs.

Club or treasurer accounts

These are designed for use by clubs and associations which are not registered charities. Typically, such associations do not need a normal bank current account because they do not have many payments into or out of their accounts, and they also want to earn interest on their balances.

Instant access accounts

These permit withdrawal of capital without notice, though there is usually a restriction on how much can be withdrawn in cash on any one day. The interest rate is variable. Interest may be credited yearly, half-yearly, quarterly, monthly or daily. With most accounts, the rate depends on the amount invested. Many can be opened with as little as £10 but the interest rate may be very low on deposits of under £1,000.

Internet accounts

These have to be set up over the internet. The initial transfer is made from your current account and future transfers are also to and from your current account. Interest rates are usually higher than on branch-based accounts.

Mini-Isas

The Individual Savings Account comes in two forms, the mini-Isa and the maxi-Isa. A mini-Isa can contain cash, equities (stocks and shares) or insurance, while a maxi-Isa can include all three. You can take out a mini-Isa of every kind each year or a single maxi-Isa, but you cannot invest in both a mini and a maxi in the same year. Most banks and building societies offer mini cash Isas into which you can invest up to £3,000 in each tax year up to 5 April, 2006. Regardless of your personal tax status, no tax is payable on the interest you earn in an Isa – whether you draw it out or leave it in the plan. Cash Isas usually offer instant access and a variable rate of interest, which is often higher than on other types of account. If you have large sums to invest, though, it will be to your advantage to open a maxi-Isa rather than a mini. The minimum age for a cash mini-Isa is 16. See Chapter 10 for more on Isas.

Monthly income accounts

These may have a minimum notice period for withdrawal. The income is usually paid direct by bank transfer to your current account. There is usually a minimum investment of £2,500 or more.

Notice accounts

Money can be withdrawn without penalty by giving the appropriate period of notice. Common terms are seven days, 30 days and 90 days. If you withdraw money without giving this notice, you will lose interest, often the amount that would have been paid during the notice period. Minimums are usually £1,000 or more.

Postal accounts

Some building societies offer these accounts, where deposits and withdrawals can only be made by post. Interest rates are variable and may be higher than on instant access accounts, as are the minimum investments required.

Telephone accounts

The initial deposit is made by cheque. You set up a direct debit arrangement with your current account and can then transfer money between it and your telephone account. You have to set up a security code and every time you call to make a transfer the code is used to identify you. Interest rates may be variable or fixed and are usually very competitive. Only instructions by telephone will be accepted.

Time deposits

Here the interest rate is fixed for the period of the deposit, often 30 days, 90 days or even six months. There will be a penalty for early withdrawal. Interest is usually added to the account at maturity without deduction of tax. Minimum investments may be as low as £1,000 or as high as £50,000.

Fixed-rate investments

The majority of the accounts discussed so far pay a variable rate of interest that alters in line with short-term rates in general. Ultimately it is the Bank of England that sets the level of short-term rates through its money market operations.

If you know you will need a certain sum in two, three or four years, you can also consider placing it in a fixed-rate investment that will mature just when you need it. This is a more complex decision, because at the time you commit your money you cannot be certain you will get more interest this way.

A fixed rate of, say, 7% may be on offer for a three-year period at a time when variable rates are only 5.5%, making it seem attractive. But the variable rate may rise at any time. If it rises sharply soon after you have made your investment, you would obtain less interest over the three years than in a variable rate account. Of course, the variable interest rate could also fall, and if it became, say, 4% after you had made your fixed-rate investment at 7%, you would be sitting pretty.

What this shows is that you have to consider the outlook for interest rates before committing yourself to fixed-rate investments. Much will hinge on the outlook for inflation: is there any reason to expect it to rise or fall? If inflation looks more likely to rise than fall, a fixed-rate investment is unlikely to be profitable.

Unfortunately, the evidence of numerous surveys is that even highly qualified economists' predictions of future interest rates are no better than random guesses. So you should not have too high an expectation of getting your interest rate decisions profitably right.

You need to look at the downside as well as the upside. Maybe you will not make a big profit by fixing your return at 7% when variable rates are 5.5%. But look at the situation in terms of risk. Suppose you are counting on getting a minimum rate of interest over the three-year period. If you invest at a variable rate you might not get it because rates could fall sharply. Fixed-rate investment assures you of reasonable returns.

Short-term fixed-rate investments

Escalator bonds

These are issued by building societies and pay a rate of interest that rises each year for a fixed period. A typical pattern would be to get interest of 5% in year one, 5.5% in year two, 6% in year three and 8% in year four. An enticingly high rate is often paid in the last year, but this may be balanced by a below-average interest rate in the first year or two. Since these are fixed-rate accounts, once your money is committed you cannot usually get it back early, or if you can there is a significant financial penalty (except in the event of death). These bonds often have minimum investments of £1,000 or more.

Fixed-rate bonds

These bank or building society accounts pay a flat fixed rate of interest for a fixed period from one to five years. Early withdrawal may not be permitted, but if it is there will be a penalty. Minimum investments vary from £500 upwards.

Guaranteed growth bonds

Issued by insurance companies, these guarantee a fixed rate for a specified period, usually between two and five years. The bonds pay out a lump sum at the end of the term. The return is treated as having borne income tax at the basic rate, so only if you are a higher rate taxpayer will there be any additional tax liability. Non-taxpayers and those paying tax at 10% cannot reclaim the tax paid by the insurance company.

Guaranteed income bonds

These pay a fixed income for a specified term, usually two to five years. The tax treatment is the same as that of guaranteed growth bonds.

Maxi-Isas

Some companies offer maxi-Isas with a fixed rate of return for periods of up to five years. The returns are tax-exempt. Sometimes a rate of income is guaranteed, but at maturity you do not get all your capital back unless a stock market index is above a certain level. Examine such plans carefully and be absolutely clear about what you might stand to lose.

National Savings Certificates

These grow in value at a fixed rate over a period of up to five years. The profits are exempt from tax. Usually there is a limit on the amount you are allowed to invest.

National Savings Pensioners Guaranteed Income Bonds

These pay a fixed rate of income over a two- or five-year period. The interest is taxable but is paid without deduction of tax at source.

Longer-term savings plans

If you succeed in getting 1% or 2% a year extra on your short-term savings and deposits, you are entitled to feel that you have done well. But you should not over-emphasise the value of a higher return over short periods. Refer back to the compound interest table on page 6. It is over the long term – ten years or more – that the benefit of a higher rate of return really shows up.

As we saw in Chapter 1, over the long term the highest rates of return have always come from equities (stocks and shares). So it makes sense to link your long-term savings to this type of asset. There are several ways of doing so and if you are saving more than £100 per month it will probably make sense to use more than one type of plan.

Isa savings plans

Maxi-Isas, in which you may invest or save up to £7,000 in each tax year up to 5 April, 2006, are well suited to regular savings. They are exempt from income tax and capital gains tax. They give access to a range of unitised investment funds and offer considerable flexibility. Minimum savings are usually £30 to £50 a month.

Both unit trusts and investment trusts can be held within Isas. (See the separate sections below on these and, for more details, Chapter 10.) Provided the amount you are saving is large enough, you can usually divide it between two or more different funds run by the same manager. There is no fixed period or maturity date. You are free to cash in all or part of your plan at any time. Usually, you can add a lump sum (within the annual limit) whenever you like.

Costs are between 1% and 5% of each contribution plus an annual charge on the assets of the fund of between 0.5% and 2%.

Isas may not be joint accounts but must be held in the name of one individual. You cannot take out a maxi-Isa in a child's name; the minimum age is 18.

Unit trust savings plans

Unit trusts and open-ended investment companies (Oeics) are similar in having a pool of money which they manage on behalf of investors. The pool expands or contracts depending on whether investors are adding to or withdrawing from it. The value of a unit or share is the value of the investments in the pool divided by the number of units or shares in issue.

A wide variety of funds are available, investing in different types of share and different areas of the world. (For more information see Chapter 10.) Minimum monthly savings are from £30 to £50. There is no fixed term or maturity date. You are free to cash in at any time, or add lump sums if you wish.

The income received within the plan is taxable. It will bear tax at source and basic rate taxpayers will have no further liability. Higher rate taxpayers will receive an annual certificate showing what they have paid by deduction at source and will be liable to extra tax. The profits from the plan may be liable to capital gains tax if they exceed your annual exemption.

Costs vary from 1% to 5% of each contribution with an annual charge of 0.5% to 2% of the value of your assets. You can take out a plan in the name of a child.

Investment trust savings plans

Unlike unit trusts or Oeics, investment trusts do not issue new shares to savers in their regular savings plans but buy existing shares for them through the stock market. This is because investment trusts have a fixed pool of assets and the price of a share in the market may be higher or lower than its net asset value (Nav). Its Nav is calculated by dividing the value of the investments by the number of shares in issue. For more information on investment trusts, see Chapter 10.

Savings schemes are run by investment trust managers. They usually subsidise the costs of the plan, which are much lower than the normal cost of buying investment trust shares through a stockbroker. The annual charges on investment trusts are between 0.5% and 1.5%. The taxation rules are the same as for unit trusts. You can take out a plan in the name of a child.

With-profits savings plans

With-profits savings plans are in the form of endowment policies issued by insurance companies. Though they are life policies, they provide very little life cover. Most of the premiums that you pay are used to invest in the company's with-profits fund, which is a giant pool of assets often worth several billion pounds.

The fund will hold a wide variety of assets including fixed-rate investments,

UK and overseas shares and property. Policyholders may also benefit from profits made by the company on other (non-profit) policies, such as term assurance.

The with-profits policy has a sum assured, which is the minimum amount that will be paid on death or at the maturity date. Two types of bonus are added to the sum assured. Reversionary bonuses are added each year, often at quite a low rate of 3% or so. At maturity (or death), a terminal bonus is added which can be equal to all the reversionary bonuses paid. Once a reversionary bonus has been added to a policy, it cannot be taken away, but terminal bonus rates are not guaranteed and can be varied at any time.

With-profits policies are of two types. Some have one fixed maturity date, while with a 'flexible' policy you can encash it at several different dates, usually at five-year intervals. The charges for with-profits policies are typically about 12% to 15% of premiums over the term. This may seem high, but over longer periods it can compare favourably with a unit trust levying a 2% annual charge.

The key factor about with-profits policies is that if you encash them in the early years, you are likely to get back less than you have paid in, because the costs are loaded onto the early years. These policies are only suitable if you are very confident you can sustain your savings for the period you have chosen. The minimum term is ten years and the normal maximum is 25 years. The maturity proceeds are free of tax.

Friendly society plans

Friendly societies are permitted to run tax-free savings schemes with low minimum and maximum investments. Some are of the with-profits type, while others are unit-linked. Some plans have high costs and charges which wipe out the value of the tax concessions, so study the small print closely. The plans have a minimum term of ten years. There may be stiff penalties for early encashment, and if you do make a profit it may be subject to tax.

Some of these plans are marketed as ways to build up a nest egg for children. But the only advantage they offer over a unit trust savings plan is the low monthly saving. Every child has a tax allowance and if your child cashes in a unit trust savings plan that is theoretically taxable, if he or she is a non-taxpayer at the time of encashment, no tax will be payable.

Past results of long-term plans

The table shows the results of different types of savings plan over various periods. These are the averages for all funds of a particular type available over the relevant period. Note that there were substantial differences between the best and worst.

Over short periods, returns vary more dramatically from one year to the next than they do over longer periods. A £50-per-month savings plan linked to UK smaller companies maturing after ten years in March 2000 would have paid out more than £17,000, or almost double a ten-year plan's payout in March 1999. The performance of Japan-investing unit trusts was spectacularly good in the 1980s and equally bad in the 1990s. Over longer periods, these variations are far less noticeable.

One surprise is that over long periods the with-profits policy still produces returns as good as those from many types of unit trust. Since with-profits funds include investments other than shares, and shares produce the best long-term results, you might expect unit trusts to outpace them, but this is not the case.

The long-term investment trust results are very good, though over this period a reduction in average 'discounts' was probably responsible for much of the extra return. For more on this topic, see Chapter 10.

The results from different types of savings plan

Final plan values and annual returns on £50 per month, maturing spring 2000

Type of plan	Period of years				
	5	10	15	20	25
With-profits endowment	n/a	£10,000	£21,800	£47,520	£101,490
		9.4%	10.4%	11.6%	12.4%
Unit trust savings plans					
UK equity income	£3,610	£10,520	£21,690	£60,350	n/a
	7.2%	10.7%	10.8%	14.2%	
Europe	£5,780	£17,930	£28,240	£95,900	n/a
	26.0%	20.3%	17.2%	17.8%	
Global growth	£4,410	£12,680	£25,680	£59,270	n/a
	15.1%	14.0%	12.6%	13.7%	
UK smaller companies	£5,925	£17,330	£37,260	£79,170	n/a
	26.6%	19.5%	16.9%	16.4%	
Investment trust savings plans					
UK general	£4,260	£13,300	£27,880	£72,620	n/a
	13.5%	15.0%	13.7%	15.5%	
International general	£4,300	£12,990	£29,560	£79,130	n/a
	13.9%	14.5%	14.4%	16.3%	

Source: With-profits policies: Money Management survey, April 2000, results to February 2000. Unit and investment trust savings plans: Money Management survey, May 2000, results to March 2000.

The results on the previous page were those up to 2000. Results for periods up to 1990 would have shown unit and investment trusts in a far worse light. The substantial rises in share prices worldwide from 1994 to 2000 boosted unit and investment trust savings plan payouts more than those from with-profits policies. If share prices fall over a period of several years, the reverse will probably happen: with-profits policy returns are likely to remain relatively stable, while those from unit and investment trusts fall.

These are all, in a sense, minor points in relation to the splendid long-term returns shown here. Average returns of 10% to 17% over 15 years and 11% to 17% over 20 have far outpaced inflation and produced real wealth for investors. Long-term savings plans linked to stock market investments are probably the only fail-safe method of becoming wealthier. You may regret not saving enough, you may make lump-sum investment decisions you regret, but in ten or 15 years' time you are most unlikely to look back and have any regrets about putting money into this type of long-term savings plan.

Costs and charges

The costs and charges referred to above are those you will pay if you buy through the normal routes. If you buy a with-profits policy from a representative of the life insurance company, or through an independent financial adviser, commission will be paid to the adviser. This commission accounts for between 20% and 30% of the overall cost of the policy over its term.

If you buy a unit trust savings plan through the unit trust management company, you will usually pay the full initial charge of 3% to 5% on each contribution. Charges on Isas for regular savings are similar.

If you are prepared to make your own choice of plan, you will be able to deal at lower costs via intermediaries who arrange with the plan providers to receive a lower rate of commission. The difference between this and the higher normal commission rate will then be invested on your behalf.

In the case of investment trust savings plans, the special schemes run by their managers are already very cheap because they subsidise them to attract more investors, so you will not be able to save on these charges.

Choosing the right long-term plan

The type of long-term savings plan you should choose will depend on a number of factors.

Timescale

The shorter the timescale, the bigger the likely variations from year to year in the payouts of plans linked directly to the value of shares. If you want a greater degree of certainty in your return over a ten-year term, the with-profits policy provides this. As the table shows, over long periods with-profits policies have done well, but there is certainly scope for unit or investment trust plans to do better if you pick the right funds.

Tax

Isas are the only tax-exempt savings vehicle, so it makes sense to put in as much capital as you can. If you have no capital to spare, use one as your first savings vehicle. This should boost the return by at least 0.5% a year because of the tax savings (for details see Chapter 10), and these will be greater if you pay higher rate tax in the future. If you are already using up your annual Isa allowance, the with-profits policy has attractions because payouts from those with a term of more than ten years are free of tax. With-profits policies are, therefore, especially attractive to higher rate taxpayers.

Purpose

The purposes for which you may want to save are many and varied. The following points are relevant to some of the more common savings objectives.

◆ **Retirement income** If you plan to use your accumulated capital to produce retirement income, Isas are a very good way to do this. Not only are they tax free, but within the Isa you can hold a set of different funds to provide the balance of capital growth and income that you want. You can adjust this when you reach retirement by selling your existing funds and buying new ones within your Isa.

◆ **Children's education** Whether you are saving for private school fees or to build up a fund to help pay your children's way through college, you probably want a reasonable degree of certainty about what you will get. This makes with-profits policies well suited for this purpose.

◆ **Debt reduction** If you think of your savings plan as a means whereby you can, if you choose, reduce your mortgage or other debt at some point in the future, you do not need to be so concerned about the value of the plan at any one time. If the stock market goes down, you can wait for a year or two before encashing it. So a unit or investment trust plan may be most suitable.

◆ **General purpose** If you do not have any specific need for the money you are saving but could end up using it for one or more different purposes, there will be an argument for having both a with-profits policy and a plan directly linked to the value of shares.

Your savings strategy

Long-term savings plans linked to equities are the easy way to grow rich slowly. Set up your plan or plans and add to them whenever you can afford to. Use different types and choose funds from different managers, or invest in different areas, to spread the risk. Once you have a basic plan in place, preferably a with-profits plan or one linked to a widely spread general fund, then consider a more volatile type of fund for your next plan: one linked to emerging markets, say, or smaller companies.

Use the flexibility of the Isa, unit trust or investment trust savings plans. Instead of feeling gloomy when prices fall, be courageous and add whatever lump sums you can afford. On a long-term view, this is almost certain to pay off.

The tax exemptions of the Isa under existing legislation will end in 2009. By then there will be so many Isa savers that it seems unlikely any political party would risk voters' wrath by abolishing the tax breaks. So the tax concessions could well end up being extended indefinitely. As long as they remain, you will be better off keeping your money within the Isa. When it comes to taking money out of savings plans, you will, therefore, usually do better to withdraw from taxable plans, leaving your tax-free Isa untouched.

3

Borrowing Money

We are all borrowing more. According to the Office of Fair Trading, consumer credit increased by 60% between 1996 and 2000 and is now running at £159bn a year. But if you can avoid credit, it is better to do so. It will save you money. Buying goods on credit usually means you have to pay considerably more for them. Goods or services priced at £5,000, for example, will cost you nearly £2,000 extra if you pay for them with a five-year loan at 15% interest. But avoiding credit is easier said than done when it is so freely available.

In some situations, you will have little choice but to borrow money. An important item, such as a car or a washing machine, may need to be replaced before you have time to save for it. And few students nowadays are able to go through college or university without accumulating some debts along the way.

If you do have to borrow, the important thing is to make sure you get the cheapest possible deal. It is surprising how few people look beyond their existing bank or building society or the provider of the goods. Yet, there are plenty of lenders competing to offer you credit these days and wide variations in the cost. If you shop around you could save hundreds of pounds in interest.

Before you borrow

Before you borrow it is worth considering whether you really need to. Do you have savings you could use instead? Many people are tempted borrow money even when they have savings. This does not normally make financial sense. Although it may be useful to keep a small amount of cash for genuine emergencies, it is rarely economic to pay for credit if you have savings. The interest you have to pay on your borrowings will invariably be higher than the return you get on cash deposits. If you have investments in the stock market, your returns may exceed the cost of borrowing but they are uncertain.

If you do not have savings, think carefully about whether you really need to spend the money now. If you waited a little longer, you could save all or part of it in a dedicated savings account. This could at least reduce the amount you need to borrow and so cut the interest you have to pay. It would also be a useful discipline and give you a good idea of how much of your income you could afford to devote to loan repayments if you did have to borrow. Some people over-estimate their ability to pay back loans and then find it very difficult to keep up the repayments because of other demands on their income.

If borrowing really is a necessity, it is important to know exactly what repayments you can afford, as this will determine how fast you can clear your loan and help you decide which type of credit arrangement to go for. The quicker you can clear your debt, the less interest you will have to pay. But there is no point agreeing to a higher level of repayment than you can realistically manage. You may need to work out your budget in detail to arrive at this amount, especially if you are someone who tends not to know where your money goes each month.

Before deciding on the right type of credit, it is also worth being honest with yourself about what kind of person you are. Flexible forms of borrowing such as credit cards are attractive and can be low cost for short-term purposes, but if you will be tempted to let your outstanding balance run and run, a personal loan, which has a set repayment period, may be more appropriate.

Comparing costs

Any lender will be happy to give you credit, providing they deem you creditworthy. So find out who is offering the best deal. Don't just restrict yourself to your local high street. Look in the money pages of national newspapers which appear mid-week or at weekends, where you will usually find tables showing which institutions are offering the 'best buys' for credit. The internet is also a useful tool for shopping around for loans.

To find the cheapest credit you will need to compare different lenders' interest rates in the form of their APR (annual percentage rate). The APR is designed to show the true cost of borrowing, and all lenders must calculate it in the same way.

Arrangement fees and any other charges must be included as well as interest. How and when payments are made is also taken into account. This enables you to make direct comparisons between different forms of borrowing, so check you are being quoted the APR and not the monthly or flat rate of interest, which is likely to sound a lot less.

Generally, the lower the APR, the lower the cost of the credit, but make sure the deals you compare are for the same repayment period. The APR, as its name implies, is the cost of credit over one year at a time. If you spread the repayment of a loan over two years, the total cost will be more than if you were repaying over one year, even if the APR is lower. For example, if you borrow £1,000 at an APR of 15% for one year, you will pay a total of £1,078 including interest. If you borrow at an APR of 10% but spread the repayments over three years you will end up paying a total of £1,154 including interest. To find out how much loans cost over different periods at different rates, check the ready reckoner below.

APR ready reckoner
Total cost of a £1,000 loan at different rates and over different periods.

	1 year	3 years	5 years	10 years	15 years	20 years
			Length of Loan			
5%	£1,027	£1,077	£1,129	£1,266	£1,413	£1,569
10%	£1,053	£1,154	£1,262	£1,557	£1,887	£2,248
15%	£1,078	£1,231	£1,398	£1,867	£2,404	£2,995
20%	£1,102	£1,308	£1,536	£2,191	£2,947	£3,773
25%	£1,126	£1,385	£1,675	£2,523	£3,502	£4,557
30%	£1,149	£1,461	£1,815	£2,860	£4,058	£5,333

Source: OFT

However, the APR may not be the only factor to take into account when comparing loans. A lender may make a low APR conditional on you taking out payment protection insurance, but the cost of this cover may not be as competitive as that available from other lenders. So you could be better off going elsewhere.

You will also need to consider whether the interest rate is fixed or variable. Fixed rates make it easier to budget because you know exactly what your payments will be. You are protected against rising rates but your payments won't fall either if the general level of interest rates goes down. Conversely, with variable rates, you will have to be sure you can cope with the repayments if interest rates rise.

Flexibility is another important factor. Check whether there are any penalties if you want to repay your loan early.

Payment protection insurance

With many types of credit nowadays you will be offered payment protection insurance to cover your repayments if you are unable to work due to accident, sickness or unemployment. If you would have trouble repaying a loan in these circumstances, insurance is worth considering, but check carefully that it meets your needs. If you are self-employed, on a short-term contract or have a pre-existing medical condition, the policy may not pay out when you expect it to.

Some loan companies offer competitive interest rates but then overcharge for insurance, so ask more than one lender what your monthly repayments would be with and without insurance so you can make a true comparison.

Borrowing to pay off other loans

This is a tricky one. Some people just end up borrowing more if they manage to reduce the cost of their existing credit. However, it can make sense to shift from an expensive to a cheaper form of borrowing. But try to restrict yourself to conventional lenders.

Beware of credit brokers who offer to bring down the cost of your credit significantly. They may achieve this by switching you from unsecured to secured credit. These are loans where you home or other assets are used as security. They can be cheaper because lenders know they can recoup their money by repossessing your home if necessary. They may also appear to be cheaper because your debt is spread over a longer period.

With this type of loan you need to check carefully for penalties if you are late with your payments or want to pay it off early. If you are prepared to use your home as security, you will normally find a remortgage is cheaper than a secured loan.

Overdrafts

If you want to borrow for a short period, an authorised overdraft can be a good option, providing your bank offers competitive terms. Unauthorised overdrafts, on the other hand, will cost you dear. Some accounts will automatically let you go into the red by, say, £50 or £100 without penalty, but normally you will need to agree an overdraft limit in advance.

Before you go ahead you must check your bank's terms. Some charge arrangement fees for setting up an overdraft facility and apply relatively high rates of interest. It may also levy a monthly usage fee of between £3 and £9 and charge for cheques and direct debits while you are overdrawn. This can make borrowing small amounts very expensive and if you regularly go overdrawn it is worth considering switching to a bank offering more competitive terms.

Newer entrants to the banking market, such as building societies, ex-building societies and telephone or internet banks, which are competing for market share, tend to charge less for authorised overdrafts.

However, no lender likes you to overdraw without permission. The interest rate charged will typically be 50% or 100% higher than for authorised overdrafts, and you may have to pay a penalty fee and other charges.

The advantage of overdrafts is that they are flexible, but the amounts you can borrow in this way are usually limited. Also, if you are constantly overdrawn they can become expensive.

Credit cards

Credit cards are one of the most popular ways of borrowing money nowadays thanks to their convenience and flexibility. The maximum credit limit you will be given initially will range between £500 and £5,000, depending on your income and other outgoings, although you can usually apply for it to be increased later. Once you have your card, you are free to run up credit whenever you want to and you can repay your outstanding balance as quickly or as slowly as you wish, subject to a minimum monthly repayment, typically 3% or £5, whichever is lower. However, if you are late with your payments or exceed your credit limit, you may be charged a penalty of £10 to £15.

If you clear your monthly balance in full, you will not be charged any interest on the cost of any goods or services you have purchased. This means you may have gained up to 59 days' interest-free credit between the time the transaction took place and when you paid your bill. If you do not pay the balance in full, interest will normally be applied from the date the item was charged to your account. However, if you use your card to obtain cash or foreign currency, you will usually have to start paying interest immediately, even if the balance is cleared in full at the next statement date.

Interest rates on credit cards vary considerably. If you have a card issued by one of the main high street banks, you will usually be charged a rate towards the top end of the scale. This may not bother you if you usually clear your balance. However if you want credit, you should look for a more competitive deal. There is nothing to stop you having more than one card. You could use a low-cost one for a specific purchase and set yourself a monthly repayment.

Many card companies try to attract customers from competitors by offering reduced rates of interest on balance transfers. Some give these low introductory rates on new purchases as well. So if you have run up a large balance or need to spread the repayments for a new purchase over a few months, it is worthwhile switching. The introductory rate will normally last for six months, after which it will revert to the card's standard rate, so make sure you check what that is. There is nothing to stop you swopping after six months to another card with a low-rate introductory offer.

Even if you don't want to borrow money, buying goods and services by credit card can make sense. If you use your card to buy something worth between £100 and £30,000, you will normally qualify for extra protection under Section 75 of the Consumer Credit Act, which makes the card issuer jointly liable with the supplier if there is a problem with the goods. Other perks may also be offered by the card supplier such as free purchase protection, travel accident insurance and various reward schemes.

Gold or platinum cards

These work in the same way as ordinary credit cards but are only available to those with an above average annual income, typically over £20,000 to £30,000, so they may be seen as something of a status symbol.

There are relatively few practical differences from ordinary cards except that they will normally allow you credit of up to £10,000 or £15,000. Other differences are that they include travel accident cover (though this is still no substitute for ordinary travel insurance) and you may get further travel-related perks. The rate of interest charged is much the same as for ordinary cards and on some occasions you may even find better deals on the latter.

Store cards

Many retailers offer their own branded credit cards these days. Customers are usually offered the inducement of a hefty discount on the first purchases they make using the card plus other special offers such as sale previews. However, with a few notable exceptions, such as John Lewis and Marks & Spencer, the interest rates on these cards are much higher than on ordinary cards – often double the rate on the most competitive. So unless you clear your balance every month, they are best avoided.

Affinity cards

A large number of special interest groups also offer credit cards. Many are linked to charities, arts, sporting or educational organisations. They receive a donation of £5 to £10 from the credit card company for every card issued and a percentage, typically 0.25%, of the value of all purchases made. The interest rate charged for credit is usually around average.

Personal loans

Personal loans are offered by a wide variety of institutions nowadays. Banks, building societies and finance companies are the main providers, but you may find your local supermarket or affinity group can also offer favourable terms.

For a major purchase, such as a new kitchen or furniture, your supplier will probably offer to arrange a loan. This may be convenient but will not normally be the cheapest option. By arranging a loan independently, you may also be able to drive a better bargain for the goods you want and get a discount as you would if you were a cash buyer.

Personal loans are a useful way of borrowing over the medium term or if you need more than you can get from an overdraft or credit card. Between £500 and £25,000 can normally be obtained over terms of one to ten years. This type of loan can usually be arranged through the post, over the phone or on the internet, and the money will be sent to you by cheque or transferred to your bank account.

When you are comparing the rates on these loans, note that most lenders charge differently for different amounts. The more you borrow, the lower the APR. Lenders will normally advertise their lowest rate, but don't be misled. Terms on smaller amounts may not be so competitive. So check the rate for the exact amount you want to borrow.

Repayments on personal loans are calculated to ensure you clear your debt over the agreed period and interest rates are normally fixed so you know exactly how much to budget for. This type of structured repayment is useful if you find overdrafts and credit cards hard to clear. The disadvantage is that there is often a penalty of one or two months' interest if you want to settle your loan early.

If you need a borrowing facility you can re-use, rather than a one-off lump sum, some lenders offer flexible loans where you agree a monthly payment and are allowed to borrow a maximum multiple of, say, 25 times that amount at any time.

Secured or unsecured?

Most personal loans are unsecured. This means if you fail to make repayments, a lender may take you to court but does not have an automatic right to any of your assets. With a secured loan, assets such as your property or investments are used as security. If you already have a mortgage and take out a secured loan from another lender, this is known as a second charge loan.

Bear in mind that if you default on payments, a lender with a second charge can take you to court and demand repossession of your property even if you have managed to keep your first lender happy. Nowadays, there is little advantage in taking out a secured loan unless you have a poor credit rating, as you will probably be able to find a cheaper unsecured one if you shop around.

Interest-free or low-start credit

Interest-free credit often seems too good to refuse. But you should look carefully at what you are being offered as there may be a sting in the tail. You could find that what you are signing up to is actually an interest bearing loan which has an initial interest-free period. If you make full repayment before the end of the initial period no interest will be payable.

The payments collected during the initial period will not cover the full cost so you will have to pay off the balance at the end of the period. If you miss the deadline, interest becomes payable not just from the end of the interest-free period, but from when you signed the credit agreement. The interest charged can be significantly higher than for ordinary personal loans. So if you are offered interest-free credit, make sure you know exactly what it involves.

Another ploy used by some suppliers such as car companies is to offer credit deals which start off with very low interest rates in the first year or two but shoot up thereafter. Check this before you commit yourself as it may be cheaper to take out an ordinary personal loan.

Endowment policy loans

In general, using savings is preferable to borrowing money. However, if your savings are tied up in a with-profits endowment, you will lose out if you surrender early. A better alternative is to ask your insurer for a loan secured against the value of your policy. This way it can continue to grow until its usual maturity date.

Interest rates on endowment policy loans are variable but they are usually less than those on overdrafts or personal loans. The loan can be repaid from the proceeds when the policy reaches the end of its term. It may also be possible to roll up the interest and pay that off at the end of the term too. However, if your policy is being used to repay your mortgage, a loan will not be available.

Some banks and building societies will also provide cheap loans secured against endowment policies.

Hire purchase

Hire purchase (HP) is still one of the most common forms of car finance. There are several important differences between personal loans and hire purchase. First, unlike a loan which can cover the whole cost, a cash deposit is normally required under a hire purchase agreement or the part exchange value of your current car. Second, you are effectively hiring the goods rather than taking over the ownership as you would when you buy with a personal loan. This means that until the final payment is made, they remain the property of the seller. You cannot dispose of them until the agreement has ended. If you fail to make payments on time, the provider of the hire purchase can also repossess the goods, though a court order would be required unless you give your permission.

Personal contract purchase schemes

If you are buying a new car, you may be offered a personal contract purchase (PCP) scheme instead. PCPs were introduced by a number of major motor manufacturers to make their cars more affordable. They are designed so that the monthly repayments are much lower than under a conventional hire purchase agreement. Each plan is slightly different but they do have some common features.

Typically they run for two to three years. When the car is purchased, the manufacturer sets a guaranteed future value (GFV) which the dealer will pay if you return the vehicle at the end of the agreement, subject to reasonable wear and tear and mileage. The GFV is then deducted from the price of the car, minus your deposit, and the monthly repayments are based on the balance. The interest, though, is calculated on the amount outstanding including the GFV. So if you bought a car for £15,000, putting down a £5,000 deposit, you would normally need to borrow £10,000. However, if the car has a GFV of £7,500 after three years, you would only have to make repayments on the balance of £2,500, plus interest on the £10,000.

After three years, you will have three options. You can pay the outstanding balance and keep the car; you can return it and pay no more (though there may be penalty payments if you have exceeded the agreed mileage), or you can trade it in for a new vehicle and start the process again.

Although these schemes may seem attractive because of the low monthly payments, they are not comparable with an ordinary loan or HP agreement as you will still owe a substantial amount when you reach the end of the term. However, if you like to have a new car every two or three years, they can be attractive.

Remortgages and flexible mortgages

Mortgages are one of the cheapest forms of borrowing because the lender has the security of your property to fall back on. So if the market value of your home exceeds your current mortgage by a comfortable margin, it is worth considering increasing your loan if you need extra funds. This type of borrowing is particularly suitable for home improvements, but most lenders are happy to advance money for other purposes such as education fees and car purchase.

A further advance will normally be arranged at the lender's standard variable rate and over the same term as your existing mortgage. The only snag is that you may have to pay for another valuation. So if you are considering a further advance, it may be best to switch to another lender altogether. Increasing competition in the mortgage market means you may be able to bring down the cost of your mortgage despite increasing the size of your loan. Your new lender may also be happy to help with the cost of the valuation and legal fees.

New style flexible and bank account type mortgages make accessing further loans even easier. Flexible loans allow you to pay off your debt faster than conventional mortgages but they also allow you to borrow money back at any time if you have made overpayments. Bank account mortgages, which work like giant overdraft facilities, can be even more flexible.

Credit unions

Credit unions are becoming increasingly important as a source of low-cost credit, particularly for people who find accessing conventional sources of credit difficult. Essentially they are financial co-operatives set up and run by people with some form of common bond. Members may work together or belong to the same profession, live on the same estate or belong to the same club.

Members who save regularly are able to get cheap loans. Apart from cost, the advantage is that you don't need an established credit record to borrow. Your savings record and ability to pay will be the main factors which determine whether you can obtain a loan. To find out if there is a credit union you can join or how to set one up, contact the Association of British Credit Unions (see Appendix 2).

If you are turned down for credit

Lenders cannot refuse credit on the basis of such factors as your race, gender, religion, sexual orientation or address, but they can turn down your application if they think you might not be able to repay your debt. Lenders usually make a decision about your creditworthiness by means of 'credit scoring' and/or by contacting a credit reference agency.

Credit scoring

After you have filled in an application for credit, lenders will score you on the basis of the answers you give. They will award varying points depending on factors such as your age, occupation, salary and whether you live in rented accommodation. After the marks are added up, only those applicants who have scored above the lender's pass mark will be given credit. However, since lenders have different methods of scoring, you could find that you pass with one but not another. If your application has been turned down due to this process, you will be told but you may not be given the exact reason why.

Credit reference agencies

There are a number of specialist organisations which collect factual information about individuals which they will pass on to prospective lenders. Their data comes from the electoral roll, the courts and other lenders. This enables potential lenders to find out whether you have defaulted on any other credit agreements, have any county court judgments against you or are bankrupt. Negative information stays on record for six years. Lenders will also find out what other credit agreements you have, whether your payments are up to date and if you have made other applications for credit recently. If you make several applications in a short space of time this could affect your credit rating even if you don't actually take out credit.

If you are refused credit on the basis of information from a reference agency, the lender will give you the name and address of the agency used. You can then write to it, giving your full name, current address and any other address you have lived at over the past six years, and ask for a copy of your file. A small fee of, say, £2 will normally be charged for this service. If you find the information is incorrect, you can ask for it to be corrected and the agency must send your updated file to any organisation that has asked for information about you in the past six months.

Debt problems

If you are having problems keeping up with credit repayments, it is important to contact lenders as quickly as you can. The sooner you do so, the more sympathetic they are likely to be. Your first priority should be to notify your mortgage company, followed by credit card companies, banks and finance houses with whom you have credit agreements.

If you have a legitimate problem such as having lost your job, fallen ill or suffered a marital breakdown, they will normally be prepared to reduce or freeze your payments until you have sorted yourself out. This is better for them as well as you, as they will avoid the expense of chasing you for money and having to take you to court.

If you think you need help sorting out your debt problems, call your local Citizens Advice Bureau or the National Debtline (see Appendix 2).

As soon as you are able to get back on track with your repayments, do so. The longer the time you can put between debt problems and any subsequent application for credit the better. If you have defaulted on a loan or had a county court judgment against you, try and pay this off and then obtain a Certificate of Satisfaction. This should be noted automatically on your record at the credit reference agencies, but check before reapplying for credit.

4

Protection Policies

Woody Allen once said his idea of hell was to be trapped in an elevator with a life insurance salesman. Most of us would instinctively sympathise with the view – but why? What is it about life insurance that triggers such reactions? After all, this sort of protection is vital for us and for our families' well-being.

Perhaps that is precisely the point. When the salesman starts his spiel, he reminds us of our own mortality. He makes us confront uncomfortable subjects that we would rather not have to think about. So we ridicule him – doing so helps us laugh off our fears and anxieties about the fragility of life.

This is a natural human response. But if it stops us actually considering that salesman's wares, problems can arise. If we don't buy adequate insurance – and not just for our lives, but for our health – we face the threat of financial difficulties while we are alive and risk making our dependants suffer hardship when we die.

So, while it might not be the most pleasant of tasks, it is important to review the various protection policies and to get adequate cover. This chapter looks at the different forms of life insurance, medical fees cover, illness and accident insurances, income protection insurance, and policies designed to help meet the costs of old age. It also details the wide range of places you can buy from – although you might think twice about taking insurance from someone that you meet in a lift.

Life, or should that be death, insurance?

At its most simple, life insurance pays out if you die during a specified period. It might more properly be called death insurance, but then it would be even harder to make it attractive to potential buyers.

A small point: is it insurance or assurance? If there ever was a proper distinction between the two, it has been lost in the mists of time. In this book, we will talk about 'insurance'. If you come across the word 'assurance' elsewhere, don't worry – it means the same thing.

There are various types of life insurance. The most basic is term cover, but note there are a range of policies on offer – and it is important to get the right one.

Term insurance

Term policies pay out if you die within a specified term, which might be five, ten or more years. If you survive to the end of the term, the policy simply expires – you don't get your money back if you don't claim. Many people buy term cover to match a debt so that it will be cleared if they die. For instance, many mortgage lenders insist you have term insurance.

You can arrange decreasing term insurance, which means the amount of cover falls over time in line with the reducing debt. A policy which provides the same amount of cover throughout its term is known as level term insurance. If you opt for the policy to provide an income rather than a lump sum, it will be referred to as family income benefit.

The good news about term insurance is that it is getting cheaper. In 1994, a policy providing £300,000 of cover to a 30-year-old man for 15 years cost, on average, £37 a month. Today, the premiums are around £20, a fall of some 40%.

Premiums are falling because we're living longer, both in terms of recovering from illnesses and accidents, and in reaching greater ages. This means the chance of your dying during the term, and your dependants claiming on the policy, has reduced.

Competition is also driving down prices. The traditional insurance company establishment has been boosted by new players such as Marks & Spencer, Virgin and Direct Line.

Get the right amount of cover

The price of insurance is determined by, among other things, the amount of cover you have (known as the sum insured). There will clearly be a limit to the amount you need to buy. When working out how much to get, make sure you have enough to meet outstanding debts, particularly your mortgage. If you die owing money to your mortgage lender, it could repossess the property and sell it to recover the debt. That may be acceptable for those who do not have dependants, but anyone with a family will want to protect their interests. If you are paying off your mortgage with an endowment policy, life insurance cover will be built in.

Once your debts are covered, you should think about buying enough insurance to provide for those you would be leaving behind. Calculate how much income they would need each year, then think about how much would have to be invested to generate that income. At the moment, someone looking for £10,000 a year would need an investment of around £200,000.

Cover through your pension

If you are in a pension scheme, you can get tax relief on your term insurance premiums. As a basic rate taxpayer, if the monthly premium was calculated at £100, you would pay only £78, because the insurer would reclaim basic rate tax at 22% from the Inland Revenue. A higher rate taxpayer would be able to claim a further £18 through the self-assessment procedure, thus securing the full 40% relief and bringing the premium down to £60.

There is a limit on how much insurance you can buy in this way – you can spend only up to 5% of your earnings on these premiums. Your employer or pension provider will be able to give you more information on this.

What determines the cost?

The level of term insurance premiums is determined by a number of factors, such as your age, sex, health, whether or not you smoke, the amount of cover you require and the length of the term – the period for which you will remain insured.

The younger you are, the lower the cost. A man aged 30 wanting £100,000 of cover for 25 years would pay around £10 a month, but at 50 he would pay around £29 a month for just £50,000 of protection.

Women, on the whole, pay less because they tend to live longer. The lowest premium for a 30-year-old non-smoking man wanting £300,000 of cover over 15 years is around £20 a month. A woman of the same age could pay as little as £16.16.

If you are seriously ill or suffer from a condition such as diabetes, you will have to pay more – and smoking normally bumps up the cost dramatically (although a few companies charge the same for smokers and non-smokers). As an example of the impact of diabetes, a 50-year-old non-smoking man who was insulin dependent wanting £50,000 of cover for 20 years would pay around £50, but the premium would fall to just £22 if he did not have the illness.

As you might expect, being insured for a higher amount for a longer period will always cost more.

If you smoke and want cheaper insurance, the message is simple: kick the habit. If you can state you have not smoked for a year, you will enjoy substantially lower premiums. According to Swiss Re, a 30-year-old man wanting £100,000 of cover over 15 years would pay around £8 a month if he was a non-smoker and

£11.60 if he smoked. A 30-year-old woman wanting the same policy would pay £6.70 a month if she didn't smoke and £9 if she did. At 45, the figures would be £17 and £29 respectively.

Writing your policy in trust

Life insurance should always be written in trust. This ensures that, if you die during the term, it pays out to the chosen beneficiary straight away. If the policy is not written in trust, the proceeds will go into your estate and potentially become liable to inheritance tax. If your total estate exceeds the 2001-02 nil-rate band of £242,000, tax is payable at 40% on the surplus.

When you buy life insurance, the salesman should raise the issue of trust and provide the necessary paperwork. If you already have any policies, check they are written in trust.

Term insurance can be used in inheritance tax planning. This can be a complex area, so if you are sufficiently wealthy to think this tax will be an issue – and remember, your estate is everything you own, including the value of property – you should get inheritance planning advice. For more details on inheritance tax planning, see Chapter 14.

Review cover regularly

If you look at your policies on a regular basis, you will ensure the premiums are competitive and the cover is adequate. Term insurance has no investment value, so if you find a cheaper deal, you simply stop paying premiums with one company and start with another.

Remember, however, that age and medical conditions help determine the size of the premium, so if you start afresh after a number of years and have suffered a deterioration in health, you may struggle to find a cheaper quote.

Sally Forrester moved her term insurance to Direct Line and saved £28 a month on the premium. She now pays £81 a month for £156,000 of protection and is insured for the next ten years. The policy is to cover the mortgage on the house she is buying with husband Charles, a local government worker. Over ten years, paying the lower premium will save Sally £3,360.

Direct Line is one of the growing number of firms which sell over the telephone and Sally was impressed with the service she received: "It couldn't have been easier. I had to have a medical because of the size of the sum insured, so they arranged for a doctor to visit me at home. Everything was fine and the policy came through in a matter of days."

Where to buy term insurance

You can buy term cover direct from the company or through an independent financial adviser. It is worth shopping around for the best deal because of the variations in price. An independent adviser will provide access to the bulk of the market, but with firms that only sell direct, you will need to call them yourself.

IFA Promotion (0117 971 1177) provides details of independent advisers. Direct sellers include Direct Line Life (0845 3000 233), Marks & Spencer (0800 363422) and Virgin Direct (0845 6102 040). You can also trawl the internet for a good deal. Useful sites include www.find.co.uk, and www.financial-discounts.co.uk.

Sample quotations for term insurance

Age 35 – £100,000 over 20 years

Male, non-smoker Provider	Premium	Female, non-smoker Provider	Premium
Tesco PF	£9.74	Legal & General	£7.70
Legal & General	£10.00	Scottish Widows	£8.40
Swiss Life	£10.57	Tesco PF	£8.82
Scottish Widows	£11.20	NFU Mutual	£9.12
Norwich Union	£11.40	Zurich Life	£9.30
Royal & SunAlliance	£11.69	Norwich Union	£9.40
Standard Life	£11.70	Scottish Amicable	£9.50
Zurich Life	£12.10	Marks & Spencer	£9.55
Scottish Amicable	£12.50	Standard Life	£9.55
Eagle Star Direct	£12.70	Eurolife Assurance	£9.76

Male, smoker Provider	Premium	Female, smoker Provider	Premium
Legal & General	£17.20	Legal & General	£13.60
Swiss Life	£18.47	NFU Mutual	£14.04
Tesco PF	£18.56	Tesco PF	£14.45
Standard Life	£18.78	Royal & SunAlliance	£14.49
Royal & SunAlliance	£19.09	Scottish Amicable	£14.50
NFU Mutual	£19.15	Standard Life	£14.64
Scottish Amicable	£19.50	Swiss Life	£15.20
Zurich Life	£20.50	Marks & Spencer	£15.25
Norwich Union	£20.80	Norwich Union	£15.50
Ecclesiastical	£21.00	Scottish Widows	£15.50

Source: MoneyExtra

Other forms of life cover

Life insurance and investment are very closely linked. Many policies offer a core of insurance but also aim to make you a profit (unlike term cover, which has no investment element). Products of this type include endowment policies and whole-of-life plans.

Endowments

Most endowments are sold to homebuyers. The insurance cover is there to clear the debt if the policyholder dies, while the investment portion is designed to repay the loan at the end of the mortgage term. These contracts have come in for severe criticism in recent times because of fears that investment growth might not be as strong as hoped for – which could leave policyholders with a shortfall. As a result, many insurance companies and lenders have stopped selling them.

If you already have an endowment, your insurance company will keep you informed about how it is performing. The message is: don't panic. The majority of endowments will meet their stated objectives.

If, for any reason, you want to get at the value of your endowment before the end of the term, consider selling it on the traded endowment market. You are likely to get a much better deal than if you surrender it to the insurance company. The Association of Policy Market Makers (see Appendix 2) will send you a list of firms who can help.

Whole-of-life insurance

While term insurance protects you for a certain length of time, a whole-of-life policy covers your entire life. With term cover, there is a good chance you will not make a claim. With whole-of-life cover, the policy will, sooner or later, pay out. The inevitability of a claim makes whole-of-life cover more expensive, although the actual cost is determined by the same age and health considerations that apply to term insurance.

Whole-of-life cover is heavily investment oriented and is designed for those who want to build up a legacy. The best way to protect your dependants against financial difficulties following your untimely death is term insurance.

Critical illness insurance

◆ Over 250,000 people a year in the UK develop cancer. A third of all people will contract cancer at some point. Some 35% of men and 46% of women who get cancer will live at least five years.

◆ Every year in the UK, 120,000 people will suffer a stroke. Over 80,000 will survive for a year.

◆ More than 100,000 people in the UK today have suffered kidney failure and survived.

◆ Over 5,000 people a year in the UK require major organ transplants.
◆ Around 25% of men and 20% of women suffer a serious illness before reaching 65.

Taboo subjects such as death and serious illness tend to trigger the ostrich reaction. The prospect of suffering a major medical problem can be too horrible to contemplate, so we stick our heads in the metaphorical sand.

Such matters, unpleasant though they may be, are facts of life. If we ignore them and the financial catastrophes they can unleash, there is a serious risk that life might become very unpleasant indeed.

Basic life insurance pays out when we die. Critical illness cover pays out when a major medical problem is diagnosed – something which happens to hundreds of thousands of people every year. This sort of insurance is needed thanks to advances in medical science. A diagnosis of cancer, for example, is no longer an automatic death sentence. Many people recover from heart attacks and strokes and live happily for many years.

How critical illness cover works

Critical illness insurance pays out a pre-agreed, tax-free lump sum if the policyholder contracts a serious illness, suffers a debilitating affliction or becomes disabled. The money can be used for any purpose and is there to ensure financial worries do not add to the anxiety and stresses that inevitably accompany a severe medical problem.

Many people use the money from their insurance to pay for private nursing care, to adapt their home to take a wheelchair or stairlift or to buy a suitable car. Convalescent holidays are another popular option.

The most common serious illnesses – heart attacks, cancers, kidney and other organ failure and transplant, and multiple sclerosis – are covered. Policies will also pay out if total permanent disability is diagnosed. Insurers have different ways of determining this condition. For example, they may require that you be unable to carry out your job or any other form of work, or they may apply a test linked to what are termed 'activities of daily living'. These include such tasks as washing and moving around the house. If you cannot manage these by yourself, the policy will pay out.

Conditions such as Aids, addictions, depressive illness and self-inflicted injuries will usually be excluded. Insurers also have different attitudes to illnesses such as Alzheimer's and Parkinson's, perhaps only paying out if you have reached a certain age. The product literature will explain what is provided and you can choose accordingly.

The insurers' trade body, the Association of British Insurers (see Appendix 2), has issued a code of conduct so its members explain clearly what is covered. This will hopefully avoid the problem, which has arisen in the past, of someone falling ill and claiming on their policy, only to find their particular illness is not insured.

When you buy critical illness insurance, you have to choose the amount of cover (or sum insured). This will play a large part in determining the size of the premium.

This insurance is not designed to replace your income. It pays a single lump sum and, once it has done so, the policy comes to an end. If you contract two illnesses, you will receive only one payout. You can either have critical illness cover for a specified number of years or for the whole of your life. The first of these options is the cheaper.

The cost of nursing care or adapting your home may make it unrealistic to expect to live off the proceeds of a critical illness policy if you are unable to work again. To receive a regular income if you are forced to stop work by injury or illness, you will need income replacement insurance.

Combination covers

Critical illness insurance is available either as a stand-alone policy or in combination with another type of insurance. For example, you can buy term cover – life insurance that pays out if you die before a certain date – which also has a critical illness component. If you fall ill within the term, the policy will pay out (but it will not pay again if you die).

You can also link critical illness cover to whole of life insurance. This policy guarantees to pay out when you die, whenever that may be, and you can enhance the protection to take account of illness as well. It is also possible to link your critical illness cover to a specific debt.

Covering your mortgage

You can build critical illness cover into an endowment policy so that it pays off your mortgage if you fall ill. Endowments already provide built-in life insurance cover to clear the debt if you die. With critical illness protection on top, if you become ill, you will not have the worry of meeting your mortgage: it will be paid off and the house will be yours.

Additional options

When choosing a policy, consider paying a little extra for what is known as waiver of premium benefit. This pays the premium on your behalf if you are temporarily unable to work because of illness or injury (if you do not pay your monthly premiums, the policy will lapse and have no value).

Another option is to index-link the sum insured. This means the potential payout will increase to take account of inflation. Again, if you choose this, your premiums will be higher.

Where to buy

As with any form of insurance, it pays to shop around. An independent financial adviser or insurance broker will obtain quotations from a number of companies on your behalf, but some organisations – such as Lloyds Abbey Life, NatWest Life, Barclays Bank and HSBC – either sell direct only or through a branch outlet.

Remember also that cheapest is not necessarily best. The policy with the lowest premium may have the narrowest range of medical conditions that can trigger a claim. You may consider it worth paying more to have complete peace of mind.

Counting the cost

The insurer will calculate your premium with reference to a variety of factors, including your age, sex, health, occupation and whether or not you are a smoker. (Gender is important because the likelihood of men and women falling ill is different at different ages.) The size of the sum insured will also be significant. So, while it is important to have enough cover, take into account your other assets when considering how you would cope with the financial consequences of a critical illness. In other words, don't pay for cover you don't require.

A stand-alone policy lasting 30 years and giving £100,000 of cover for a man aged 35 should cost around £40 a month – a few pounds less for a woman because, statistically, women are less likely to fall ill. A policy running until death (but only paying out on diagnosis of an illness) would cost upwards of £60 for a man and, this time, a few pounds more for a woman. This is because women live longer and have more time to contract an illness.

A policy linked to term insurance running over 30 years would cost a 35-year-old man at least £40 a month; a woman would pay pretty much the same.

Income replacement insurance

◆ At any given time, around 7% of the working population is claiming state sickness benefits. Ten years ago the figure was under 4%.

◆ At the moment, two million people have been ill and off work for more than 26 weeks. Over one million people have been claiming state invalidity support for over a year, and of these, over 600,000 have been sick or disabled for longer than three years.

◆ Twenty-five per cent of men and 20% of women suffer a serious illness before reaching 65. One in five of us will be off work for three months through disability at some point in our career.

◆ An individual is 20 times more likely to have a breakdown in health lasting more than six months than he or she is to die before reaching 65.

If you find yourself off work for a protracted period because of illness or injury, money troubles can only make a bad situation worse. One solution is income replacement insurance. This pays a regular, tax-free income all the time you are off work and continues, if necessary, until you reach retirement age.

It is valuable cover because statutory sick pay and state benefits are far from generous, and it is preferable to using up your savings. You may have a rainy day fund, but if you are seriously ill for a prolonged period, it might not last long.

Some insurers call income replacement cover permanent health insurance, or PHI. This is easily confused with medical fees cover (often referred to as health insurance), so more firms are changing over to income replacement.

What to look for in a policy

This type of insurance is intended to replace some of your earnings while you are off work through sickness or injury. You choose the amount of cover you require, but insurers will only provide enough cover so that, when added to any benefits you receive, it makes up about two-thirds of your salary. The idea is to limit any payments you receive so you are not better off staying at home instead of going back to work.

Employers are obliged to pay statutory sick pay (SSP) for the first 28 weeks of incapacity, at the rate of £60.20. Those not eligible for SSP (because they have not paid National Insurance contributions) can claim the short term, lower rate of Incapacity Benefit. Once SSP comes to an end, full Incapacity Benefit can be claimed (see table).

Some firms pay more than the statutory minimum, especially to senior staff. If you are thinking about buying insurance, ask your employer what its attitude is. You might also be able to insure through the firm's group scheme, which would probably offer a competitive premium rate.

If you're self-employed, you should make provision for yourself.

What about state benefits?

There are three types of Incapacity Benefit:
◆ Short-term benefit at the lower rate is paid if you can't get sick pay.
◆ Short-term benefit at the higher rate is paid if you have been sick for more than 28 weeks and fewer than 52.
◆ Long-term benefit is paid if you have been sick for over 52 weeks.

Extra help may be available for those with children and/or dependent adults. Leaflet GL23 from post offices has full details of these and other benefits.

Incapacity benefits
Short-term lower rate (first 28 weeks)
Basic rate   £50.90
Adult dependency increase   £31.50*

Short-term higher rate (weeks 29-52)
Basic rate   £60.20
Adult dependency increase   £31.50*
Child dependency increase
     for the first child   £9.85*
     for any subsequent child   £11.35*

Long-term rate (week 53 onwards)
Basic rate   £67.50
Adult dependency increase   £40.40*
Child dependency increase
     for the first child   £9.85*
     for any subsequent child   £11.35*

Age addition to long-term rate
Incapacity before 35   £14.20
Incapacity between 35 and 44   £7.10

* Payment made only if there are dependent children or there is a dependant over age 60.

The cost of cover

Premium levels depend on age, sex, health, whether or not you smoke and your occupation. Older people pay more because they run a greater risk of becoming seriously ill and disabled. Those with an existing medical condition might be refused cover.

Women pay more because statistics show they are more likely to be off work as a result of illness. It does not matter that they are often off work looking after other members of the family that are ill, the insurers merely work from the employment statistics. Those in hazardous jobs also have to pay higher premiums.

Another major factor in determining the cost is the length of the 'deferred' period. This is the time you must be off sick before benefit is paid. The premiums are lower the longer you are prepared to wait. This is because there is more likelihood of your recovering before benefit becomes payable.

The choice of deferred period is usually four, 13, 26 or 52 weeks. You have to balance the length of the wait with the effect on the premium. Most people are prepared to dip into savings and rely on statutory allowances to see them to the 26-week stage.

The cost of income replacement cover

Monthly premiums for a healthy 35-year-old, non-smoking accountant on an 'own job' basis
Benefit: £15,000 a year/£288 a week (50% of salary) with policy terminating at the age of 60

Male premium

Deferred period	4 weeks	13 weeks	26 weeks	52 weeks
Level benefit				
Canada Life	£54.99	£23.89	£18.51	£15.49
Permanent Insurance	£33.42	£21.25	£14.11	£12.79
Zurich Life	£43.23	£27.08	£23.28	£20.58
Index-linked benefit				
Canada Life	£63.14	£27.30	£20.35	£18.63
Permanent Insurance	£38.45	£24.70	£16.49	£15.16
Zurich Life	£49.28	£30.73	£26.24	£23.16

Female premium

Deferred period	4 weeks	13 weeks	26 weeks	52 weeks
Level benefit				
Canada Life	£81.85	£34.26	£26.12	£21.66
Permanent Insurance	£61.47	£37.65	£24.16	£21.51
Zurich Life	£73.26	£44.99	£38.37	£38.18
Index-linked benefit				
Canada Life	£93.06	£39.37	£29.01	£26.39
Permanent Insurance	£74.43	£46.39	£29.71	£27.34
Zurich Life	£83.81	£51.39	£43.56	£38.18

Details to watch out for

Some policies provide a no-claims discount, while others have an investment element. Another important point is the insurer's attitude to what is known as the 'own job, any job' distinction. The cheaper option is 'any job' cover. Here, the benefit is paid when you are unable to do any sort of work.

The 'own job' cover pays out when you are unable to do your own job. This is more expensive because it means you have only to demonstrate that you cannot do your own work. With 'any job' cover, if you are physically able to do something else, the benefit will stop. In other words, you might have to take alternative employment. Thus someone off work from a high-pressure management job because of stress might find he or she has to work as a car park attendant.

This 'own job, any job' distinction also applies to state benefits. After 28 weeks, Incapacity Benefit is paid only to those judged unfit to do any job, not just their own. Decisions about entitlement are made by government inspectors rather than the individual's GP.

When you take out your policy, you can arrange for the benefits to be index-linked so that, if you make a claim, the payout will increase with inflation. As you might expect, this cover is more expensive.

An income replacement insurance policy keeps going as long as you pay the premiums and you can claim as many times as you need to. For this reason, premiums should be paid even while you are claiming. This can be taken care of with waiver of premium, which pays your premiums while you are off work. This is very important cover and well worth having.

Making a claim

You can claim once you have been signed off work by your doctor for the length of the deferred period. You will then receive benefits until you return to work or reach retirement age. Insurers are entitled to check that those claiming are genuinely unfit to work – they employ representatives to make regular visits to ensure convalescence is not being unduly extended.

Among the top income replacement insurers are Canada Life (0345 226232), Permanent Insurance (0345 228800) and Zurich Life (01793 405359). You can contact a broker via the British Insurance Brokers Association (020 7623 9043).

Accident, sickness and unemployment insurance

Accident, sickness and unemployment (ASU) insurance, sometimes called mortgage payment protection, covers your mortgage repayments when you are unable to earn. It is primarily sold by lenders at the same time as the loan is arranged, although some insurers, such as CGNU and Royal & SunAlliance, sell it over the telephone. If you already have a mortgage, you can still apply for cover.

State help – or the lack of it

This insurance contract has grown in popularity as the amount of state help for borrowers who lose their income because of unemployment, sickness or disability has reduced. Previously, if someone applied for Income Support, 50% of the interest on a loan would be paid for the first 16 weeks of a claim. After 16 weeks, the full amount of interest was paid.

Now, however, those who have had a mortgage since before October 1995 and who make a claim for benefit receive no payment for two months and then receive 50% of the interest for the following four months. Full interest payments are made after six months.

Those who have taken out their mortgage since October 1995 and who have subsequently become eligible for Income Support receive nothing towards the cost of mortgage interest for the first nine months of the claim.

Income Support is means tested, so anyone with savings and investments of more than £3,000 will receive reduced benefit, while anyone with more than £8,000, or a spouse or partner who works more than 24 hours a week, or another source of income will not qualify. It is estimated that 80% of borrowers would not qualify for the benefit for one reason or another.

Also, Income Support only pays the interest on the first £100,000 of any mortgage. In other words, if you have a £150,000 mortgage, you will get no help on the interest due on £50,000 of the loan. And remember Income Support only pays the interest. It makes no contribution towards repayment of the capital debt or to any investment policy that is being funded to repay an interest-only loan.

How ASU policies work

When you buy insurance, you pay a premium each month. If you become unemployed or unable to work because of an accident or sickness, the policy will pay your mortgage for you.

Generally, you must have been in continuous employment for a certain period, which ranges from six months with some insurers to a year with others, and you must work a minimum number of hours – usually 16 – each week. You must not know of any impending cause of unemployment and you must be in good health.

Payments will normally be made until you find work or for 12 months, whichever period is shorter. Some policies stretch the payments to 24 months, while others cover claims for unemployment for 12 months and claims for other reasons for longer. According to insurance company statistics, the average length of claim is five to six months.

Qualifying for payment

Not surprisingly, insurers want to avoid claims from people who take out policies knowing they are about to lose their job. For this reason, there is a qualifying period for which a policy must be in force before a claim will be accepted. This varies and may be as short as 30 days or as long as 180 days.

Again, some policies make a distinction between unemployment and disability, with a qualifying period applying for claims following redundancy but not for those caused by accident or sickness. Policies also require a period of time to elapse before benefits will be paid; it will be 30 to 90 days depending on the insurer.

Many policies specifically exclude the self-employed. This is because insurers are worried they might not be able to prove the policyholder is genuinely unemployed. Those working on fixed-term contracts may also find it difficult to obtain unemployment (but not accident and sickness) cover, although some policies cover redundancy if the contract is cancelled mid-term.

There is a limit to the amount of cover you can buy. The maximum is normally 120% or 125% of your total mortgage commitments each month, which includes capital and interest payments, contributions towards an investment plan to repay the loan and life and household insurance premiums.

Most policies are sold on a fixed-rate basis, which means that if your application is accepted, you pay the going rate charged by that particular provider. Premiums do not vary from individual to individual. They start as low as £2.50 or £3 a month for every £100 of monthly cover.

Private medical insurance

Private medical insurance pays for the cost of treatment when you are ill. The cover provided by different policies varies widely. Sometimes the literature will specify or exclude certain treatments and dictate which type of hospital must be used. It is clearly important to read documentation thoroughly to make sure you are getting the cover you require.

Some insurers, such as Bupa, run their own hospitals. In some instances, you will be able to use a private ward within an NHS facility. The amount you are willing to spend on premiums will determine the flexibility, scope and luxury of the service you receive if you have to make a claim.

Whatever you spend, you are unlikely to get cover for long-term illnesses or degenerative diseases associated with old age. Aids, self-inflicted conditions such as suicide attempts and drug or alcohol abuse will not be covered. If you have pre-existing medical conditions, they may either be excluded completely or subject to a moratorium which states you will not be able to claim for that particular problem for a given period, perhaps two years.

When you arrange cover, always tell the insurer everything that might be relevant to your application. If you do not disclose a fact which emerges later on, perhaps when you make a claim, your entire policy might be invalidated, leaving you with a hefty medical bill.

You can buy an individual policy or one which extends to your spouse or partner or whole family. Many people, of course, enjoy private medical cover as a benefit of their employment. It is, however, taxable.

How premiums are calculated

Your premium will reflect your age, occupation, health and medical history – and, as ever, smokers have to pay more. You can save money with a budget scheme, which will cover you only if your treatment is not immediately available on the

NHS. You can also control the cost by opting to pay the first part of any claim – something the insurers call the excess. The bigger the excess, the greater the premium saving.

The main areas of cover under a standard private medical policy are:

◆ **Professional fees** This pays for consultants, specialist physicians, anaesthetists and surgeons.

◆ **Hospital charges** This is the cost of accommodation and nursing, either in a private hospital or in a private bed within an NHS hospital.

◆ **Specialist treatments** These include physiotherapy, chemotherapy, radiology, which may be taken as an in- or out-patient.

◆ **Also covered** Drugs, tests, X-rays, dressings and treatments, out-patient treatments and home nursing.

◆ **Cash benefit** This is a sum (typically £50) paid for every night the policyholder receives treatment from the NHS. Some policies, known as hospital cash plans, concentrate solely on providing this type of benefit.

The most common exclusions are:

◆ Fees payable to a general practitioner.

◆ Treatments not recommended by a GP.

◆ Dental treatments (except those requiring an operation).

◆ Cosmetic surgery (except when made necessary by an accident).

◆ Routine tests and examinations (such as for sight and hearing).

◆ Vaccinations.

◆ Pregnancy and childbirth (although complications arising in pregnancy may be covered).

◆ Termination of pregnancy.

◆ Infertility treatment.

◆ Self-inflicted injuries.

◆ Alcohol and drug dependence.

◆ Aids.

◆ Injuries sustained in war.

Why are premiums so high?

Many people have been forced to give up their private medical insurance because of spiralling premiums. In some cases, the price leapt more than 30% in 2000.

Premiums have been rising well above the rate of inflation for several years. The reason, according to the insurers, is that the cost of providing cover is itself increasing rapidly because of new technology and high demand. As more procedures become available, insurers receive more claims. At the same time, the increased sophistication of the procedures themselves increases the costs.

Tom Bradby, a communications consultant, bought cover for himself and his wife Sara with a leading insurer in 1995, when the premium was £39.30 a month. When he renewed in 1998, it had already increased to £59.22 a month and his 1999 renewal notice quoted a figure of £72.84 per month – up by over 23% year-on-year and by 85% in five years.

"This level of premium increase certainly makes me want to shop around to see if I can get a better deal. We have not made a claim in five years, but the cost just keeps going up anyway," Tom says.

Denise Shreeve decided to change her insurance company as she neared her 40th birthday. Most insurers impose age-related premium increases, which means cover costs more as you get older, with the trigger points usually being 30, 40, 50 and so on. This is because older people represent a worse risk from the medical insurance point of view. For Denise, however, the rise in premiums was just too steep.

After shopping around, she opted for Healthcare 4 Life, which differs from most insurers in that it imposes just one age-related premium increase. So, whatever age you are when you join, the only age-related increase you face is when you reach the next decade birthday. Thus, if you join at age 39, as Denise did, your premiums will only increase at 40.

"I left my old insurer after 14 years as its premium became so high. I spent six weeks looking at all the alternatives and chose Healthcare 4 Life, as after the first age-related increase there will be no others," she says.

Dental insurance

Dental charges can be substantial, even if you use one of the increasingly rare NHS facilities. One way to plan for these costs is to join a dental health scheme. This allows you to visit a private dentist and have routine and emergency work done at no extra cost. You pay a monthly subscription that is worked out in advance by the dentist and which reflects your dental history and the state of your teeth. As part of the arrangement, you are required to visit the dentist on a regular basis.

This concept is known as 'capitation'. Unlike other forms of insurance, you do not pay a premium and then make a claim if and when you need treatment. Instead, you pay a regular subscription which entitles you to check-ups and any routine work required.

The cost of capitation

The monthly costs vary. If your teeth are in a very bad state, expect to pay the top rate. That said, if regular visits to the dentist result in an improvement in their condition, your subscription should come down. Likewise, if they deteriorate, the cost will increase. Monthly prices range from £10 to £25.

There will also be a one-off registration fee. Denplan (0800 401402), the main company in this market, makes a charge equal to your monthly subscription. Your dentist may use another provider with a different pricing structure, so ask for details.

Schemes such as this cover routine, preventative care, accidents and emergency treatment, oral cancer treatment and wisdom teeth extraction. They can also cover major restorative dentistry such as crowns, bridges and dentures. They do not pay for everything, however. You may, for example, have to pay for the materials used in crowns, bridges and dentures. There might also be a bill if your dentist has to sub-contract work to a laboratory or refer you to another dentist. Purely cosmetic work will not be included.

If you have a dental emergency, you should be covered to go to any dentist worldwide and have any costs you incur refunded to you. Should you need to go into hospital overnight under the care of a consultant dental surgeon, you will receive a cash benefit. Denplan pays £60 for every night spent in hospital due to dental treatment.

These schemes are effectively run by the dentist and it is through the dentist that you join. You need to arrange an assessment with one who participates – you may be charged separately for this. You may then be required to undergo a course of further treatment to ensure you are dentally fit before joining.

NHS dental treatment

Of the 29,000 dentists in the UK, almost half have either gone completely private or have stopped accepting new NHS patients. If you track down an NHS dentist, you will still have to pay 80% of the cost of treatment, up to a maximum of £354. Who gets free treatment?

◆ Children under 18.
◆ Those under 19 in full-time education.
◆ Women who are pregnant or who have a child under 12 months.
◆ Anyone receiving Income Support, Family Credit or Job Seekers' Allowance.
◆ Families with a certificate for full help with the cost of NHS services.

Pensioners, the unemployed and students get free treatment only if they fall into one of these categories or if they have low income. Anyone on a low income may be eligible for free treatment or may pay a reduced amount. Ask the dentist for form AG1 or get booklet AB11 from your local post office.

The cost of NHS treatment

Check-up	£4.92
Check-up and two X-rays	£8.32
Check-up, scale and polish	£12.68
Check-up, two X-rays, scale and polish	£16.08
Filling (silver in back tooth – medium)	£13.56
Filling (white in front tooth)	£9.88
Extraction (one tooth)	£8.80
Crown (precious metal)	£63.84
Dentures (full set, upper and lower)	£107.60

An NHS dentist may charge for a broken appointment if reasonable notice is not given.
Source: British Dental Association

Long-term care insurance

◆ In 1990, the proportion of the UK population aged 60 or over was 20.8%. By 2030, the figure will be 30%. In that year, there will be 6.3 million people over the age of 75 in the UK. Today the figure is 3.9 million.
◆ In 1901, a new-born baby boy had a life expectancy of just under 46 years. In 1992, the figure was 74 years. Women live an average of five years longer.
◆ In 1901, a 60-year-old man's life expectancy was 13 years. By 1992, he could reasonably expect to survive for 18 years.
◆ More than 40% of those over 60 suffer from a limiting long-term illness.
◆ Almost 50% of people over 85 have some form of dementia. On average, sufferers have the disease for eight years and can live with it for 25 years.
◆ Forty thousand houses a year are sold to fund the care costs of the elderly.
◆ Every day 315 people need long-term care for the first time.

One of the major issues facing society in the 21st century is how we adjust to the increasing number of elderly people. It is quite feasible that someone currently in the workforce could spend a third of their life in retirement. This may not be an unpleasant prospect if they have their health and plenty of money. But both these things are in relatively short supply among the elderly. Physical and mental deterioration and a lack of adequate pension income can add up to a life of deprivation and misery for many old folk.

One of the problems is that, while medical science has managed to prolong life, it has not been able to eradicate all the problems associated with old age. As a result, millions of elderly people have to go into residential or nursing accommodation. The costs can rapidly eat through their life savings and destroy any plans they had to bequeath money or property to children or grandchildren.

Private nursing home fees start at £16,000 to £23,000 a year, depending on the area of the UK. Someone paying privately for only four hours of nursing care a day in their own home may face a bill of £14,000 a year. State assistance is severely restricted and is means tested, which means assets have to be used before help is given.

It is estimated that as many as one in four of us will need care in old age, but very few make any specific financial provision.

The insurance solution

Long-term care insurance meets the costs of care made necessary by disabilities that occur in old age. This might be nursing care or additional help given in the policyholder's home, or it might be fully-fledged residential or nursing home care.

Pure insurance policies have an agreed amount of benefit that will be paid each week, and this helps determine the size of the premium. If the care actually costs less, then the lesser amount will be paid.

Investment-linked plans are funded by a single premium. These contracts allow you to get your money back by encashing the policy.

You can also buy an immediate care contract if you need care straight away. Here you invest a lump sum into an annuity which generates a guaranteed monthly payment for the rest of your life which can be used to settle the bills.

Get the cover required

When you buy a long-term care policy, you specify how much benefit you want. This decision will be influenced by the cost of nursing or residential care costs in your area (or the area you want to move to). You can index-link the premiums and benefits to ensure they keep pace with inflation.

Your broker or insurance company should be able to help with the necessary figures. On the point of getting advice, consult a broker who knows the market thoroughly, not one who sells the occasional policy. Check that he uses a range of companies and understands the issues. This is a complicated area of insurance and warrants far more attention than arranging cover for your house or car.

The role of the state

Widespread outrage at the plight of elderly people struggling to meet the cost of their care in old age has made this issue a political hot potato. Successive governments have delayed making firm proposals, primarily because they realise that guaranteeing to meet costs universally would simply be too expensive – and admitting this would alienate the increasingly powerful 'grey lobby'.

The Labour government set up a Royal Commission on the subject, to which it finally responded in July 2000. It decided to adopt the majority of the commission's recommendations but crucially said it would not implement the main one – that the state should pick up the cost of both personal and nursing care. Instead, it proposed to pay only for nursing care in a nursing home.

Further confusion has been brought about by a decision by the devolved Scottish executive to pay for both personal and nursing care in Scotland.

The main funding proposals at present are:

◆ The means-test threshold will increase from £16,000 to just over £18,000 with effect from 6 April, 2001.

◆ For the first three months after admission into a residential care or nursing home, the value of a person's home will not be included in a means-test assessment. This means the local authority may have to meet some of the care costs during this period if a person's assets (excluding the value of their home) are less than the means-test threshold. This change will be made from April 2001.

◆ Nursing care in a nursing home will be free. This is expected to be introduced in October 2001. The details remain sketchy, but what seems clear is that the amount of nursing care covered will depend on an individual's medical condition. A person who has Alzheimer's, for example, may not get any nursing care or assistance with fees.

Clearly, there remains a role for long-term care insurance – especially as the state's ability to pay bills will diminish in a low tax environment. Indeed, the government has highlighted this insurance as a way for people to protect their assets against the costs of long-term care. This signals that anyone over the mean-test threshold should consider this form of protection very seriously.

Payment of a long-term care claim

Insurance companies judge whether a claim should be paid according to the policyholder's ability to carry out certain 'activities of daily living' (ADLs). Six of these are normally listed:

◆ Getting in and out of the bath or shower.
◆ Dressing.
◆ Eating and drinking.
◆ Using the toilet and coping with continence.
◆ Moving to or from a bed or chair.
◆ Moving around the house.

If the person cannot manage a certain number of these tasks, benefits will be paid for the appropriate level of care. Payment will also be made if the care is deemed necessary by a doctor. Some insurers impose more stringent ADL tests than others, and some require an inability to perform three from the above list while others settle for only two.

Insurers also measure cognitive ability, which may be affected by ailments such as Alzheimer's and other conditions causing senility. Again, they will adopt varying attitudes, but a claim will normally be paid when it is no longer safe or practical for a person to continue living in his or her own home.

Among the leading long-term care providers are CGNU, Royal Skandia, Scottish Widows, Scottish Amicable and PPP Lifetime Care.

5

General Insurance

Buying insurance is nobody's idea of fun. After all, you only use a policy when something goes wrong. If nothing does, you get no return on your outlay. What's more, with most types of insurance, you have to pay insurance premium tax at the rate of 5% – and up to 17.5% in some cases, such as travel insurance. But the sort of protection provided by insurance policies is essential for peace of mind. It makes sense, therefore, to get the cover you require at the best possible price.

Everyone with a car or motorbike must have a policy. If you own your home, you will need buildings cover. Wherever you live, you need contents insurance to protect your belongings. Then there is travel insurance, insurance for pets, legal expenses cover… the list goes on. This chapter looks at the main covers and gives an idea of what to look out for with each. It also considers the various ways you can buy insurance: over the telephone, via the internet, direct from the company or through a broker.

Home insurance

There are two types of insurance for the home. The first, known as buildings cover, protects your bricks and mortar. The second, contents cover, is for your possessions. Many companies sell both and will offer a discount if you buy both sorts from them. That said, it can be worth shopping around as some insurers specialise in one or the other and offer a better deal.

Many householders buy their buildings cover through their bank or building society at the same time as they apply for their mortgage. Lenders earn massive commissions from selling this sort of insurance (up to 40% of the premium) and they deter borrowers from renewing with another insurer by levying an administration fee of £25 on anyone who moves companies.

Also, some special mortgage offers have only been available to those who take insurance too. This has outraged rival insurance companies and encouraged the government to step in and ban this kind of conditional selling.

If you have insurance through your mortgage lender, you will almost certainly save money by switching to another company. Some firms, notably Direct Line, even offer to pay the £25 administration fee on your behalf. You should expect to trim a fifth off the annual premium.

Cost factors

Leaving aside the shenanigans of some mortgage companies, the price of buildings insurance is determined by three main factors: the rebuilding cost of the property (not its market value), its type and its location. If your area is prone to subsidence or flooding, your premiums will be higher. If you live in a thatched or listed property, you will pay more.

As far as contents insurance is concerned, premiums are determined primarily by the value of your belongings and the area where you live. If your neighbourhood suffers from high burglary rates, cover will be more expensive, although you can mitigate this to a certain degree, as you will see.

Not all contents policies are the same. Some are aimed at the wealthy, providing cover for objets d'art and antiques, garden furniture and students' possessions while away from home. These contracts often include a host of extras, such as protection for business equipment, built-in travel insurance and all manner of telephone advice services and helplines.

At the other end of the scale, there are budget deals, providing a bare minimum of cover to keep the premium as low as possible.

In between, policies offer a menu of covers that you can add to the core protection. For example, you can include items of expensive jewellery. You might also be able to insure your bicycle, but note that there will be a limit on its value of, perhaps, £250. If your bike is more expensive, you will need a special policy.

People who work from home need to ensure that they have appropriate cover. There are an increasing number of policies which cater for tele-workers and home-based craftsmen. These include such covers as liability insurance and money to help you restore your records if they are destroyed in a fire or lost when a computer is stolen.

Wherever you live, whatever you do and whatever you own, make sure your policy suits your needs. If you do not have adequate cover, you will not get as much as you need if you have to make a claim. Equally, there is no point in paying premiums for insurance that you do not require. In any case, you can control the cost of cover in a number of ways.

Security

There are over 1.25 million burglaries in the UK every year. Even the best insurance policy will not eradicate the anger and sense of violation, but it can at least help repair some of the material damage. Prevention, however, remains better than cure. Insurers recognise this and will reduce the cost of contents insurance if you take steps to keep the burglars at bay.

◆ **Locks** Some insurers offer a discount if you have locks of a certain standard fitted to all your doors and windows, or at least to those on the ground floor. Others will even insist that they are fitted (and used) as part of the policy conditions. If this is the case, you may find that your policy is 'endorsed' – which means it won't pay out if a burglar gained access through an unlocked entrance while you were out.

◆ **Safes** If you possess valuables, a safe may be required. Again, the policy might be endorsed so jewellery is covered when worn or in the safe. Some wealthy householders fit two safes – a decoy containing a modest amount of cash and jewellery, and a main one for the more important items.

◆ **Alarms** Fitting an alarm may also secure a discount. Make sure you use an installer approved by the insurer. The proposal literature will include a list. Heat-sensitive lighting also enhances security. If you live in a large property, the insurance company may send a specialist to advise on improving the overall security.

◆ **Neighbourhood watch** Membership of the local neighbourhood watch may trim a few pounds off your contents premiums.

Weather risks

There is not much you can do about extreme conditions, but keeping your property in good repair will reduce the likelihood of routine problems. For example, drains and guttering should be cleared regularly. During the winter, heating the house round-the-clock and lagging the system can prevent frozen pipes.

Most insurers will provide advice on how to look after your property so as to reduce the chances of a claim. If you live in an unusual property, such as a thatched cottage or a listed building, you will need a special policy designed for your particular needs.

Long-term deals

Cover is traditionally arranged for 12 months, with the premiums reviewed at renewal. Policies are now being developed which last three or even five years, with the premium guaranteed throughout provided there is no change to the sum insured (the amount of cover you buy). By locking into a price in this way, you effectively insulate yourself from premium inflation, which is thought by industry watchers to be around 5% a year.

No-claims bonus

Ask about a no-claims bonus on your household cover. If you do not claim for several years, you may be able to build a discount of up to 30% – not as much as the 60%-plus you can get on a motor insurance policy, but worth having nonetheless.

Excess payments

All policies require you to contribute towards the cost of any claim you make – this is the mandatory excess (also known as the deductible). Normally, this will be £50 or £100 and is levied to deter small claims and keep premiums down. If you live in an area prone to subsidence, you may have an excess of £1,000 or more on your buildings cover. It is possible to increase your excess. The higher the amount you volunteer to pay towards a claim, the larger the reduction on your premium. The policy literature should provide details.

Instalments

As with motor insurance, paying in monthly instalments can make a hefty insurance premium easier to digest. But watch out for insurers that add up to 6% to the cost if it is paid monthly. A growing number of insurers make no charge. Insurers like instalments because they create inertia – you are less likely to change company if you have to change your direct debit. However, when renewal time comes around, you should check that a better deal is not on offer elsewhere.

The flood menace

It is estimated that four million people in 1.3 million properties around the UK are routinely at risk of flooding. In 1999, the Environment Agency launched a £2m awareness campaign which urges people to contact a special telephone information bureau for help with planning for the worst. The service, called Floodline (0845 988 1188), tells callers what risks they face and how to reduce them. Stark statistics also ram the message home: in recent years, the cost of flooding in the UK has been estimated at more than £2bn.

The areas deemed most at risk from flooding include those around rivers flowing into the Severn, Thames, Humber and Tees estuaries, the Wash and the east coast of England, from Lincolnshire south to Essex.

If you are flooded, your contents policy should pay for temporary accommodation, such as a hotel, while your home is made habitable again. The bills will be paid until a pre-set amount is reached. This is usually 10% or 15% of the total sum insured.

In November 2000, the Dalton family of Shrewsbury found out at first hand how devastating a flood can be when the River Severn burst its banks and swamped the town's drains.

"We had some inkling that there might be trouble so we put down sandbags," says Chris Dalton. "The next morning, I saw that the whole street was awash and when I went downstairs, water was coming in under the door. For the first time in my life I felt completely helpless. Inch by inch the carpet was getting soaked and there was absolutely nothing I could do."

With the carpets and fitted kitchen appliances ruined and the electricity shorted out, Chris, his wife Pat and their children Elizabeth and Max went to stay with Pat's parents in Wales. When they telephoned their insurer, they were told to return home to meet the loss adjuster.

"I told them we couldn't go home because we had nowhere to stay," says Chris. "But when we met the loss adjuster at an hotel in Shrewsbury, he said we could stay there. After four days, we moved to a rented house nearby and stayed there for six months while the house dried out, all the damage was repaired and our ruined possessions were replaced. The policy picked up the tab for everything."

Motor insurance

Drive a car without insurance and you immediately become a criminal. What is more, if you have an accident while uninsured you could face financial ruin, especially if someone else – including a passenger in the vehicle – is injured or killed.

Few of us would contemplate driving without insurance. But if we are going to buy a policy, we quite reasonably want to get the right cover without spending more than we have to. So can we simply get a range of quotations and pick the cheapest? Or are there features and benefits that make it worth paying that bit extra?

If you choose to spend a bit more than you have to, you can buy a policy that includes roadside assistance, a courtesy car if yours is off the road and legal helplines. Most of us, however, just want good, solid cover for the smallest premium we can find.

Controlling the cost

You can reduce your motor insurance premium and ensure you get the best protection in a number of ways. Taking action could be important, because the early years of this century will see insurers trying to recoup some of the loss they made in the last.

It might not feel like it, but we have enjoyed good value motor insurance in recent years. This is because lots of companies have been competing for our business, which has kept a lid on prices. But there are clear signs that premiums are on the way up again. Surveys by the AA and RAC showed that price rises of 15% were the norm in 2000, pushing average premiums for comprehensive cover to around £500 a year. Some motorists suffered increases of 25% to 30% and further increases are in the pipeline.

Remember also that when you buy a motor policy – or any of the policies outlined in this chapter – you pay insurance premium tax. In 1999 IPT crept up to 5%.

Shop around

Don't be seduced by the first advertisement you see. There are literally hundreds of places you could buy cover and just a few minutes on the telephone will give you a feel for a typical price. Call companies that sell direct and also make sure you contact a broker who can scour the market on your behalf.

Improve security

Theft is a major headache for insurers, so they offer lower premiums to drivers who fit security devices to their cars and who park off-road at night.

Alarms and immobilisers can be a good investment. Any reduction in the premium may not cover the cost, but if you can deter a thief, you will save yourself having to make a claim. A tracking device will also secure a discount because it virtually guarantees that, if stolen, your car will be recovered by the police.

Parking in a garage or in your garden will also trim a few pounds off your premium. Be warned, however, that if you take such a policy, your vehicle may not be insured if you leave it in the street.

As well as physical security, you can make yourself a better driver by completing an advanced driver or defensive driver course. Some companies offer a discount in such cases, the theory being that you are less likely to have an accident.

Avoid claims

Motor insurers reward policyholders who do not make claims with a no-claims discount (or bonus). Obviously, if you have an accident or your vehicle is stolen, you will have to claim. But with many smaller knocks and scratches, it can make sense to pay for the repair yourself, rather than jeopardise your bonus.

The bonus as a percentage of your premium increases for each claim-free year

Years	Bonus
1	25%
2	35%
3	45%
4	55%
5	65%

If you decide to change insurer, the new company will honour your existing discount. If you are buying insurance for the first time after driving a company car for some years, you should be able to find a company that offers an introductory bonus of, say, 25%.

You can protect your no-claims bonus by paying a small amount extra on your premium. This is called a protected bonus and means that, if you have a claim (or perhaps three in two years), you will not lose the discount you have built up.

Pay an excess

Motor insurance policies include an excess (sometimes called the deductible). It comes in two forms: compulsory and voluntary.

Nearly all policies will have a compulsory excess of £50 or £100. This is the amount you must pay towards any claim you make. With a £50 excess, for example, the insurer will pay only £550 towards a £600 claim. The idea is to deter people from making small claims.

If you volunteer to have a larger excess, you will cut the size of the premium. You are trading a saving in your initial insurance costs against the risk that you will have to pick up a large bill if you ever have to make a claim.

Live somewhere safe

What you pay in motor insurance (and household insurance, for that matter) will be determined in part by where you live. Insurers charge less to those who live in rural areas for a number of reasons. First, there are fewer vehicles per mile of road, which means there are fewer accidents. Second, motor crime tends not to be such a problem as in cities.

However, while you might cut your premium in half by moving to the countryside, it is hardly likely to be a practical option. But if you are weighing up the pros and cons of living in different areas, it is a factor to take into account.

Find a sympathetic insurer

Your age and sex will affect your motor premiums. Women usually pay less because, statistically, they are safer drivers than men. By the same token, young men pay more because they tend to have more accidents. Middle-aged people pay lower rates because they are viewed as safe drivers in safe cars. But premiums creep up again for those aged 60 or more.

Clearly, sex and age are not variables that you can do much about. But some insurers reflect differences in their prices more acutely than others, so it is worth shopping around for those that are sympathetic to your particular circumstances.

Get the cover you need

When you buy insurance, you will need to specify the type of cover you want. To save money, buy only the cover you need. For instance, if you insure the vehicle so anyone can drive it, you'll pay more than if you have a 'named driver only' policy. If you are already a member of a road-rescue service, don't buy a deluxe insurance policy that duplicates the benefits.

The legal minimum level of cover is third-party only. This is cheapest but will provide nothing towards your costs if you are to blame for an accident – it will only meet your legal liabilities towards the others involved. Third-party, fire and theft cover costs more and will pay for repairs or a replacement in a limited number of circumstances.

Comprehensive insurance is the most expensive option, but it allows you to claim whatever the cause of the problem – even if you simply bump the car against a wall and cause the damage yourself. Remember, though, you can cut your premiums by building up your no-claims bonus.

Drive an ordinary car

The bigger, flashier and more expensive your car, the bigger your premium will be. One reason is that thieves target highly prized vehicles, often stealing to order. Another is that high-performance vehicles driven by inexperienced or inexpert motorists are more likely to be involved in accidents. Parts for rare and exclusive vehicles are harder to come by, which inevitably increases the cost of repairs. This also applies to many imported cars.

If you want the lowest possible premium, therefore, you need to drive an old banger. Realistically, you should at least be aware that, if you want a classy model or fancy marque, it will come at a price in terms of higher insurance costs. That said, if you buy a new car, you may be entitled to free insurance for a year or more. But when the year is up, the high cost of cover might come as a shock.

Pay by instalments

With most motor premiums easily into three and even four-figure territory, the option to spread the cost over 12 months is often extremely welcome. But most insurers levy a charge for this – perhaps as much as 6% of the premium will be added to the total cost. That said, some companies offer interest-free instalments. If you need to pay monthly, quiz each firm on its approach and specify to your broker that you do not want an instalments charge.

Cover for classics

Many people are surprised at the definition of a classic car. They tend to think of purring E-type Jags and stately Rolls-Royces, but while these are undoubtedly classics, they are just a small part of the classic car community. Insurance companies define a classic by its age. For some it is any car over 20-years old, but for others it need only be ten or 12.

If you have a vehicle which qualifies, it could be worth considering a specialist classic car policy. The protection offered might suit you better than a conventional deal, and you could save money. As with any car insurance, the cost will be determined in part by where you live and the type of vehicle, but there are a host of other factors to be taken into account.

For example, the vehicle's annual mileage is very important. If you never take your car out on the road, you will pay a lot less than someone who is driving to shows and rallies every weekend. Some insurers have mileage bands of, say, 1,500 miles a year, so you pay more if you drive 3,000, 4,500 or 6,000.

You can trim your premium by increasing the vehicle's security. Older cars can be easy prey for thieves. To qualify for fully-fledged classic car insurance, you will usually have to keep it in a garage overnight. If the car is particularly valuable – say, worth £25,000 or more – the insurer may insist on an immobiliser being fitted.

The value of the car is important in determining the premium. The insurer may want to see photographs to check on its condition. It is also worth keeping abreast of fluctuating prices to ensure your valuation is up to date. Once you and the insurance company agree the valuation, this is the amount you would receive after a write-off. Remember that your vehicle may be worth less than the total amount you have spent rebuilding and renovating it. If you make a claim, you'll only get the market value.

If you keep a collection of vehicles or hire out your car for weddings or other events, a classic car policy can be adapted to your needs. Cover is also available for classic motorcycles.

Terry Colter insures all his family's cars under a single policy. The Colter fleet consists of a BMW 3 Series, a Jaguar XJ6, a Ford Orion, a Ford transit and a Honda Goldwing motorcycle. The annual premium is £2,500, which is considerably less than the aggregate of the separate policies that were previously in force.

He says: "I reckon we must have saved around £700. I like the fact that we have just one renewal date, one set of paperwork and one direct debit. And the policy is flexible in that any named member of the family can drive any car."

These family fleet policies, which are becoming increasingly common, are suitable for collections of at least three vehicles.

Caravans

As with cars, theft is a major problem for caravan owners. Caravans are seen as soft targets by many thieves, both in terms of the vehicle and its contents. Over £12m of theft claims are made by caravanners every year. For this reason, caravan insurers encourage their policyholders to look after their vehicles, both while they are at home (or in storage) and on tour.

Research undertaken by the insurance industry shows thieves tend to target two particular situations:

◆ unattended storage areas, such as fields rented out by a farmer where there is no round-the-clock security guard;

◆ driveways in heavily populated areas.

However, it seems, nowhere is absolutely safe. In a recent case, a caravanner was towing his vehicle along the motorway when it suffered a puncture. He pulled over, removed the wheel and put it in the boot of his car, which he unhitched and drove to the nearest garage for a repair. He never thought the caravan would be at risk – after all, it was sitting on the hard shoulder, minus a wheel. But when he returned, it was gone.

Insurers recommend that, if your caravan is in storage, it should enjoy 24-hour, 365-day security. If you are touring, or siting the caravan permanently, you are advised to go to a proper holiday park where there is decent protection.

Wherever the vehicle is parked, even if it is on your own driveway, you are urged to use either a wheel clamp or a hitchlock. Indeed, some policies will only provide cover if such a device is used. Other, cheaper policies provide cover only while the vehicle is on the road or in a holiday park. This can trim the premium substantially, but remember that your vehicle is at risk while parked anywhere, including outside your house.

Another option might be to ask your household contents insurer whether the policy can be extended to the caravan. But if it can, an extra premium will probably have to be paid and you may be required to upgrade the level of security.

When arranging cover, there are a few points to bear in mind. For example, if you hire your caravan to others or if it is used as a permanent dwelling, you may need a specialist contract.

Those towing their caravan should also check the cover provided by their motor policy to see that protection is provided in case of an accident. It is essential to have at least third-party cover so that, if you are involved in an accident in which people are hurt, you are covered for any claims made against you. Also look out for any geographical restrictions on cover. Most policies will indemnify you against loss within Continental Europe for up to 60 or perhaps 90 days a year. If you are going further afield or are touring for longer, you may once again need a special policy.

In all instances, it is as well to check with your insurance company or broker. This cover is sold by specialist companies who will be able to advise on the best product for your circumstances.

Tim MacPherson's caravan is sited on an estate in West Lothian. Despite the presence of security patrols, it was broken into, with the thieves stealing over £500 worth of goods and causing £1,200 of damage.

Tim says he is glad he resisted the temptation to save money by insuring his caravan only for the holiday season: He says: "It just isn't worth the risk of not insuring the van for the whole year round. You are just as likely to need protection outside the holiday period as within it."

Motorcycles

Motorcyclists have a poor image. No matter that many are respectable professionals (of both sexes) who indulge their passion for speed on expensive machines, they are seen, not least by the insurance industry, as bad boys. And this is reflected in the premiums charged.

There is, of course, plenty of justification for insurers to be wary of covering motorbikes. The statistics suggest that you are six times more likely to be killed or injured while riding, than driving in a car. And thieves love motorbikes – they are relatively easy to steal and there is always a ready market for powerful machines.

As with mainstream motor insurance, younger people pay the highest premiums for motorcycle cover. But attitudes are changing, albeit slowly. Back in the early 1990s, Norwich Union, a principal insurer in this market, stopped offering theft cover to anyone under 28. Improvements in security devices later persuaded the company to reintroduce theft cover for all ages with its Premier Bike policy.

You can also get a no-claims bonus on your motorcycle policy, although the maximum is likely to be 30% or 40% – you can almost double that if you are claim-free for long enough with your car policy. Further discounts might be forthcoming if the bike is garaged overnight and if an approved immobiliser is used.

Some policies still target the mature market, perhaps specifying those aged over 30. Bikes above a certain engine size are excluded from some policies (400cc is a typical cut-off point) while others turn away those doing more than, say, 5,000 miles a year.

The cost of cover, as might be expected, is also determined by where the policyholder lives. In some cases, those living in inner city and urban districts will find they can get cover only if the bike is garaged overnight. In the other areas, cover is available but the premium increases by, say, 10% if the bike is kept outdoors.

Motorbike policies also include the excess (or deductible) that is found in other types of insurance – this is the amount you pay towards the cost of any claim you make. The compulsory excess will be £50 or £100, depending on the policy, but you can volunteer to pay more to secure a lower premium. For example, a £250 voluntary excess might trim the cost by 7%, while a £1,500 excess could save as much as 20%.

Cover is also available to those with vintage machines, which must usually be over 15 or 20 years old to qualify. Riders will be expected to insure on an 'agreed value' basis, which means the owner and the underwriter will decide between them how much the motorcycle is worth and how much it might cost to repair. The Vintage Motor Cycle Club will often assist by providing independent verification. The club also offers its own policy to members.

The terms of a vintage motorcycle policy will restrict the annual mileage to perhaps 3,000 or 5,000 and require the bike to be kept in a garage or protected by certain other security measures. If the bike is hired out for special occasions, the insurer will expect to be told and will adjust the premiums accordingly.

Travel insurance

There has been little short of a revolution in the travel insurance market in recent years. Previously, most people bought cover for a specific journey at the same time as they arranged the trip itself – and travel agents made good money from the commissions generated by these sales.

Indeed, as the number of people taking holidays overseas mushroomed, some operators were thought to be using the profits they made as insurance intermediaries to subsidise the package deals they offered. The government has now decided travel agents can no longer force holidaymakers to take out their insurance policy in order to qualify for a special deal on the holiday itself.

Increasingly, travellers are being offered annual, multi-trip policies which offer protection for the whole family for all journeys undertaken during a 12-month period. The majority of these new-style plans are sold direct by insurers and brokers through the travel pages of national newspapers and on the internet.

Annual policies have a distinct edge on single-trip deals because they offer more protection for less money. When buying an annual deal, you choose whether you want European or worldwide cover and state the number of people to go on the policy: they are available in single, two-person or family variations.

The only real restrictions are that any single journey might be limited to, say, 31, 60 or 90 days and certain hazardous activities, such as winter sports, might be excluded or require the payment of an additional premium. Business trips are included in most cases, although you may need a special policy if you take important documents or valuable samples with you.

Prices for an annual travel policy begin at around £45 to £60 for individuals, with family policies costing up to around £130. A family buying single-trip insurance from a travel agent might face a premium well in excess of £200.

As with most types of insurance, the least expensive policy will not necessarily be the right one for you. For instance, with some of the cheapest annual policies, you can get a rock-bottom price by not including your luggage – but only if your belongings are covered worldwide under your house contents policy.

At the other end of the scale, deluxe contracts will provide additional benefits, such as a home-watch service while you are away – this is where someone is employed to keep an eye on your property to deter burglars.

Legal expenses insurance

Most people acquire legal expenses insurance as an add-on to another policy such as motor or household. It is also available as a stand-alone product but it has never sold in meaningful numbers in the UK. (Elsewhere in Europe, particularly in Germany, it is extremely popular.)

The policy pays any legal costs you incur for civil actions. If it is included with your motor insurance (or if you pay a few pounds extra for it), it will be known as uninsured loss recovery (ULR). You would use it, for example, to prove an accident wasn't your fault and that you should be reimbursed for out-of-pocket expenses incurred as a result, such as the cost of a hire car.

With a household policy, you might be able to claim if you get involved in a legal dispute with a neighbour or there is some disagreement over your status as owner of the property, or the boundaries of the property itself. You might also use the cover if you were in a dispute, either with a retailer or a manufacturer, over the purchase of goods or services.

Stand-alone legal expenses cover caters for all the problems in motorists' and householders' versions as well as the legal costs associated with:

◆ Claims against other people for personal injury damages;
◆ Disputes with your employer over your contract of employment;
◆ Disputes with the Inland Revenue over personal taxation assessments;
◆ Disputes over inheritance.

Free legal advice will probably be included with all types of legal expenses insurance. This can be valuable in helping you decide if you have a valid case.

All policies will have a limit – usually £50,000 – for each claim. There will also be an aggregate limit for the amount that may be spent on all claims in any one year. The payment will cover solicitor's fees and expenses, barristers and expert witnesses, court costs and your opponent's costs if these are awarded against you.

Pet insurance

Advances in veterinary techniques have helped domesticated animals to live happier, healthier, longer lives. But vets' bills can be extraordinarily steep. Pet insurance offers a solution to this. It pays medical fees and other occasional expenses associated with owning a pet. Not surprisingly, vets are keen on pet insurance because it allows them to treat the animal according to its needs rather than according to the pocket of the owner. Most vets' surgeries will have literature on insurance.

Note that insurance is for illness and injury. Policies do not cover the cost of vaccinations or of neutering or spaying.

Premiums range from £60 to £80 a year for a cat and £100 to £120 for a dog, according to the breed. In both cases, the animal will have to be within a certain age range – such as over ten weeks and under ten years. Cover for other animals, such as rodents, birds and fish is harder to find – unless you have an expensive ornamental breed such as Koi carp, which can cost thousands of pounds. Here, you will be buying theft cover rather than anticipating vets' bills.

Horses and ponies need a special equine policy, where the cost is determined by the value of the animal. This might also cover tack and other equipment. It should certainly provide liability cover in case you cause an accident on the road or otherwise injure someone who subsequently makes a claim for damages.

In addition to veterinary fees, pet insurance will pay for:

◆ **Third-party liability** This covers you if your pet causes an accident that results in injury or damage and you are found to be legally liable.
◆ **Death** Policies will usually pay a death benefit up to the purchase price of the animal if it dies from an illness or accident. Death from old age would not trigger a payment.
◆ **Boarding fees** If you have to go into hospital, your policy might pay for accommodation for your animal while you are away. If you would rather leave

the pet with a friend, it might pay a certain amount for each night you are indisposed.

◆ **Advertising and reward** If your animal is lost or stolen, your policy should contribute towards the cost of advertising for its return in the local newspaper and for the payment of an appropriate reward to the finder. If you have a horse or a pony, the policy may cover the costs of fetching it home.

◆ **Loss by theft or straying** If the animal is lost, the policy will refund the purchase price. Different policies require different amounts of time to elapse before the animal is certified as lost. If a claim is paid and the animal is subsequently discovered, you may be required to pay the money back.

◆ **Holiday cancellation** If you are forced to cancel your holiday because your pet needs urgent treatment, the pet policy would reimburse the cost of the holiday. This cover would not be available from a travel insurance policy.

◆ **Accidental damage** This covers any damage caused by your pet, either to your own property or someone else's. This is important if your house contents policy does not offer such protection.

Boat insurance

If you take a boat onto a river or canal, you are obliged to have liability insurance so that, if you cause an accident, you will be able to meet any damage claims made against you.

In addition to this mandatory cover, you can buy insurance to protect your craft and its contents from damage and theft. Modern vessels are equipped with costly navigational systems, which are highly portable and, therefore, attractive to thieves. It is relatively easy for a thief to break into a typical boat, unless you take additional precautions such as fitting extra locks and an alarm, or removing gear when the boat is left unattended for any length of time.

Insurance companies usually require policyholders to note the serial numbers of valuable items to help their recovery if they are stolen. Premium discounts may be available if security measures are implemented. Small boats may have to be kept in a locked building, while if a larger vessel is attached to a trailer this should be fitted with wheel clamps.

The cost of insurance depends on the type of craft and its value, but a rough rule of thumb is that the annual premium will be around 1% of the value. A £75,000 cruiser would attract a premium of between £700 and £800, while a £30,000 Westerley sailing yacht would be nearer to £300. A powerful speedboat worth £12,000, however, would cost around £500 to insure because of the higher potential risks.

If you sail out of UK territorial waters, check the scope of your cover. Some policies only provide protection in certain areas and then only for a certain number of days a year.

Miscellaneous insurances

There are a wide range of policies that you can take to cover specific events or eventualities. The best place to find out more about these is through an insurance broker, who will have contacts with the specialist insurance companies offering this sort of protection.

Special events

Organisers of outdoor events who want to protect themselves against the possibility of a downpour keeping the crowds away and reducing their takings or even resulting in cancellation can buy contingency cover. The cost varies according to where the event is taking place, the season and the amount of money involved.

This type of cover provides other sorts of protection for those organising events such as fetes, sports days and outdoor concerts. For example, the organiser has certain liabilities with regard to the safety and security of those who pay to attend. The policy will cover you for any claims for damage, injury or death and pay your associated legal costs.

Special events insurance can also protect you against the normal risks of damage to your equipment and theft of any takings, both at the show and (since many events of this type are held at the weekend) until the next banking day.

Weddings

If you are organising a wedding, you can take out insurance to cover a number of risks, such as weather damage to a marquee, double booking of a reception venue or the theft or loss of presents. A top-of-the-range home contents policy might provide protection for wedding gifts kept at the parents' house prior to the event.

Twins

Those trying for a baby can insure against the risk of a multiple birth. The idea is to provide funds to meet the additional costs if more that one child is born.

Funeral plans

Funerals typically cost over £1,200, so it is easy to see why many people want to plan for the event. With a funeral plan, you either lodge a lump sum with an insurance company or make monthly payments for the rest of your life. You stipulate the sort of funeral you want and at what cost, and the payments are worked out for you.

There are a number of points to watch out for with these plans: does the policy guarantee to pay all the costs associated with burial? Will the cover be valid if you move and die in a different area of the country? Does the policy leave your family with a choice of undertaker or oblige them to use a certain firm?

Also, it is important to ensure that your heirs and the executors of your estate are aware of any arrangements you make.

Where to buy insurance

As a nation, we spend over £25bn a year on protecting ourselves and our belongings. That is a lot of money, which is why insurance companies advertise so heavily on television and in the press and spend so much sponsoring sporting events, from the FA Cup (Axa) to cricket matches (Cornhill, NatWest, CGNU), tennis (Guardian) and athletics (Prudential). This intense competition helps to keep premiums in check, but it also means a bewildering range of options when it comes to identifying the right policy at the right price.

With the internet playing an ever-larger part in our lives, more companies will attempt to sell motor, household and travel insurance over the world wide web.

Also, it would be wrong to think of insurance companies and brokers as being the only institutions selling insurance. You can buy it in the bank or building society. Most supermarkets offer policies, as do utility companies such as British Gas. Clubs and associations often act as agents, selling policies to their members.

There is, however, an important distinction between companies which recommend their own products and those offering a choice. As with any service, independent advice from a skilled and experienced professional broker can be valuable in identifying the right way to proceed. But such advice has to be paid for – in the case of insurance, through a commission.

That is not to say brokers are always more expensive. Companies that don't use brokers still have to pay for advertisements and employ staff to answer the telephones. The onus is on you, the buyer, to check out as many suppliers as you can to find the best deal. Yellow Pages or a similar directory will contain details of companies and various intermediaries in your area. The British Insurance Brokers Association (020 7623 9043) will provide a list of local brokers.

Brokers consult a range of companies but by no means all – you will have to research those that do not use brokers yourself. Some companies only sell through brokers, so you can find out what they have to offer only by asking one.

When it comes to buying insurance, there has never been so much choice. You can buy over the telephone, by clipping a coupon, by visiting a broker's office, by surfing the internet or when you buy your groceries. The important thing is to decide what you want and then shop around for the best value for your money.

The golden rule is not to spend more than you have to, but don't spend less than you need either.

6

Buying your Home

Everyone wants to own their own home – and most of us end up achieving that ambition, although there is usually a good 20 or 25 years' worth of hard graft involved in paying off the mortgage first.

Starting out on the homebuying process can be a daunting prospect: it is said that buying a house is the third most stressful event after a death in the family and getting divorced. First, there are the actual mechanics of making the purchase, which can take weeks or even months. Second, there is the decision on how to pay for it. With hundreds of different mortgage deals available at any one time, it is very hard to feel certain you have made the best choice.

But this does not – and, indeed, should not – put potential buyers off. In the long run, buying a home pays off handsomely for most people, and not just in financial terms. Finding a place you are happy to live in and having the security of knowing that you cannot be thrown out by a landlord count for a great deal.

House prices

Until a decade ago, it seemed as if house prices only ever moved in one direction: upwards. The housing boom and then bust of the late 1980s and early 1990s destroyed that comfortable certainty once and for all. Now we know that house prices can fall, sometimes; but it is still true to say that the long-term trend is inexorably upwards. Ultimately, the level of prices is governed by people's ability to pay, and as long as average earnings keep rising, so will house prices.

Mortgage availability

Not that long ago, borrowers used to go to the building societies cap in hand, grateful to be offered any sort of mortgage, and meekly accepting queues and rationing. Those days are gone and attitudes have changed. Mortgage lenders need borrowers at least as much as borrowers need them, so you should not feel you must accept the first offer that comes along. You can afford to pick and choose, and should not be reluctant to question anything that seems unsatisfactory or unclear.

How much can you borrow?

The most important question, at least for many first-time buyers, is how much money they can borrow. Lenders have two separate criteria they work to before deciding how much to lend. The first is based on a multiple of the borrower's income, the second on the value of the property.

Income

If you are buying on your own, most lenders will offer a loan of up to 3.25 times your annual income.

If you are buying as a couple, there is usually a choice, and you can pick the one which works out best for your circumstances:

◆ 3.25 times the first income plus once the second, or
◆ 2.5 times joint income.

The first formula gives the highest figure when one partner's income is much greater than the other's, while the second comes out on top if you earn similar amounts.

John Martin earns £40,000 a year and Jane Green earns £10,000. Using the 3.25 plus one formula gives a maximum loan of £140,000. Using the 2.5 times joint income formula gives a maximum loan of £125,000.

Bob and Linda Moore both earn £25,000 a year. Using the 3.25 plus one formula gives a maximum loan of £106,250. Using the 2.5 times joint income formula gives a maximum loan of £125,000.

The 'first income' is always the highest, irrespective of whether it is earned by the man or the woman.

These income multiples are the typical ones operated by most high street banks and building societies, but it may be possible to find lenders that will stretch them a bit more, especially for people who can demonstrate they are good credit risks. You may be able to get as much as four times the first income plus once the second, or 2.75 times joint incomes. If you need to borrow this much, it is probably best to consult a mortgage broker.

Most lenders will also credit score their applicants, which means taking a closer look at their income and outgoings. Borrowers who have other debts could find they are allowed to borrow less than the maximum.

Property value

However much a lender is prepared to lend on the basis of income, it will still not offer more than a certain percentage of the property's value. The highest is generally 95% of the lender's valuation, although some special mortgage deals stipulate a maximum loan of less, perhaps 80% of the value.

Except for a very few special deals, no-one will lend more than 100%, and where borrowing is above 75% or 80% of the value, borrowers usually have to pay an extra fee – see the section below on mortgage indemnity guarantees.

How much will it cost?

The table on the next page shows the monthly cost of a £100,000 mortgage at various interest rates. The first section shows the monthly cost of a repayment mortgage over 25 years – the typical length of time that a mortgage is set up for. You can choose to borrow over a shorter or a longer term if you wish, though many lenders prefer to see the mortgage paid off by normal retirement age. The shorter the term, the higher the cost – the next chapter gives details.

Note that if you are buying a leasehold flat, the lender may stipulate there should be at least 25 years left on the lease after the end of the mortgage term, so with shorter-term leases this may affect the length of mortgage it is prepared to grant. However, now that leaseholders have the right to buy their freehold or extend their lease, this may be less of a stumbling block than it used to be.

The second section shows the monthly cost of an interest-only mortgage, where no capital is paid off. Loans of this sort are usually taken out in conjunction with a savings plan – either an endowment policy or an Individual Savings Account (Isa) – so remember this section does not represent the whole of your monthly outgoings.

The next chapter goes into the pros and cons of the different ways of repaying your mortgage.

Until April 2000, borrowers got some tax relief on their mortgage interest, but that has now been abolished.

At the time of writing, the standard variable mortgage rate was between 7% and 7.74% (although there are always plenty of special deals available for new borrowers which undercut the standard rate). However, interest rates do vary over time, depending on bank base rates, so it is important to be aware of how the monthly cost might change.

The monthly cost of a £100,000 mortgage

A repayment mortgage over 25 years

Interest rate	Monthly cost
5%	£591.27
6%	£651.89
7%	£715.09
8%	£780.66
9%	£848.39
10%	£918.07

An interest-only mortgage

5%	£416.67
6%	£500.00
7%	£583.34
8%	£666.67
9%	£750.00
10%	£833.33

Source: Halifax

Mortgages for the self-employed

The general rule is that self-employed people must produce three years' audited accounts as proof of income. However, in certain circumstances this may be reduced to one or two years, if it is accompanied by a report from your accountant.

Some lenders offer 'self-certified' mortgages to people who cannot or do not wish to produce proof of their income. These are generally at a higher interest rate than the standard offers. However, it may be worth consulting a mortgage broker in such circumstances as they can often arrange better deals. The best special offers are likely to be available to those who can provide a deposit of 25% or more of the purchase price.

Impaired credit mortgages

There are now a number of lenders which specialise in lending to people with bad credit records, including those who have county court judgments against them. Interest rates are usually significantly higher than on the standard deals.

These loans can generally only be arranged via a mortgage broker. It can be worth shopping around among brokers to see if you would, in fact, be eligible for a loan from a mainstream lender – it will depend very much on individual circumstances. If you are obliged to use one of the specialist lenders, check how easy it would be to remortgage at a better rate in due course, once you have established a good payment record. Some arrangements make it very expensive for borrowers to change.

Mortgage indemnity guarantees

Most lenders charge an extra fee for lending above 90% of their valuation of the property and a few charge for lending more than 75% to 80%. The traditional name for this charge is a mortgage indemnity guarantee, but it goes under a number of different names, such as a higher loan to value fee or additional mortgage security fee. There are two ways it may be imposed. Some lenders require a one-off payment, others load the mortgage interest rate.

The key point to be aware of is that where payment is made by a lump sum, the cost can rise steeply according to the percentage borrowed. Lenders can charge one rate for borrowings of 90% to 94.9% and a higher rate for loans of 95% plus.

Taking typical current rates, the cost of borrowing £94,000 for a £100,000 property works out at £1,280. Borrowing £95,000, however, would involve a fee of £2,400. In other words, it costs £1,120 to borrow that extra £1,000. Wherever possible, therefore, borrowers should avoid borrowing just above one of the stages at which the fee rises.

If the money cannot be saved, or perhaps borrowed privately from relations, it may be worth splitting the mortgage and seeking a smaller top-up loan elsewhere. A good mortgage broker should be able to advise. In the last resort, it can actually work out cheaper to borrow the excess by credit card.

Buying in England and Wales

The government is proposing to make radical changes to the way houses are bought and sold in England and Wales by introducing 'seller's packs'. The new system is designed to simplify and speed up the process. One of its main aims is to discourage the practice of gazumping, whereby a seller accepts an offer from one buyer, only to renege on it later to accept a higher offer from someone else. This is not illegal, but it can cause considerable heartache as well as expense for the original buyer, who may have paid legal and survey fees. These proposals require new legislation and are likely to come into force in 2003.

The current system involves a number of distinct stages and, on average, takes ten to 12 weeks, even if there are no chains involved.

Making an offer

Offers made on property in England and Wales are always subject to contract and valuation or survey. If there is negotiation to be done on the price, some buyers are happy to do this directly with the seller, others prefer to conduct such negotiations through the estate agent.

It is common to make an initial offer somewhat lower than the asking price and, if need be, negotiate upwards from there – but this depends on circumstances. When property markets are booming, it may even be necessary to offer more than the asking price, especially if you are in competition with other potential buyers.

It is important to remember that the estate agent acts for the seller, not the buyer, so you must use your own judgment rather than rely on the agent's advice.

This initial offer is not binding on either party. It is common for agents to ask for a small deposit, perhaps £100, at this stage, as a sign that you are serious.

The valuation or survey

The lender must then carry out its own valuation or survey before making a formal mortgage offer. It is not uncommon for the valuation to be at a lower price than the one you have agreed to pay. In this case, you can either try to renegotiate a lower price with the seller, or resign yourself to borrowing a higher percentage of the value than you had originally planned.

The legal process

Once the formal offer of a mortgage is secured, you should instruct your solicitor to proceed with the purchase. This may take several weeks. The solicitor must, among other things, check that the buyer has proper title to the property, and that there are no local developments planned which will affect the house or its value in the future.

Exchange of contracts

This takes place once the legal preliminaries are completed and it is only at this stage that the contract becomes binding on both parties. A substantial deposit is paid – typically 10%, but it can be lower by negotiation – and this money is forfeited if the buyer then fails to complete. The seller is also entitled to sue the buyer for any other costs.

On exchange, the risk regarding the property passes to the buyer, who must make sure it is properly insured (this is generally carried out by the solicitor).

Completion

Completion generally takes place between one week and one month after the exchange of contracts. The rest of the money is handed over, the seller moves out and the buyer moves in.

The government's proposals

Under the government's proposals, before putting a home up for sale, a seller will be required by law to put together a seller's pack of standard information for prospective buyers. This is likely to include:
◆ Title documents;
◆ Replies to standard preliminary enquiries made on behalf of buyers by their solicitors;
◆ Copies of any planning, listed building and building regulation consents and approvals relating to work done on the property;
◆ A draft contract;
◆ Replies to local authority searches;
◆ A house condition report based on a professional survey of the property;
◆ A copy of the lease and ancillary documents where the property is leasehold.
At the same time, buyers will be encouraged to obtain a mortgage offer in principle before making an offer, and local authorities and others involved in the process, such as solicitors, lenders and surveyors, will be encouraged to provide a faster service.

Buying in Scotland

The same stages have to be worked through in Scotland as in England and Wales, but the key difference is that once an offer is made and accepted, both parties are committed.

Initially, a buyer will have his interest in the property 'noted' by the seller's solicitor. He must then arrange a valuation or survey, plus mortgage finance, before making a formal offer. Following acceptance, his solicitor then carries out the appropriate legal work.

Buyers must pay for a survey and preliminary legal work before knowing if their offer will be accepted – or take the risk of committing themselves to purchase before they know the results of a survey.

Sellers in Scotland will generally stipulate a minimum or 'upset' price, and invite bids above that figure, in contrast to the practice in England where sellers invite offers and may agree to one below their asking price. Often a closing date is set, on which the seller will decide whether to accept one of the bids.

There are some firms of estate agents in Scotland, but much of the residential property market is handled through property centres run by solicitors.

While there are no firm proposals to change the house-buying process in Scotland, it is being suggested that it may in due course follow the new system outlined for England and Wales.

The costs of buying and selling

One effect of the new proposals may be to shift some of the costs of the transaction, such as a survey fee, from the buyer to seller. At present, however, the buyer pays most of the expense, except for the estate agent's fee.

Some lenders will meet some of these costs in conjunction with a special mortgage deal. Whether this will be worth accepting will depend on whether you could have got a better deal elsewhere without the free offers.

The costs of buying

The main costs of buying a property are:
◆ Legal fees;
◆ Land registry charges;
◆ Stamp duty;
◆ Valuation or survey;
◆ Removals;
◆ Fees in connection with the mortgage – for example, an application fee;
◆ Insurance costs (home and contents).

These might add up to between £1,500 and £2,000 for a property costing up to £100,000.

Legal fees

Solicitor's fees for buying a home are likely to be in the region of £250 to £500, depending partly on the cost of the property, as well as on whether any complications emerge during the transaction.

Buying a leasehold flat may be relatively more expensive than buying a freehold house, as the lease needs to be checked. Borrowers must also pay the lender's legal costs, but these may well be included in the overall total. You may be able to save money by shopping around, asking different legal firms for quotations.

Land registry charges

These are payable at the same time as the solicitor's fees. Most property in England and Wales is already registered, and the fees for transferring the title are on a sliding scale depending on the property value.

For example, the charges are £40 for a £40,000 property, £100 for £70,000 to £100,000 properties, £200 for £100,000 to £200,000 properties, and £300 for those costing between £200,000 and £500,000.

Scotland has a separate land registry system.

Stamp duty

Stamp duty is payable on all properties costing more than £60,000, as follows:

Property price	Stamp duty rate
£60,000 to £250,000	1%
£250,000 to £500,000	3%
£500,000-plus	4%

Valuation and survey

All lenders insist that a basic property valuation is carried out before they make a formal mortgage offer, and the borrower pays for it. Many offer three types of valuation or survey: the basic valuation, whose purpose is simply to establish a current market value for the property; a homebuyer's report, which includes a basic structural survey; and a full survey, which includes a valuation but will also go into full detail on the structural condition of the property.

Experts recommend buyers choose the homebuyer's report or a full survey, because it may reveal problems they would otherwise miss. The new system proposed for England and Wales may make it unnecessary for buyers to commission a full survey, as they may be happy to rely on the one in the seller's information pack, but it will still be necessary to pay for the lender's valuation. The cost of these reports varies according to the property purchase price.

Typical survey fees

Property price	Valuation	Homebuyer's report
£50,000	£160	£300
£100,000	£195	£375
£150,000	£225	£405
£200,000	£255	£455
£250,000	£285	£505
£300,000	£315	£555
£350,000	£345	£605
£400,000	£375	£655

The costs of a full survey are likely to be above those for a homebuyer's report but are usually by negotiation.
Source: Halifax

The costs of selling

If you are selling as well as buying, you must add an estate agent's fee to the total, unless you decide to sell privately. Most act on an agency basis, which means they collect their commission only if you end up selling the house through them. Their fees for a sole agency are likely to be between 2% and 3% of the purchase price for properties in London and the South-east of England and perhaps a little less – say 1.5% to 2.5% – elsewhere. If you instruct more than one agent, the rate is likely to be 0.5% higher.

Make sure you read the small print of the contract though, as some agents now work on a 'sole selling rights' basis. This means they are legally entitled to their fee even if you go on to sell privately, rather than to a buyer introduced by them.

Agents may also reserve the right to charge a fee so long as they introduce you to a buyer who is willing and able to proceed with the purchase at a price acceptable to you – even if you don't go ahead with the sale. This could happen if, for instance, you withdraw the house from the market because your own purchase has fallen through.

If these terms are clearly spelled out in the contract, you have no choice but to abide by them – so look before you leap.

Insurance and your home

You are obliged to buy buildings insurance when you take out a mortgage. It would be sensible to take out insurance for the contents as well and, at the same time, to get life insurance to cover the mortgage debt in case you die within the term. If you decide to take out an endowment mortgage (see Chapter 7) such insurance is automatically built in, but it is not with other types of mortgage.

Buildings insurance

Many mortgage lenders encourage borrowers to take out buildings insurance through their own insurance department or subsidiary. While they do not usually insist on this, they will sometimes charge a fee of, typically, £25 or £30 if you elect to buy a policy from a different company.

Despite this fee, it may well be worth shopping around. Insurance costs vary according to the rebuilding cost of the property and also the area in which it is situated; areas prone to subsidence or flooding attract much higher premium rates. Insurance companies set their rates according to their claims experience in different areas, so it can be beneficial to get quotations from a number – it is always possible one has a better claims experience than another.

If you are shopping around, points to watch out for include:

◆ Does the policy cover the cost of alternative accommodation if the house is destroyed?

◆ To what extent does it cover fences, driveways and garden sheds?

◆ What excess (the amount a policyholder must meet from his own pocket) is charged in the event of claims for subsidence?

Specialist buildings insurance may be required for unusual properties such as thatched cottages or listed buildings and it may save money to use an insurance broker to arrange it.

Typical annual premiums for mainstream property range from £14 to £42 per £10,000 of rebuilding cost. Note that the rebuilding cost (which excludes the value of the land) may be higher or lower than the price you have agreed to pay.

If you are buying a flat, the buildings insurance is likely to be arranged by the managing agent for the whole block.

Contents insurance

It is not obligatory to buy contents insurance, although many lenders will encourage you to take a combined contents and buildings policy. You may do better by buying separate policies. Premiums vary according to the area you live in, but in this instance, the biggest factor is the likelihood of burglary. The range could be anything from about £3.50 to £23.50 per £1,000 insured.

Life insurance

Life cover is especially important if you have dependants who would find it impossible to keep up the mortgage payments if you died. However, you do have a choice: most lenders do not insist it is taken out. The cheapest form is a mortgage protection policy, also known as decreasing term insurance. This will pay out the amount outstanding on the mortgage if you die within the term. Because capital is being paid back over the term, the amount of cover required declines over the years.

Alternatively, with level term insurance the same sum insured will be paid out on death within the term. This type of policy is appropriate for borrowers taking out an interest-only loan, or one linked to a savings plan such as an Individual Savings Account (Isa).

The cost varies principally according to the term and the age of the borrower. Many mortgage lenders offer their own life insurance policy, but you may be able to save money by going elsewhere.

Mortgage payment protection insurance

Most lenders will offer a special insurance policy which covers your mortgage payments if you become unable to work because of an accident, illness or being made unemployed. The policy will usually pay out for up to 12 months (no longer), starting after 30, 60 or 90 days – there is normally a choice over the length of this deferred period; the longer the delay, the lower the premiums.

It is possible to buy unemployment cover only. Premiums are likely to be around £2.50 to £3 a month for every £100 of monthly mortgage payment for this type of cover alone, and around £5 to £7.50 for a combined accident, sickness and unemployment policy.

If you are self-employed, think carefully before taking out a combined policy. The unemployment part will be of little use as you would have to go bust or cease trading altogether before it kicked in. It is possible to buy a policy covering just accidents and sickness, for a similar cost to those offering just unemployment cover, say around £3 per £100 per month. This might be worth considering, especially if you are in the sort of occupation that carries higher than average risks of accident or sickness. This is because the premiums on these policies are not individually costed, so high-risk people effectively get a bargain, being subsidised by those who are lower risk.

In general though, the self-employed need a lot more insurance than these policies offer if they are to protect themselves adequately, in which case, proper permanent health insurance (PHI) is the best bet.

You can buy mortgage payment protection insurance either through your own lender or separately from an insurance company and it may well pay to shop around for the best rates and terms.

The government is keen to encourage borrowers to take out such insurance, mainly so they won't then become a burden on the state. It is worth bearing in mind that the state does not pay any mortgage interest to borrowers for the first nine months after they become unemployed, and any help thereafter is strictly means tested – if you have savings of more than £3,000, the benefit is cut, and with savings of £8,000 or more, you are disqualified altogether. Even if you don't have any savings, you may well still be disqualified if you have a joint mortgage and your partner is earning. If, despite all these caveats, you do qualify for full benefits, they are limited to the interest on a loan of up to £100,000.

The extent of mortgage protection cover varies considerably, so make sure you read the small print carefully before taking out a policy.

See Chapters 4 and 5 for more information on all types of insurance.

Estate agents

Estate agents act as agent for the seller, but they also have some legal duties towards buyers. They should treat all prospective buyers equally, must not invent other interested parties to encourage buyers to make an offer, and must describe the property for sale accurately. However, they do not have to volunteer information to buyers that might be detrimental to the seller.

Estate agents are likely to belong to one of two professional bodies: the Royal Institute of Chartered Surveyors or the National Association of Estate Agents. Both have codes of conduct.

Many also belong to the Ombudsman for Estate Agents scheme, which also has a code of conduct and provides an independent, free service for dealing with disputes. Complaints must be made within 12 months. See Appendix 2 for contact details.

Buying through the internet

The internet is beginning to play a part in homebuying and selling. There are a clutch of search sites that pool properties for sale from various estate agents, allowing you to 'view' them without leaving home. This is especially useful for preliminary research if you are planning to move a long distance. There are also sales sites which allow people to buy and sell directly, bypassing any estate agent, and even one for people wanting to swap their homes. In addition there are specialist sites detailing forthcoming auctions or repossessed properties for sale.

The process is still in its early days – probably only a fifth of properties for sale at present are listed on the net – and experts predict the number of websites will contract over the next year or two as the industry consolidates. Appendix 2 lists useful websites active at the time of writing.

Buying at auction

Occasionally property is sold by auction rather than through estate agents, solicitors or privately. The Royal Institute of Chartered Surveyors can provide a list of property auctioneers, together with an explanatory leaflet on the subject. The drawback is that successful bidders are obliged to buy the property and must generally put up a 10% deposit on the day of the auction, with the balance within 28 days.

This means that usual preliminaries – such as organising mortgage finance, carrying out legal work and having a survey done – have to be completed before the bidding starts, and you may not, of course, be successful. Experts recommend buyers interested in property auctions should attend a few as observers before bidding.

Home improvements

It is a fact of life that most home improvements will not recoup their cost in terms of adding value to the property. The best 'investment' in property is routine maintenance work, keeping it in good general condition.

As regards specific improvements, the most likely to recover its full cost is the installation of central heating. A new kitchen or bathroom may also pay for itself, as long as the cost is not disproportionate to the value of the property. For example, you are unlikely to get your money back if you put in a very expensive, top-of-the-range kitchen in a modest terraced house.

Adding a garage can certainly add value, but it depends very much on location.

For many properties in the centre of cities, for example, garages are like gold dust – and worth a small fortune – but at the same time impossible to build because of the lack of space.

Extensions and loft conversions are, perhaps surprisingly, less popular – especially loft conversions – and if they are not carried out properly they can actually decrease the property's value. New windows, if they are not in keeping with the style of the house, can have the same effect. Improving home security may add to peace of mind and cut insurance premiums, but the cost is unlikely to be directly recouped in terms of a higher selling price.

Paying for home improvements

If the cost is substantial, the simplest and cheapest way of covering it is to add to the mortgage, assuming you have sufficient equity in the property to allow this. A more expensive alternative is to use a personal loan, which is generally repayable over a shorter time span, perhaps five years. Chapter 3 gives more information on short-term borrowing.

If you want to add to the mortgage this may well involve paying for a new valuation, and it may be worth considering remortgaging the whole loan as you may be able to pick up a cheaper deal elsewhere. Borrowers with flexible mortgages (see Chapter 7) are better placed in that they can usually arrange the extra finance immediately without extra cost.

Buying the freehold or extending the lease

Leaseholders now have certain rights to buy the freehold of their property in conjunction with others in the same building, or to extend their lease. The legislation current at the time of writing is the Leasehold Reform, Housing and Urban Development Act of 1993, but a new bill, the Commonhold and Leasehold Reform Bill, should be working its way through parliament in the spring of 2001.

The new bill will introduce into England and Wales a type of property ownership known as 'commonhold' (already used in Australia and the US). This means the block is owned, and managed, collectively, by all the individual flat owners. This form of ownership may be chosen by developers selling newly built blocks of flats (though it seems it won't be obligatory). Meanwhile, existing leaseholders deciding to buy the freehold will be able to convert to commonhold ownership for the future.

There are a couple of other options for leaseholders. Both are available under the 1993 legislation, but should become easier under the new rules.

Buying the freehold

◆ Leaseholders can join forces to buy the freehold. They have the right to do so, currently, if two-thirds agree. Of those two-thirds, at least half must have lived in the flat as their main home for the last year (or at least three years in the previous ten). If the freeholder and leaseholders cannot agree a price, the leaseholders must apply to the Leasehold Valuation Tribunal. The freeholder can subsequently appeal to the Lands Tribunal, whose decision is normally binding on both parties.

◆ The new bill proposes three main changes to these rules. In future, only half the tenants will be required to buy the freehold rather than two-thirds (as long as they own at least half the flats in the block).

Second, there will no longer be a requirement that half the buyers have lived in the flats as their main home for the last year, or three in the previous ten.

Finally, a new rule will be introduced on the maximum price they can be asked to pay. Most of the cost of buying a freehold may be represented by the 'marriage value' – the amount ownership of the freehold adds to the value of the property. Under the new rules this value must be split equally between freeholder and leaseholders. Also, where leases have more than 80 years to run, buying the freehold will no longer create a marriage value.

Extending the lease

◆ If you cannot get sufficient numbers of leaseholders to agree to buy the freehold, the alternative is to extend your lease by up to 90 years. Currently, you are entitled to do this only if you have lived in the property full-time for the last year or during three years in the past ten.

◆ Under the new rules, you will be entitled to extend the lease if you have simply owned the property for two years.

The Leasehold Advisory Service, a private company but fully funded by the government, provides free advice on all aspects of buying a freehold or extending a lease. See Appendix 2 for contact details.

Buying property to let

Many investors are attracted by the idea of buying to let and using the rent to cover the mortgage interest. If all goes well, it can be a rewarding investment. The property continues to grow in value, while rents should rise at least in line with average earnings. Many individuals see it as a good alternative to a pension plan.

There is an Association of Residential Letting Agents (see Appendix 2) which can provide initial advice and put borrowers in touch with both professional letting agents and mortgage lenders which specialise in the market. Rates on buy-to-let mortgages tend to be slightly higher than those for owner occupiers. Lenders will usually take into account the expected rents when deciding how much to lend, rather than relying on your earned income. However, most insist on a minimum deposit of 20% to 25%, and it is worth noting that many loans include early redemption penalties. Buyers with plenty of equity in their own home can remortgage instead and so get a lower rate. They must let the Inland Revenue know the loan is to buy letting property so they can claim tax relief on the interest.

The risks of buying to let

While the attractions of the buy-to-let market may seem obvious, it also involves risks, as does any investment involving borrowing to invest. Experts suggest rents of between 130% and 150% of the mortgage interest must be achieved to cover your costs. These include general maintenance, insurance, and paying a letting agent to find tenants and collect the rent. A basic letting service is likely to cost 10% of the rent and a full management service, 15%.

Agents suggest buyers should work out their figures on the basis that the property may be vacant for one month in 12. They also warn that the criteria for choosing a good buy-to-let property can be very different from those you would use to buy your own home. Many suggest the ideal buy-to-let property is a recently built studio or one-bedroom flat rather than a typical family house.

While rising house prices benefit those already in the market, they are, of course, not such good news for those seeking to buy. In recent times, rents have not moved upwards at the same pace as house prices and buyers may find it hard to cover their mortgage interest and other expenses from the rent.

There has also been evidence recently in some areas of a surplus of rented properties, leading to falling rents and the greater likelihood that landlords will fail to find tenants.

You should, therefore, approach the idea with caution and be fully aware of the risks involved. It should always be treated as a medium to long-term investment and is not for those who may need to realise their capital in a hurry.

Tax and your home

Mortgage interest

Until April 2000, tax relief at the rate of 10% was automatically given on the interest relating to the first £30,000 borrowed to buy your main home. This has now been abolished. The effect of it was to keep mortgage payments slightly lower than they are now, but for many borrowers the difference will have amounted to no more than a few pounds a month.

Profits from your home

Your own home is exempt from capital gains tax (CGT), which means any profits realised when you sell it are tax free. In tax terms, it is only your 'principal private residence' which qualifies for relief from CGT, and you are only allowed one such residence at a time.

However, if there is an overlap between buying a new home and selling your old one, some relief is granted: you are allowed up to a year (two years in 'exceptional circumstances') to sell your old home. If the delay is longer the full profits on the old home become liable to CGT.

If you have two homes, you can elect which one is to be treated as your principal private residence. It does not have to be the one you live in most of the time. However, if you refuse to elect one, the tax inspector can decide for you, which he will do on the basis of which one you spend most time in. You can change the election at any time, but it cannot be backdated by more than two years.

Many people may own a main property and a country cottage, for example, which they use initially as a holiday home but then move into full-time after retirement. If they eventually sell the country cottage to move elsewhere, there will still be some CGT to pay on the sale, depending on the respective lengths of time it counted as a second home and a main home. For instance, if it functioned as a holiday home for ten years and then as a main home for ten years, half the profits are taxable.

If the property does not qualify for private residence relief, CGT of up to 40% may be payable on the profits, depending on how long you have owned it.

Working from home

If you use one part of your home – say, a single room – exclusively for work, there may be a CGT bill to pay on the appropriate proportion of profits. If you use one room in six, for example, one-sixth of the total profits may be liable – or the tax inspector may decide to calculate on the basis of total floor area. The tax will only be payable if you have been claiming a similar proportion of the home's costs as deductions against your earnings.

Many accountants suggest you should not make such claims. They may result in relatively small savings in income tax each year and the price of having to pay a significant CGT bill when you finally sell is too high.

Inland Revenue booklet CGT1, *Capital Gains Tax*, explains the main provisions of the tax and includes further details on tax and your home.

Income tax and rented property

Tax is payable on rent received after certain allowable deductions such as mortgage interest, general maintenance, on-going repairs, advertising for new tenants and agent's fees.

If you are renting out a room within your own house, gross rent of up to £4,250 a year may be enjoyed tax free, but you cannot claim any expenses against this. If you prefer, you can choose to pay tax on the net rental income after expenses such as those listed above.

Profits on sale are liable to CGT. Inland Revenue booklet IR150, *Taxation of Rents: A Guide to Property Income*, provides further details.

7

Choosing a Mortgage

When it comes to choosing a mortgage, there are two main factors to consider:
◆ whether to opt for a fixed, capped or variable interest rate, and
◆ what method to use to repay the loan.
The first and most important rule is don't accept the first mortgage offer that comes along. Nearly all mortgage lenders (who are mainly the high street banks and building societies, but there are other providers as well) have a 'standard variable rate' for their mortgages, but no new buyer should have to pay this initially: there will always be better deals around.

At the time of writing, the standard variable rate charged by most of the big mortgage lenders was between 7% and 7.74%. But the best buys available included fixed rates from 3.89%, discounted rates from 4.2% and capped rates from 5.69%. These offers do not apply for the lifetime of the loan, but only for limited periods – in these examples from two to three years – so buyers may well have to pay the standard variable rate at some point. However, no ordinary borrower need start out paying at that level.

The initial choice is whether to opt for a fixed, capped or variable rate. Each has its advantages.

Fixed and capped rates

Fixed rates

Fixed rates are just that: fixed for a specified period. This may be anything from one to five or even ten years. The most common terms available at present are two to five years. Occasionally lenders have offered rates fixed for a full 20 or 25 years, but they have been unpopular with buyers and are rare these days.

A fixed-rate loan has the advantage of certainty, and may prove an especially good buy if interest rates rise after you have taken one out. By the same token, it will be expensive if interest rates turn out to have been at a high and fall later. In that case, you will be stuck paying the higher rate at a time when variable rates are lower.

Given the uncertainty of interest rates, it is hard to predict whether you will win or lose by taking out a fixed-rate loan at any one time: the main reason for choosing one should be the certainty it provides.

Capped rates

Capped rates also provide the certainty that mortgage payments will not rise for the duration of the term, but they have the extra advantage that if interest rates fall below the initial capped level during that term, your monthly payment will also move down.

Capped rate offers are generally very close to fixed rates. If the general consensus is that the interest rate trend is downwards, capped rates may be slightly more expensive than fixed, but there is usually little in it. At the time of writing, a five-year capped rate was available at 6.22% compared to a five-year fixed rate of 5.99%. On a £100,000 loan, the difference in interest would be £230 a year.

Fixed and capped rates are always limited offers, and the most competitive may be available for only a short time. While some are available direct from lenders, others are made only in conjunction with a particular mortgage broker.

Redemption penalties

Nearly all fixed and capped offers carry early repayment penalties. Some last for the duration of the fix; others continue beyond the fixed-rate period, tying the borrower into paying the lender's standard variable rate for a certain period. If you decide to remortgage, or even if you only want to pay back some of the capital early, you must pay the penalty, and this could cost you several thousand pounds. The size of penalty varies considerably: it may be anything from three months' interest to 6% or more of the loan.

In general, the better the initial deal, the higher the penalties will be and the longer they will last.

Redemption penalties have been heavily criticised, especially those that extend beyond the fixed or capped period. It is, frankly, unrealistic to expect all penalties to be abolished. Without them lenders would find it hard to offer fixed rates at all: they generally hedge their exposure by buying in fixed-rate money themselves from the money market. If there were no redemption penalties, borrowers would desert the fixed rates as soon as they became uncompetitive, leaving the lenders still committed to paying fixed interest on the money they had raised.

Arrangement fees

Many fixed and capped deals charge a one-off arrangement fee, typically £300 to £400. This is usually payable only if the mortgage is completed. Sometimes, however, it is described as a 'booking fee' and must be paid even if the mortgage does not eventually go through.

Compulsory insurance

It used to be common for lenders to offer special deals which required the borrower to buy buildings or house contents insurance from them. This is tantamount to an extra annual cost, as such policies are usually considerably more expensive than the cheapest insurance available. Such deals are rare but beware – despite an earlier promise to ban them outright, the government has now decided not to, and they could make a comeback.

Variable rate mortgages

Variable rate loans divide into two main camps. Many high street lenders operate a 'standard variable rate' which they set with reference to the general level of interest rates but which has no explicit link to any external interest rate. The rate at any one time will depend partly on the rates the bank or building society feels it must offer to its savers to retain their deposits.

The alternative is a base rate tracker mortgage. With these, the mortgage rate is linked to the Bank of England's base rate, generally at a fixed margin of perhaps 0.75% to 1% above base.

The main advantage of tracker mortgages is that they provide an element of transparency and certainty. Borrowers can be confident that lenders are not covertly raising their margins each time the base rate changes. They cannot fail to pass on the full impact of a rate cut or raise their own rates by more than the increase in base rate. Any downward movement in rates is immediately reflected in the amount you pay, whereas lenders in the past have often delayed implementing cuts in the standard variable rate.

The disadvantages of tracker mortgages may become more apparent should we experience a prolonged period of interest rate rises. In such times, borrowers on the standard variable rate may be insulated for a while and may never face their full impact. For those with tracker loans, there is no such protection.

It is instructive that tracker-type mortgages first made their appearance in 1987-88. They enjoyed a brief moment of popularity before interest rates rose markedly. They then disappeared, and it was only in the late 1990s that they became available again.

Discounted rates

Many lenders offer special deals for new borrowers involving a discount on their variable rate for a fixed term, lasting for anything from months to years. The size of the discount is fixed, but the underlying interest rate will vary.

Discounted offers may involve early redemption penalties and, as with fixed rates, there may be an arrangement fee.

Cashback mortgages

Some lenders offer immediate cash rebates on their mortgages, which may be a few hundred pounds or a percentage of the total loan. Cashbacks have an immediate attraction, especially for first-time buyers who may be facing all the costs of furnishing a home for the first time. There is, inevitably, a price to pay: most cashback deals are available only with the more expensive mortgage offers.

Using a mortgage broker

Around half of all new mortgages are arranged direct, by borrowers who walk into a building society or bank branch. The rest go via brokers. Brokers often arrange exclusive deals with lenders at better terms, so it can be worth using one. Good brokers should also help to guide you through the maze of different offers. That is not to say you should rely on them entirely – some brokers may be more keen to sell you a lucrative savings scheme than find you the best deal. But on the whole, and especially if you are a 'problem' case – newly self-employed, for example, with no income track record – using a broker can be beneficial. If you decide you don't like what is being offered, you can always go direct to a lender instead.

Many brokers don't charge a fee as they get paid by the lender. If they do, they must tell you in advance exactly how much it is. If you decide not to go ahead with the deal, the broker can only keep £5 of your fee and must refund the rest.

How to repay the loan

The other main decision borrowers must make is how to repay the loan. There are two broad choices:
◆ a repayment loan, where capital is paid back during the term, or
◆ an interest-only loan, often set up in conjunction with a separate savings plan which, it is hoped, will pay off the capital at the end of the term.
These two methods are not mutually exclusive. Just as there is nothing to stop repayment mortgage holders setting up their own savings plan, so there is nothing in theory to prevent a borrower with an interest-only loan paying back part or all of the capital during the term. You should, of course, check if there are any redemption penalties before making a decision.

Repayment loans

Repayment mortgages are conventionally set up to last 25 years, but it is possible to arrange a shorter or (sometimes) longer time period.

While capital is paid back each year, the rate at which this happens rises markedly during the term. This is because the loans are organised so that (if interest rates do not change) the monthly payments stay level during the term. At the beginning, nearly all of the monthly payment goes to pay interest on the outstanding debt. Consequently the amount available to pay back capital is very small. Gradually over the term, the balance shifts and more of each payment consists of capital repayment rather than interest.

£100,000 repayment mortgage over 25 years at an interest rate of 7.5%
Monthly payments: £747.59

Year	Debt at end	Year	Debt at end
1	£98,529	10	£79,189
2	£96,948	15	£61,578
3	£95,248	20	£36,296
4	£93,420	21	£30,047
5	£91,455	22	£23,329
6	£89,344	23	£16,108
7	£87,073	24	£8,345
8	£84,633	25	Nil
9	£82,009		

The half-way point – when £50,000 of the capital has been paid off – is only reached half way through the 18th year of the mortgage.
Source: Halifax

How the interest is calculated

Most mainstream mortgage lenders operate a rough and ready system of calculating interest known as 'annual rest'. The amount of interest is based on the debt outstanding at the beginning of the year. This interest is then divided by 12 which borrowers then pay month by month.

However, this method takes no account of the fact you are repaying some of the capital during the year, so you are paying more interest than you actually owe.

Other lenders make more frequent calculations: some use a monthly and others a daily rest system. If the interest rate is identical, lenders using monthly or daily rest will charge less interest than those using an annual system.

In the early years of a mortgage, the difference between the two ways of charging interest is very small, and it is only in the last five or so (of a typical 25-year loan) that it really begins to bite. This is because you are paying back only small amounts of capital during those early years, so the delay in crediting it has relatively little effect. Up to year ten of a 25-year mortgage, the difference amounts to an average of 0.1% extra on the interest rate for an annual rest loan.

So you should not be deterred from choosing a mortgage with an annual rest system, if its terms are competitive in all other respects.

But there are two circumstances in which the annual rest system does start to cost you serious money:

◆ if you decide to make extra lump sum repayments at any time, and
◆ during the last five years of the term.

Most annual rest lenders are prepared to make an exception and credit extra lump sum payments immediately (or at least within a month) and then recalculate the interest on the reduced capital outstanding. But they usually require a minimum lump sum to be repaid – either expressed as three or four times the monthly payment, or a flat sum of perhaps £250 to £1,000. You should also inform the lender when you are making such a payment.

If you do not want to pay as much as this minimum, extra payments should be made towards the close of the lender's financial year (often, but not always, the calendar year) as this will mean the shortest delay in crediting the capital.

In the last few years of the mortgage term, the amounts of capital paid back each month rise significantly. In the first year of a £100,000 repayment mortgage, for example, around £120 of each monthly payment goes to repay capital, but by year 23, this has risen to £600 or more.

The total interest for the year is worked out on the balance outstanding at the beginning of the year, making the annual rest system progressively more expensive. This means it is a good idea to consider repaying the whole of the mortgage a year or two early, if you have the means.

John McKay has a 25-year £50,000 mortgage which has one year to run at a variable interest rate of 7.5%. His loan is with a lender which uses the annual rest system of charging interest. The capital outstanding on the loan is £4,173. Instead of letting it run for the full term, he decides to withdraw the £4,173 from his building society savings account and pay off the loan early. Doing this means he loses one year's worth of interest. Assuming a savings rate of 5% gross (4% after basic rate tax) this means losing £167. However, he has saved mortgage interest of £313, making an overall saving of £148.

Choosing your term

Repayment mortgages are usually set up to last for 25 years, but you can choose a shorter or (sometimes) longer term. The shorter the time, the higher the monthly payments, but the overall savings can be substantial, as the table shows.

£100,000 repayment mortgage at an interest rate of 7.5%

Term	Monthly payment	Total interest paid
10 years	£1,214	£45,686
15 years	£944	£69,930
20 years	£817	£96,183
25 years	£748	£124,277
30 years	£705	£154,012

Source: Halifax

Borrowers can usually change their repayment term during the course of the mortgage, although the lender may make a charge for this. While lenders will not object to shortening the term, they may not agree to lengthening it if this means taking it beyond your normal retirement date. However, if you are expecting a good occupational pension, the lender would be unlikely to refuse.

Flexible mortgages

Flexible mortgages have been developed in recent years to meet borrowers' demands for a much greater degree of control over how and when they borrow. While the conventional repayment mortgage does have a limited degree of flexibility – allowing you to make extra payments or to alter the term – organising this is often complicated and may involve charges.

There are some 50 different products available which claim to be 'flexible' mortgages, although their terms vary considerably. At the minimum, a flexible mortgage allows you to make overpayments whenever you want, without penalty. Subject to certain conditions, they also allow 'borrowing back' of sums previously repaid.

The most flexible products allow you to cut your regular payments for a time or to take a payment holiday. Some link the loan to a full current account. This means all money flowing through the account goes to pay off the mortgage, which cuts down the total interest due, even though much of this 'repayment' may be temporary, as the money is then drawn out for normal expenditure.

Using a flexible mortgage requires a completely different attitude on the borrower's part. Most people treat their mortgage as a self-contained part of their overall financial planning, not to be tampered with or altered in any way. With a flexible loan, instead of being kept rigidly separate, it becomes the central part of your finances.

For example, self-employed people who make income tax payments twice a year can 'save' their tax money in the mortgage account, and take it out again when the tax becomes due. Those planning a career break may be able to take a complete payment holiday for a time.

Anyone who normally keeps a short-term float in a building society or bank account for expenses such as an annual holiday can pay the cash into their mortgage account. Instead of earning perhaps 3% or 4% after tax in the deposit account, the money is in effect earning 6% or 7% by saving interest on the mortgage.

How to choose a flexible mortgage

If you are attracted by this type of mortgage, it is worth considering carefully the degree of flexibility you want. Nearly all flexible loans are on a variable interest rate, so it means giving up the certainty fixed rates can offer. That said, many of the providers have been charging interest rates well below the standard variable rates of the high street lenders.

Key questions to ask are:

◆ Does the product provide full current account banking facilities?
◆ Does it permit overpayments, and if so is there a minimum amount?
◆ Does it permit regular underpayments, and in what circumstances?
◆ Does it allow you to draw out lump sums and, again, in what circumstances?
◆ Does it allow payment holidays?

Some providers let you agree a 'loan facility' at the outset, based on a percentage of the property's value. You do not have to borrow the full amount initially, but can draw on it as required for home improvements or any other expenditure such as school fees, for example. The maximum loan or loan facility is likely to be between 80% and 95% of the property's value.

Other lenders only allow you to borrow back sums that have already been paid off the mortgage, so if you want a payment holiday, to make underpayments or draw out a lump sum, you must already have 'overpaid' at least the sum involved.

Most people with flexible mortgages use them mainly to speed up the repayment of their loan. The savings can be considerable, as the examples show.

Nigel Watt has a flexible mortgage of £100,000 set up for 25 years. He decides to make regular overpayments of £50 a month. This means the loan is paid off four years, 11 months early, saving interest of £20,540.

James Hendry uses a £100,000 25-year flexible mortgage with current account facilities. He earns a salary of £35,000 all of which he spends, in equal stages, throughout the month. He makes no specific overpayments. But thanks to the temporary overpayments made from his salary each month, the loan is paid off eight months early, saving total interest of £6,101.

Mortgage interest rate: 6.8%
Source: Virgin

Interest-only mortgages

The alternative to a repayment mortgage is an interest-only loan, which is usually coupled with a regular savings scheme. These days, borrowers are most likely to be offered a loan linked to an Individual Savings Account (Isa) or to a low-cost endowment policy.

In either case, there is no guarantee the plan will produce sufficient funds to repay the loan in full; it depends on the performance of the savings plan. If it does not grow as fast as predicted, borrowers will be asked to pay more, or they may have to pay back extra amounts off the capital. The only other alternative is to keep the mortgage (and the savings plan) running for longer than the original term.

Isa mortgages

The Individual Savings Account (Isa) was set up in 1999 as a replacement for the Personal Equity Plan (Pep). The scheme is designed to encourage people to save by giving useful tax breaks, and the government has promised Isas will continue until April 2009. After that, it is anyone's guess what will happen. It is possible they might be abolished, but it seems more likely that either an extension to Isas will be announced, or a similar tax-favoured plan could be set up to take their place, just as Isas replaced Peps.

An Isa is really no more than a tax-sheltered 'wrapper' around another investment, such as a cash deposit or a unit trust. If the Isa is abolished, you will still be able to continue with the underlying investment, but without the tax breaks.

You can invest up to £7,000 in an Isa each year. There are three types of plan: cash, insurance and equity (stocks and shares). The type used for mortgage repayment is an equity Isa. These are usually invested in a unit trust or other type of pooled investment fund.

The Isa is purely a savings plan. If you want to take out life insurance to repay the mortgage if you die during the term, this must be paid for separately. There is no guarantee the investments within the Isa will grow fast enough to pay off the loan within the original term.

The amount of money you will be asked to pay into the Isa for a given mortgage size is worked out by assuming those investments will average a certain rate of growth during the term. Most lenders assume a growth rate of 7%, but others may use lower or higher figures. The higher the rate assumed, the lower the monthly payments, but the greater the risk that this growth target will not be met. See Chapters 2 and 10 for more on Isas.

Low-cost endowment mortgages

Endowments are savings plans produced by life insurance companies which mix protection with investment. The most common type are with-profits endowments. They guarantee to pay back the full amount of the mortgage if you die within the term. If you survive, however, the guarantee is much more restrictive. The policy provides a 'minimum sum assured' which it promises to pay on maturity, so long as you continue paying the premiums for the full term. But this minimum sum is likely to be only half, or less, of the amount of the mortgage.

Each year annual bonuses (profits from the investments) are added to the minimum sum assured, and once added, these cannot be taken away. In addition, there is a terminal bonus, paid when the policy matures.

Broadly speaking, the annual bonus represents the income your investments have earned each year; the terminal bonus represents the capital gains achieved over the lifetime of your plan. On 25-year policies, the terminal bonus may account for about 50% to 70% of the total maturity value.

The premiums on with-profits plans are pooled together in a large fund which invests in a mixture of company shares, government securities ('gilts') and commercial property. The aim of the fund is to provide reasonably slow but steady growth, and most life companies usually keep reserves to help smooth out investment results from one year to the next. In very good years, savers do not necessarily get the full value of the investment growth achieved, but in very bad ones they may do better.

Endowment premiums are usually set on the assumption that the overall growth rate (after tax) achieved by the policies will average 6% a year for the mortgage term.

Isas versus endowments

Leaving aside for the moment the question of whether you should choose this method of covering the mortgage rather than straightforward repayment, it may be useful to summarise the differences between Isas and endowments. They are taxation, monthly cost, charges, type of investment and flexibility.

Taxation

Isas are more tax efficient than low-cost endowments. The full details are shown on the next page, but the net effect can be summarised simply: endowments are more heavily taxed, and because of this, their value is likely to grow more slowly.

The effect of this is illustrated by the growth rates the Financial Services Authority allows Isa and endowment providers to use when they are providing standard projections for new savings plans. Life companies must use growth rates of 4%, 6% and 8% for their endowment plans. But Isa providers can use growth rates of 5%, 7% and 9%. This difference is solely accounted for by the difference in tax treatment.

All income arising on endowment plans is taxed at the basic rate and profits are subject to capital gains tax (CGT). Policyholders cannot use their annual CGT exemption to set against these profits. However, higher rate taxpayers do not have to pay any extra tax on the returns, as long as the policy runs to its maturity.

With Isas, all capital gains are tax free. Income is treated in one of two ways. Interest arising from deposits or from fixed-interest securities such as gilts and corporate bonds is tax free. Income from company shares – the dividends – is treated differently. Isa managers can claim back 10% tax on the net dividends paid, but this concession is only set to last until April 2004.

Monthly cost

Because Isas are expected to grow faster, the level of monthly savings required may be lower than for an endowment, but this depends on the particular lender.

Generally speaking, lenders will use the middle rate of the three allowed by the Financial Services Authority when they set the savings level – in other words, 6% for endowments and 7% for Isas. But some are more cautious and will use a lower rate. The lower the growth rate chosen, the higher the monthly savings required. This does not, of course, mean it is necessarily worse value. If you are saving more, the plan will simply be worth more at the end of the day.

If you are comparing the cost of the two plans, remember that if you want life insurance with the Isa mortgage, you must pay for this separately. Once this cost has been added in, there may be little to choose between the two in terms of monthly cost.

The following examples show typical quotations prepared for an Isa and an endowment mortgage.

Mortgage of £100,000 lasting for 25 years, taken out by a man aged 30
Mortgage interest rate: 7.5%

Isa mortgage

Monthly premium	£167	
Life insurance premium	£19	
Mortgage interest	£625	
Total	£811	

Maturity value after 25 years

5% growth	**7% growth**	**9% growth**
£75,600	£100,000	£133,000

Endowment mortgage

Monthly premium	£189	
Mortgage interest	£625	
Total	£814	

Maturity value after 25 years

4% growth	**6% growth**	**8% growth**
£75,000	£100,000	£134,000

Sources: Woolwich (Isa mortgage), Standard Life (endowment mortgage)

Charges

Overall, there is likely to be little difference between the charges on an endowment plan and those on an Isa. But they are levied differently.

On endowment plans, more of the charges are taken out up-front, which means if you cash in the plan in the early years, you get much worse value. As a rule of thumb, if you cash it in during the first five or six years of a 25-year endowment, you are unlikely to get back as much as the premiums paid.

In addition, there may be extra tax to pay if you are a higher rate taxpayer and cash the policy in before three-quarters of the term has elapsed.

Type of investment

With-profits endowment plans are a 'one size fits all' type of investment, investing in a broad range of different securities including gilts, commercial property and company shares (both UK and some international).

Isas allow much more freedom: in theory, you can choose a fund investing solely in Japanese smaller companies or American technology shares. However, most mortgage lenders will steer you towards a more broadly invested fund, probably investing largely in UK company shares.

Flexibility

Isas win hands down when it comes to flexibility. You can increase or decrease the level of monthly savings without penalties, or even stop them altogether (though it would, of course, be foolish to do this if you are relying on the plan to pay off the mortgage). Likewise you can cash the plan in at any time without penalties, either in the way of charges or tax.

If the Isa grows faster than expected, you will be able to repay the mortgage early and save mortgage interest. With endowments, this is not a practical possibility for two reasons: first, you will be penalised on charges, and second, you will not necessarily get your fair share of the terminal bonus, which is added at the end of the policy's life. Terminal bonuses account for a high proportion of the final policy proceeds, and cashing in even a few years early could mean you lose out significantly.

Overall with endowments, you are likely to be penalised if you do not adhere to the strict terms of the savings contract. One particular problem that has surfaced in recent years is the situation of endowments on divorce. Many policies are set up on a 'joint life' basis, so if you need to divide assets on divorce, this is awkward and can be costly. To avoid this, many advisers recommend couples take out two separate policies at the outset rather than a joint one.

Other types of interest-only mortgages

Some lenders simply allow borrowers to take out an interest-only loan, leaving it up to the borrower to decide when they repay the capital. Of course, it has to be repaid at some point, but this could even be after the homeowner's death, out of the proceeds of the house sale.

Pension mortgages

Another option is to use your pension plan as the savings vehicle for repaying the mortgage. All pension schemes, whether personal pensions or company schemes, allow people to take out a certain proportion of the total as a tax-free lump sum on retirement. This could be used to pay off the mortgage.

Savings made into a pension plan qualify for full income tax relief, and the investments within a pension fund are largely tax free, so a pension plan is an attractive savings vehicle. This means that, as with Isas, lenders will usually use an assumed growth rate of 7% when setting the level of monthly premiums required to pay off the loan (as opposed to 6% for endowments).

Nevertheless, you should think twice, and possibly get independent financial advice, before going ahead. It may sound a good idea to link your mortgage to your pension in your 30s, but you may well change your mind as you approach retirement. Many people fail to save enough in their pension plan as it is to provide a reasonable income in retirement, and having to pay off the mortgage from the lump sum only makes matters worse. In addition, it means paying mortgage interest until you retire, as you cannot normally cash in a pension plan until then, or until age 50 at the earliest. Other borrowers could be free of their mortgage many years before.

A pension mortgage does, however, have one thing going for it: it forces borrowers to start contributing meaningful sums to their pension plan relatively early in life. But they will have to remember to review their pension savings regularly. In later years, it may be wise to convert the mortgage to a repayment one, so the pension plan will be free of the burden of repaying the loan – or to make extra payments into the pension plan.

On the face of it, a pension mortgage looks a much more expensive way of paying for a home loan than any other. This is because you can only take a fraction of the total pension proceeds as cash – the rest must be used to provide a regular income. The rules differ according to whether you have a company or personal pension. With a personal pension, for example, you can take out only 25% of the total fund as cash. That means the eventual pension fund has to be four times the size of the loan – so not surprisingly, the amount that has to be saved each month is larger than that required under an Isa or endowment mortgage.

Mortgage of £100,000 lasting for 35 years, taken out by a man aged 30, retiring at age 65
Mortgage interest rate: 7.5%

Monthly premium	£259 (gross)
Mortgage interest	£625
Total	£884

Maturity value after 35 years (at age 65)

	5% growth	7% growth	9% growth
Fund size	£262,000	£401,000	£626,000
Providing lump sum of	£65,600	£100,000	£156,000
Plus annual income for life	£15,400	£27,600	£49,500

This example is based on a personal pension, where up to 25% of the total fund can be taken as cash (different rules apply to company pensions). The premiums are set on the assumption that the fund will grow at an average rate of 7% a year.
The pension premiums qualify for income tax relief, so for a basic rate taxpayer, the net cost is £202 and for a higher rate taxpayer, £155.
Source: John Charcol/CGU Life

Repayment versus interest-only

A mortgage is – for 99% of borrowers – the biggest debt they will take on in their life, and it will remain a major factor in their financial lives for decades.

A repayment mortgage guarantees that it will pay off the loan in full, as long as you keep up the monthly savings. Other types of mortgage do not. Whether you choose an Isa, an endowment or a pension as your savings plan, none of these are guaranteed to produce enough at the end of the day to pay off the debt in full.

You are, in short, taking a risk. If the investments perform better than expected, there will be surplus for you at the end of the term. If they perform worse, you will have to increase your savings as you go along, or face a shortfall.

In investment terms, what you are doing when you take out an Isa or endowment mortgage is 'gearing up'. Instead of using some of each monthly payment to repay capital, you continue borrowing it (at the mortgage interest rate) and use the money to invest in the stock market.

This tactic pays off if the stock market investments grow faster than the rate of interest you are paying. But if the investments do not grow as fast, you lose out.

In the past, an investment in the stock market has, over long periods of time, outpaced mortgage interest rates. Mortgage holders have been in the happy position of borrowing money at an average rate of, say, 8%, and investing it where it achieves an average growth rate of 10% or more.

Will this state of affairs continue in the future? No-one can know, although many investment experts would say it will. If it does, you would be better off using an endowment or Isa mortgage than a repayment. You will, in other words, be rewarded for taking that extra risk.

But while, in the long run, the stock market might be expected to produce higher levels of growth than the mortgage rate, there are no guarantees it will over shorter periods. Stock markets go down as well as up and there might be several years of under-performance. This has led many experts to suggest you should consider an Isa or endowment mortgage only if you are borrowing for 25 years: they believe ten or 15-year mortgages are too short for the risks involved.

Summary

◆ A repayment mortgage is most suitable if you do not want to take any risks over the repayment of your loan.
◆ If you are prepared to take such a risk, you might be better to consider an Isa mortgage rather than an endowment, because of the greater flexibility and tax efficiency.
◆ Whichever you choose, remember you do not have to stick with it. If you have an Isa or endowment mortgage, you can start repaying capital at any time, either

by occasional lump sums or by formally converting the loan to a repayment basis.

◆ Do not base your decision solely on the different monthly payments each method requires. Remember that while an endowment automatically builds in life insurance to cover the debt if you die during the term, this usually has to be bought separately, at extra cost, if you use a repayment or Isa-linked mortgage.

◆ Using an interest-only mortgage, or linking the loan to a pension plan, is likely to be suitable for relatively few borrowers, depending on individual circumstances and financial knowledge and awareness.

If things go wrong

On paper, mortgage lenders and brokers set high standards for the services they offer. That is important, because it means that if things do go wrong, you will have clear grounds for complaint and a recognised procedure to follow.

Every mortgage lender and broker has to obey The Mortgage Code, which sets out how they should behave. They should give you a copy of the leaflet *You and Your Mortgage*, which details the main provisions and the protection offered. Every lender and broker has to have a proper internal complaints procedure in place, and if you cannot reach agreement through this, there are external bodies to complain to – Chapter 15 gives details.

In brief, the code requires all lenders and brokers to:

◆ act fairly and reasonably at all times;

◆ give information on products and services in plain language;

◆ give help if there is any area you do not understand;

◆ help you choose a mortgage to fit your needs;

◆ correct errors and handle complaints speedily.

If you want a full copy of the code, which goes into much greater detail, your lender or broker must give you one.

Endowment mortgages

Many borrowers have received letters from their life assurance companies warning that their policy may not grow enough to pay off their loan. This has caused both dismay and anger and led to calls for compensation.

If you are in this position, there are two important things you must decide. The first is whether you have reasonable grounds for complaint and possible compensation. The second is what you should do now, to make sure that you can, in fact, pay off the mortgage.

Should I complain?

There is no simple answer to this. It depends on the quality of the advice you were given when you took out the mortgage.

The Financial Services Authority has a factsheet entitled *Endowment Mortgage Complaints* (to order, call 0845 608 2372) setting out what you should have been told. For instance, it should have been made clear that an endowment is a long-term commitment that often gives a poor return if it is cashed in early. You should also have been told that it was not guaranteed to produce enough to repay the entire loan.

If your complaint is upheld, you may be eligible for compensation, but only if you have lost out financially as a result of the bad advice.

What should I do to make sure the loan is paid off?

If you have received a letter saying that your policy is likely fall short, you will probably also be told you can increase your monthly endowment premium by a set amount to put it back on track.

Alternatively, you can either start a different savings plan – perhaps an Isa – to build up extra capital, or you can begin repaying part of the mortgage every month. Talk to your mortgage lender and get it to work out appropriate figures for you. Deciding to repay capital from now onwards is probably the simplest and safest way of dealing with the problem.

8

Pensions for Employees

Pensions were first provided by employers for domestic staff in the 19th century, but the real growth in occupational pension schemes began after the First World War. Today, around 11 million people, or nearly half the working population, are members of company pension schemes. People currently retiring with membership of these schemes are among the best-off pensioners in the country.

There is little doubt that becoming a member of an employer's pension scheme is nearly always the best way of saving for retirement. It means your employer will be paying a contribution towards your pension and it can provide a low-cost method for you to add to your own savings.

Company pension schemes have not always been perfect. For example, in the past the treatment of employees who changed jobs was rather harsh. Regulation of the employers who ran the schemes was not strict enough either. Nowadays they are tightly controlled and members' interests are well protected.

However, there is still a considerable lack of understanding of the benefits of occupational schemes, how they work and how much pension they will provide. This is partly because many employers have failed to explain them properly to their employees. It has meant some people have turned down the opportunity to join a scheme.

If you don't join a scheme you can set up your own personal or stakeholder pension, but you could be losing valuable benefits, as this chapter will show.

The advantages

The ways in which you can gain from being a member of an occupational scheme include:

◆ Your employer contributes to your pension and often to the running costs of the scheme.

◆ You will receive a pension at retirement which increases every year.

◆ Many schemes will provide an enhanced pension if you have to retire early due to ill health.

◆ The majority of schemes provide pensions or lump sums, or both, for your widow/widower and other dependants on your death.

◆ Extra life insurance and health insurance may also be provided.

In case you are still sceptical about the merits of pensions, remember there are tax advantages too:

◆ You get income tax relief on your contributions at your highest marginal rate.

◆ You are not taxed on any contributions your employer makes on your behalf.

◆ Your pension fund builds up virtually free of tax.

◆ At retirement, part of your pension can be taken as a tax-free lump sum.

The ground rules

It is important to find out exactly how your own scheme works, but there are certain basic rules concerning maximum levels of contributions and benefits which apply to them all.

◆ **Your contributions** You can save up to 15% of your pay towards your pension but typically your employer will only ask you to pay in around 5% (some employers do not ask you to make any contribution at all). You can save more voluntarily if you want to.

◆ **Your employer's contributions** By law, an employer must contribute to the scheme. Indeed, on average, employers' contributions are substantially higher than their employees'. With some schemes, the employer meets the whole cost. There is no formal maximum on a company's contributions as long as they are not 'excessive'.

◆ **Pension** The maximum pension you can receive from an occupational scheme is two-thirds of your final earnings providing you have worked a sufficient number of years for your employer.

◆ **Cash sum** At retirement, a tax-free lump sum of up to one-and-a-half times your final salary can be taken, although the exact amount will be related to the length of your service. If you take a lump sum, this will normally mean sacrificing some of your regular pension.

◆ **Spouse's pension** The maximum pension your widow or widower can receive is two-thirds of your pension.

◆ **Death benefit** The maximum cash sum payable if you die before retirement is four times your earnings at the time of death.

There may be a limit on how much of your earnings can be 'pensioned'. Some years ago the government introduced an earnings 'cap'. The amount is usually changed each year in line with inflation – for the tax year 2001-02 it is £95,400. You may be offered an 'unapproved' pension scheme instead (see below) to take account of any extra earnings. The cap does not apply to those who were already members of their current scheme before 1 June, 1989.

Ajay Shah, 25, has recently started work for a new employer and is earning £20,000 a year. He has been offered membership of the company's pension scheme but is not sure whether to join. Retirement seems an awfully long way off and he wants to enjoy himself now. If he joins he will have to pay 4% of his salary, or £800, a year to the scheme.

However, his pensions administrator explains that after basic rate tax relief of 22%, his contribution will actually cost him only £624. Also, his employer will be paying the equivalent of 6% of his earnings, or £1,200, to the scheme. This means a total of £2,000 will be going into his pension at a cost to Ajay of just £624. When he hears this, he realises it is too good an offer to refuse and decides to go ahead and join.

Types of company schemes

Each pension scheme is slightly different. Retirement ages, for example, vary from one to another. However, when it comes to how much pension you are likely to get, this will depend on which of two main types of scheme you are in.

Final salary schemes

With these schemes – which are also known as salary related or defined benefit – you are promised a pension proportionate to your earnings shortly before retirement.

The amount you get will usually depend on several factors:

◆ **The rate of build up (the 'accrual rate')** This is normally 1/60th or 1/80th of your final salary for each year of pension scheme membership.

◆ **The number of years you have been in the scheme** If you are in a 1/80th scheme for 40 years you will get a pension of 40/80th, or half, of your earnings, while in a 1/60th scheme you will get 40/60th, or two-thirds, of your final earnings.

◆ **How your final salary is defined** Your pension may not be based on your pay in the exact year before you retire. It is more likely to be calculated on your best year's earnings within, say, three or five years of your retirement.

◆ **How much of your salary is pensionable** Some schemes do not include extras, such as overtime earnings. Others may be 'integrated', which means the first slice of your earnings – usually an amount equivalent to the basic state pension – is ignored for pension purposes on the basis that the state is providing you with a pension for that part of your pay.

◆ **Whether you take a cash sum** If you work in the public sector, the NHS for example, you may receive a tax-free lump sum automatically in addition to your pension at retirement. However, with other schemes you will normally be required to give up or 'commute' part of your pension if you want to take some cash.

After you retire, your pension will increase. To what extent will depend on your employer and when your pension was built up. Ex-public sector employees have long enjoyed the benefit of inflation-proofed pensions which have been increased each year in line with growth in the Retail Price Index.

Other schemes were not required to provide inflation proofing until the Pensions Act 1995 and this only applies to pensions earned after April 1997. The Act requires employers to provide 'limited price indexation', which means that pensions must be increased by either the rise in the Retail Price Index or 5% a year, whichever is lower. Some private schemes are more generous than this and give discretionary increases of more than inflation.

The benefits

The great advantage of a final salary scheme is that you have the security of knowing your pension will be a fixed proportion of your pay – you do not have to worry about investment returns or interest rates as you would if you were in a money purchase scheme (see next page). It is the trustees of the company's pension fund who must check that its investment performance is up to scratch, and your employer who must ensure there is enough in the fund to cover its liabilities to members.

The main snag is that if you change jobs frequently your pension could suffer. Any pension you leave behind will be based on your earnings when you quit the scheme. Although the value of the pension will be increased in line with prices, these tend to rise more slowly than earnings, so its relative value could decline.

How much pension?

The best way to find out how much pension you can expect at retirement is to ask your personnel department or pensions administrator. However, to get a rough idea you could use the following calculator.

Final salary pension calculator
The annual starting pension for every £1,000 of your pensionable salary (assuming no tax-free cash is taken)

	Pension per year	
Years in scheme	60th scheme	80th scheme
5	£83.30	£62.50
10	£166.60	£125.00
15	£250.00	£187.50
20	£333.33	£250.00
25	£416.60	£312.50
30	£500.00	£375.00
35	£583.30	£437.50
40	£666.66	£500.00

To work out your pension, find out whether you are in a 1/60th or a 1/80th scheme and then multiply your expected final salary, for example £25,000, by the figure shown alongside the number of years you will have been in the scheme by the time you retire, for example 20 years. In a 1/60th scheme, 25 times £333.33 gives a pension of £8,333 per year.

Money purchase schemes

When you are a member of a money purchase scheme – also called a defined contribution scheme – you build up a 'pot' of money in a pension account which must be used to buy a pension annuity at retirement.
Factors which will influence how much pension you get include:
◆ **How much you contribute** Many schemes set a fixed amount. The average is about 4% of your pay, but some employers let you choose how much you save.
◆ **How much your employer pays in** The average contribution by employers is 6% of your pay, but where the employer foots the whole bill the average is 9%. In some schemes, employers will pay more if the employee does too.
◆ **Investment growth** Investment returns will have an important effect on the amount in your pension 'pot' when you reach retirement. These returns will depend partly on general economic and stock market conditions, as well as on

the skills of the investment managers who are looking after the money. These managers are chosen by the pension fund trustees, although you may be given some choice about the type of fund in which your savings are invested.

◆ **Annuity rates when you retire** To convert your fund into a regular pension, the scheme administrator will normally purchase an annuity on your behalf. Annuity rates vary with long-term interest rates. An employee may be able to exercise some influence over the type of annuity purchased, for example whether it includes a spouse's pension or not. However, by law any pension benefits earned after April 1997 must be used to purchase an annuity which provides 'limited price indexation', that is it must increase by 5% a year or the rate of inflation if less. In future, though, it may be possible to opt for a with-profits annuity.

The benefits

Although money purchase schemes are not so advantageous for long-term employees as final salary schemes, because the size of your pension is not guaranteed, they are still attractive thanks to employers' contributions. Useful extras such as life insurance may also be provided. If you move to another employer, your fund will remain invested and continue growing. For employers, these schemes are attractive as they know what their costs will be in advance.

How much pension?

It will soon be compulsory for members of all types of money purchase schemes to be given an illustration every year of the projected value of their fund at retirement and the amount of pension it is likely to provide. However, these will be based on assumed rates of investment growth and assumed annuity rates at retirement, which means the figures will not be guaranteed. If you need the information before the annual illustration is prepared, you should be able to obtain an individual benefit statement at any time.

Group personal pensions

Not all pension schemes offered by employers are occupational schemes. Some companies offer membership of a group personal pension scheme instead. This arrangement is basically no different from having your own personal pension except that you and your workmates will all have policies with the same company, which has been chosen by your employer.

However, it can have three potential advantages over taking out your own separate pension plan:

◆ **Cost** The charges for a group personal pension should be lower than with an individual plan if your employer has negotiated a good deal with the pension company.

◆ **Employer's contribution** In the past, there was no requirement that an employer should make any contribution to a group personal pension scheme, but many did. However, from October 2001, all employers with more than five employees will have to contribute at least 3% of their pay to a group personal pension scheme, or provide access to a stakeholder pension instead.

◆ **Other benefits** Lump sum death benefits and insurance against ill-health may also be included in the deal.

Contributions to a group personal pension scheme, whether your own or from your employer, are subject to the same limits as ordinary personal pension policies. Everyone can contribute up to £3,600 a year. After that the limits will depend on your age and earnings. For details, see Chapter 9.

The amount of pension you will get at retirement is not guaranteed. As with other types of money purchase pensions, it will depend on a how big a pot of money you manage to build up and on annuity rates at retirement, when you have to convert your fund into a regular pension.

Besides the level of contributions, investment returns are vital in determining the ultimate size of your pension pot. With a group scheme, the employer chooses the pension company, but employees can decide on the fund in which they want their savings invested. There may be a wide range available depending on the pension company. Experience has shown that the best long-term growth is achieved by choosing funds that invest in assets such as shares.

As retirement draws near, it is advisable to move investments gradually into fixed-interest securities to protect yourself against a fall in the stock market or in interest rates. Some investment managers have automatic fund switching facilities for this. There is more detail about investment options in Chapter 9.

Another difference between company pension schemes and group personal pensions is that you have more control over when you purchase your annuity. The amount of tax-free cash you can take is limited to 25% of your fund, but there is no restriction on the amount of pension. In practice, however, few people build up a pension that is greater than the two-thirds of final salary allowed under an occupational scheme.

Stakeholder pensions

Many small and medium-sized employers have not offered any type of pension scheme in the past. From October 2001, this will change. Any employer with five or more employees will have to give them access to a stakeholder scheme if it does not already provide an occupational or group personal pension scheme to which it contributes at least 3% of their earnings. It will also have to offer one if there is a waiting time of a year or more before employees can join any existing scheme.

Many employers are taking action in anticipation of this requirement and introducing schemes sooner. So if you are considering starting your own pension, find out from your employer what its plans are for stakeholder pensions.

However, you may still have to make your own pension arrangements if you work for an employer with less than five employees or in a business where all employees earn less than the National Insurance lower earnings limit (currently £72 per week) as these employers will not have to provide a scheme.

Under the proposed rules, an employer will have to give details of the designated stakeholder scheme to employees within three months of their starting work. Employers will have to deduct contributions from pay if an employee wishes. You will have the choice of making flat-rate contributions, for example £50 a month, or having a percentage of your pay, say 5%, deducted and paid into your pension, and you will have the right to vary the amount you contribute to your pension at six-monthly intervals. However, employers will not be liable for the investment performance of their designated scheme. For more details of how stakeholder pensions will work, see Chapter 9.

The State Earnings-Related Pension Scheme

Even if you belong to an employer's pension scheme, you will still be building up a basic state retirement pension and you may also be contributing to the State Earnings-Related Pension Scheme (Serps). Membership will depend on whether you or your employer have decided to stay in or 'contract out'. If you are contracted out, you and your employer will be paying lower National Insurance contributions and the difference must be invested in a pension that will act as a replacement for the additional state pension you would have received.

Most final salary schemes are contracted out of Serps, and until April 1997 your employer had to guarantee that any replacement pension was at least as good as Serps. This part of the pension was known as the guaranteed minimum pension (GMP). For pensions earned after April 1997, no guarantee is necessary, though schemes have to be of a certified minimum standard. Benefits must also be inflation proofed, up to a maximum of 5% a year.

Many money purchase schemes are also contracted out of Serps, some on the same basis as final salary schemes. Others have invested the National Insurance rebates to provide a 'protected rights' pension. The size of this pension is not guaranteed – it depends on the amount in the pot at retirement and annuity rates at the time, and there are certain restrictions on what can be done with the fund at retirement. For example, the pension cannot be taken until state pension age and the annuity must be of a certain type. Rates must be the same for men and women, a 50% spouse's pension must be provided, and the pension must increase by 3% a year for service before April 1997 and 5% for service thereafter. None of this pension can be taken as a tax-free lump sum.

If you are in a group personal pension scheme, or have taken out a stakeholder plan, it is up to you to decide whether to opt out of Serps. If you do, your National Insurance rebates will be invested in your personal or stakeholder plan. The part funded by these rebates will also provide a protected rights pension.

Pensions for directors

If you are a senior executive or director running your own business, you have other pension options. You could use an executive pension plan or 'small self-administered scheme' (SSAS) to boost your retirement provision.

Executive pension plans

Although classified as company pension schemes, these are usually set up for individuals. Their main advantage over personal pensions is that they are more flexible in terms of contribution limits and benefit levels. If you have neglected your provision in the past, it may be possible to use this type of scheme to provide a larger pension more quickly than would be feasible with a personal plan.

Another attraction is that contributions are allowable as a business expense and can be offset against corporation tax, in the case of companies, or income tax, for partnerships and sole proprietors.

The maximum contributions an employer can make to this type of scheme are not a fixed annual amount. Instead they are related to the provision of the appropriate pension benefits based on the employee's length of service. This means the company can pay extra large contributions into the scheme to make up for years of service when no pension provision was made.

Sam George and his brother Tim set up their own business ten years ago when they were in their late 30s. Ever since they have been ploughing most of the profits back into the firm. Pensions were the last thing on their minds and they had no spare cash anyway. Now the business is established and their profits are improving, they want to put some money aside for their retirement in ten years' time. By setting up an executive pension plan for themselves, they will be able to make up for lost time. The company can make larger contributions now to cover those years they spent working for it with no pension provision.

As under other company schemes, the maximum pension allowed under an executive scheme is two-thirds of final salary. For plans taken out after March 1989, this can be achieved after 20 years of service on the basis of 1/30th of final salary for each year of service, subject to a cap on final earnings (£95,400 for 2001-02). Schemes taken out earlier may be able to provide higher benefits.

Part of the pension can be taken as a tax-free lump sum of up to one-and-a-half times final salary at retirement. Indeed, with a small policy, it may be possible to take the entire pension fund as tax-free cash.

Small self-administered schemes

Directors torn between investing in their own business and putting money into a pension plan may find they can achieve both objectives with an SSAS. Under this type of scheme, part of the pension fund can be used to buy assets for the business, such as an office building. The business can then rent the premises from the fund. The pension fund can also make loans to the business and acquire shares in the company, as long as the total value of shares and loans does not exceed 50% of the fund.

An SSAS will normally have a maximum of 12 members. All the members must be trustees and they are jointly responsible for running the scheme. In addition, there must be an independent trustee, known as a pensioner trustee, who is approved by the Inland Revenue. Someone to fill this role will usually be supplied as part of a package of services by insurance companies and other providers that offer these schemes.

The contribution and benefit levels are the same as for executive pension plans. Besides the potential for self-investment, another attraction of an SSAS is that the directors can retain control over how the pension fund is invested if they wish. Investments can include quoted stocks and shares, pooled funds such as unit and investment trusts, unit-linked funds, commercial property and cash deposits.

A lower cost option for smaller businesses or directors who are interested in limited self-investment is a hybrid SSAS. The insurance companies which run these schemes stipulate a minimum investment in their in-house funds, leaving the remainder for self-investment.

Topping up a company scheme

Although membership of an occupational scheme can enable you to build up an above average pension, few employees actually achieve the maximum permitted pension of two-thirds of their final salary at retirement. For most people, changes of employer, periods in jobs with no pension scheme or times spent out of the employment market will mean their pensions fall well short of the maximum.

One way of remedying this situation is to make extra savings in the form of additional voluntary contributions (AVCs). If you belong to a public sector scheme, such as the those run by the NHS or local authorities, you may be able to buy 'added years'. Alternatively, new rules mean that you may be able to use a stakeholder or personal plan to top up your occupational plan. If you are a member of a group personal pension scheme, you can simply increase your ordinary contributions.

AVCs and FSAVCs

All occupational pension schemes nowadays must offer members the facility to make AVCs. The alternative is to take out an independent, or free-standing, AVC scheme (FSAVC). The main advantage of boosting your pension in this way rather than using other forms of saving, such as an Isa, is that your contributions will be increased by tax relief.

How much?

The amount you can pay in AVCs/FSAVCs will depend on how much you are already contributing to your pension. The overall limit on employee contributions is 15% of earnings. So if you are paying, say, 5% to the main scheme, you can pay another 10% voluntarily. Sometimes employers will increase their contributions to your pension if you make additional savings.

There may be added scope for making AVCs/FSAVCs if your main scheme contributions are related to your basic pay only but you receive other income in the form of bonuses, overtime or perks, because these will count when working out your maximum contributions. Although most people tend to make regular savings into an AVC/FSAVC, it is also possible to pay in lump sum contributions, say if you get an extra bonus, if your scheme will allow this.

AVCs versus FSAVCs

AVC schemes normally work on a money purchase basis, even when you are a member of a final salary scheme. This is also how FSAVCs work. It means the extra pension generated by your contributions will depend on the pot of money you build up. This will be affected by charges and investment returns.

Unless the investment returns achieved by your in-house AVC managers have been very poor, you will normally be better off opting for an AVC scheme, because the charges are likely to be significantly lower than on FSAVCs. One of the main reasons FSAVCs are more expensive is the commission paid to the salesmen to cover the cost of the investment advice they provide. This can mean heavy initial deductions. Anyone selling FSAVCs nowadays is legally obliged to point out the potential merits of your in-house scheme. In the past, some people have been wrongly advised to take out FSAVCs. If you think you may have been mis-sold an FSAVC, you should write to the insurance company or financial adviser concerned and ask them to investigate. See Chapter 15 for more on making a complaint.

However, it may sometimes be worthwhile considering an FSAVC if you want a different investment option or you expect to change jobs. You can continue contributing to the same FSAVC in your new job or you may be able to convert it to a personal pension if your new employer does not offer a scheme (but check the potential cost of doing this).

Where to invest

You may be offered a number of investment alternatives for your AVCs/FSAVCs. Make sure you choose one which suits your needs.

◆ **Deposit accounts** These work like tax-free bank or building society accounts with interest added tax free. They may be attractive for employees close to retirement who do not want to take any risks with their savings, but they are unlikely to produce the best long-term results for younger contributors.

◆ **With-profits funds** With-profits funds offered by traditional life insurance companies invest in a mixture of shares, property and fixed-interest securities. Investment returns are added to your savings in the form of regular bonuses designed to smooth out fluctuations in investment markets. They appeal to people who want a relatively low-risk investment with some scope for growth.

◆ **Unit-linked funds** These may specialise in investing in assets such as shares or property, but the most popular choice is normally a managed unit-linked fund which holds a mixture of investments. The value of these funds will fluctuate in line with the underlying investments and can go down as well as up. They are likely to be most suitable for long-term investors.

◆ **Unit and investment trusts** These invest mainly in UK and overseas shares. Fund values will fluctuate in line with the underlying share prices. This type of scheme will tend to be most suitable for savers with a reasonably adequate main pension who want to be more adventurous with their AVC contributions and are willing to take a risk to secure a higher return.

Taking your AVC/FSAVC benefits

Your options will depend on when you started making contributions.

◆ **After April 1987** You must use the fund you have accumulated to buy extra pension, usually an annuity from an insurance company.

◆ **Before April 1987** You will have the choice of boosting your pension or taking all or part of your AVCs in the form of a tax-free lump sum, subject to the normal limits. If you were intending to take some of your pension in cash anyway, it is usually a good idea to use the AVCs for this purpose. This will leave you with a larger pension from the main scheme to benefit from future increases.

Overfunding

The benefits which you receive from your AVCs/FSAVCs must fall within the overall pension limits for occupational schemes. For most employees there is little danger of exceeding them. However, if it looks likely, your pension administrators should warn you. With FSAVCs, if your contributions are more than £200 a month, or £2,400 a year, your provider must carry out a 'headroom check' in conjunction with your main scheme administrator to ensure your benefits do not exceed Inland Revenue limits. If overfunding does occur, you will have your contributions plus investment returns refunded to you in the form of a cash sum, less tax.

Added years

Some final salary pension schemes, notably those in the public sector, give employees the option of buying 'added years' as an alternative to money purchase AVCs. Added years are not a cheap option but they do provide the certainty of a fixed amount of additional pension which will increase in line with your main scheme benefits. However, if you are considering early retirement you should check how that will affect your added years entitlement.

Stakeholder and personal pensions

New tax rules mean you can make extra savings towards your pension using a stakeholder or personal pension provided that you earn less than £30,000 a year. The attraction of this method is that at retirement you can take up to 25% of the fund as a tax-free lump sum, whereas AVCs/FSAVCs must be used to buy a pension only. Any employee can make contributions of up to £3,600 a year to a stakeholder or personal pension, regardless of how much of their income they are already paying into their occupational scheme, providing their salary is less than £30,000.

Judy Smith, 42, works part-time. She has been a member of her company's pension scheme for five years but realises she needs to save more to boost her pension. She considers paying additional voluntary contributions (AVCs), but decides to use a stakeholder pension so she can take part of the benefits as a tax-free lump sum at retirement. She also likes the flexibility of stakeholder pensions which will allow her to stop and start her contributions without penalty.

Salary sacrifice

Another way of topping up your pension, whether it is an occupational scheme or a group personal pension, is through a 'salary sacrifice'. This involves asking your employer to pay part of your earnings directly into your pension. The advantage is that no National Insurance must be paid on this money, so the employer can add the saved NI contribution to enhance the pension payment.

Unapproved schemes

Highly paid employees who have joined a company pension scheme since June 1989 may be limited on how much they can contribute to their pension due to the earnings 'cap'. The ceiling is increased each year but normally in line with the Retail Price Index, which tends to rise more slowly than earnings. For 2001-02 the cap is £95,400.

However, there is a way round this problem for employees who want to top up their pensions, if their employer is willing to set up an 'unapproved' pension scheme. These are recognised as genuine pension arrangements, but they are not granted the same tax concessions as approved schemes. They are normally 'funded unapproved retirement benefit' (Furb) schemes, under which the employer pays contributions relating to the unpensioned tier of earnings into a fund which is written in trust for the employee. There is no formal limit on either the contributions or the amount of pension that can be provided. The fund can be used to buy an annuity or it can be taken as a tax-free lump sum.

Changing jobs

If you are a member of a company pension scheme and you move to a new employer, it is important to give careful consideration to the pension rights you have accumulated in your old employer's scheme. Try to weigh up your choices dispassionately even if you have fallen out with your old employer. It may be tempting to shift your pension elsewhere so you can sever links with your old company, but this may not be to your advantage in the long run.

If you have been a member of an occupational pension scheme for less than two years, you can be offered a refund of contributions, less tax. But if you are given the option of a transfer value (see below), this will be more tax efficient.

If you have belonged to your employer's occupational scheme for more than two years, a refund will not be available. You will have three other options instead – to leave your pension where it is, to transfer the value to a new employer's scheme, or to move it to a personal scheme.

You don't have to make an instant decision. If you do not transfer immediately, you can always go back to an old employer and ask for a transfer at any time up to one year before your retirement date. But once you have made a transfer you cannot reverse the decision. This is why it is best to consult a professional adviser.

Leaving your pension where it is

If you take no action your pension will be preserved in your old scheme until you reach your normal retirement age. Other benefits may also continue, even after you leave, such as provision for a dependant's pension on death, or discretionary increases after retirement. What happens to the value of your pension will depend on the type of scheme.

In a final salary scheme your entitlement will be calculated on the basis of your earnings at the time you leave. It will then increase each year in line with the Retail Price Index, up to a maximum of 5% (with public sector schemes there is no upper limit), although some schemes may be more generous. The main drawback is that earnings often increase faster than prices so the relative value of your pension may fall. Moreover, compulsory increases have only applied to all preserved pensions since January 1991. Any pensions you may have from earlier jobs may not be increased to the same extent.

If your scheme was contracted out of Serps, different rules also apply to that part of your pension which replaced Serps prior to April 1997. That part, known as the guaranteed minimum pension, is usually revalued by the full rise in the Retail Price Index.

With a money purchase scheme your pension pot will continue to grow as before, less any charges. But no contributions will be added by your former employer. When you reach retirement, the money will be used to buy an annuity at the rate which applies at the time.

Transfer to a new employer's scheme

If you are offered membership of your new employer's pension scheme, you may be able to arrange a transfer of your benefits from your old one, but your new employer is not obliged to accept them.

If you are moving from a final salary scheme, the terms you will get in the new scheme will rarely be the same unless you are transferring from one public sector scheme to another. Although you may be offered extra years of pensionable service in your new scheme, they will probably fewer than you had before. However, such a switch may be worthwhile if you are being paid more, because your pension at retirement will be related to your new level of earnings.

> Winston Morgan, 38, is in the process of moving to a better paid job with a new employer. At his old company he had earned £28,000 a year and had been a member of the final salary scheme for 13 years. His new employer has offered him a salary of £32,000 but he is disappointed to find he will only be credited with ten years of service in the new pension scheme if he transfers his benefits. Then his pension adviser reminds him that his future pension will be related to his new higher salary and he realises it is not such a bad deal after all.

If you are transferring from one money purchase scheme to the other, it is somewhat easier. Your accumulated pension fund, less expenses, can be switched to the new scheme and will then be invested by the new scheme's investment managers. But even here it is best to take professional advice.

Transfer to a personal pension policy

If your new employer does not have a pension scheme or you don't want to join it, or you have become self-employed, you could set up your own pension plan. Your options are a section 32 'buy-out', a personal or a stakeholder pension. A buy-out policy provides greater guarantees and may be useful if a Serps replacement pension forms a large proportion of the benefits you are transferring. However, there is less scope for investment growth with this type of policy. Personal and stakeholder pensions are money purchase schemes, so the final outcome will depend on the level of charges and investment returns.

Great caution should be exercised if you are considering transferring from a final salary scheme with a guaranteed benefit. Even if your previous scheme was a money purchase arrangement, the charges on it will normally be lower than for an individual pension. Leaving your money in an occupational scheme is often a better option than transferring to a personal or stakeholder plan.

Tom Marshall, 49, has just been made redundant and is looking for a new job. He is not very happy with his old employer as he thinks it did not value his services properly. Tom was a member of the company's final salary pension scheme, but he would like to take his pension elsewhere.

He considers transferring the money to a personal pension plan but his financial adviser recommends against taking any hasty action until Tom has a new job. His adviser points out that it may then be possible for him to transfer his pension rights to his new employer's scheme. Or he could even be better off leaving his pension where it is until retirement.

If you leave a job where you were a member of a group personal pension scheme, your policy is your own anyway, so you can take it with you when you leave. Naturally, your old employer will not continue to contribute, but you may be able to persuade your new company to do so or you could increase your own contributions. Alternatively, if you move to an employer which offers an occupational scheme, you can stop the contributions to your personal pension or it may be possible to convert it to an FSAVC scheme so you can still use it to top up your company pension.

Tracing past pensions

If you have changed jobs several times during your working life you may end up with a number of pensions which you have left behind in previous employers' schemes. At retirement age you should be contacted by these schemes with information about your entitlement. However, if you have moved home and lost touch with your old employers, you may need to track them down yourself. This may not be easy if the companies have been taken over or gone out of business.

Fortunately, the Pensions Scheme Registry (see Appendix 2) should be able to provide up-to-date information about where your scheme is now located. In theory, the registry only covers pension scheme details available from April 1975, but some schemes have provided information for earlier years, so it is worth a try even if you were a member of a scheme before that date.

Divorce

A pension can become a family's largest investment and this is now recognised in divorce proceedings. Often it is the husband who accumulates the greatest pension rights. For most women, it is still difficult to build up a full pension due to career breaks to bring up a family or periods spent working part-time. Many women rely on their husbands for an adequate retirement income.

In the past, pensions were often overlooked when a couple divorced. An ex-wife could only claim part of her former husband's pension if there was a court order for maintenance.

Nowadays, it is possible for wives to get a fairer deal. The value of a couple's pension rights must be considered in a divorce settlement and rules introduced on 1 December, 2000 mean there are now three ways of dividing them up.

◆ **Offsetting** If a couple has assets such as a house, it may be possible for the wife to receive a greater share of these instead of splitting the pension. Where, for example, the husband has a pension fund worth £100,000 and their home is also worth a clear £100,000, the husband could keep the pension, while the wife takes the house.

◆ **Earmarking** Under the Pensions Act 1995, courts can earmark part of a pension for the benefit of the ex-spouse. However, this has not been a popular choice as a divorcee has to wait until her ex-husband retires before she receives any pension and when he dies her pension also ceases.

◆ **Sharing** The Welfare Reform and Pensions Act 1999, which came into effect on 1 December, 2000, means couples can now divide up pension rights at the time of the divorce. Those rights can either remain in the scheme in the wife's name for her to take at retirement or be moved to her own personal or stakeholder pension scheme. If a wife opts for a transfer, it is essential she seeks the help of an independent financial adviser.

If you are considering a divorce, the guide *I Want to Apply for a Financial Order* (D190), which is available from county courts, may be useful.

Unmarried partners should bear in mind that they have no legal right to a share in their partner's pension benefits. Women, in particular, need to consider their positions carefully to make sure they have adequate pension provision of their own, otherwise they will lose out badly if they split up with their partner.

Death

Members of occupational pension schemes often overlook the death benefits these provide. If you die before retirement, a lump sum life insurance benefit will normally be paid. An amount of up to four times your annual salary is allowed under Inland Revenue rules, and this payment is free of income and inheritance taxes. The money will usually be paid to the 'beneficiary' you have nominated. This means it can go to a common-law spouse or a same sex partner if you wish, although pension scheme trustees often retain the discretion to change the beneficiary if they believe someone else has a better claim.

Also, if you die before retirement, your widow or widower will usually receive a pension. In a final salary scheme, this is normally 50% of your rights at the time of your death plus some, or all, of the potential pension you would have earned by the time you reached your normal pension age. In addition, a pension may be provided for your children until they reach age 18 or finish full-time education.

In money purchase schemes, the approach is more varied. Some schemes pay out the value of the member's pension as a lump sum to the dependants. Others pay a pension but based only on the fund that you have accumulated at the time of your death. This may not be very much if you have not been a member for long, so you may need to consider taking out more life insurance to protect your dependants in the early years.

Problems

Fortunately, serious problems with employers' pension schemes are rare nowadays, although many people have still not forgotten the Maxwell scandal or the problems which occurred with company pension schemes during the recession of the early 1990s. However, there is much stricter regulation now.

The Pensions Act 1995 heralded a number of changes, including the setting up of a special watchdog – the Occupational Pensions Regulatory Authority (Opra) – to supervise occupational schemes more closely (see Appendix 2). It ensures any anomalies in the running of a scheme are spotted at any early stage. Also, the Act requires that one-third of pension fund trustees, who are responsible for running schemes, should be nominated by members (although members can agree to other arrangements) so they can keep an eye on what is going on on behalf of employees.

In addition, stricter rules for the investment of the assets of final salary schemes are being introduced to ensure they have the right type of investments to meet their commitments to pensioners. The Law Commission is also to investigate the legal ownership of surplus pension fund assets. In recent times there has been considerable debate about the best way of dealing with these.

At present, under Inland Revenue rules, if a scheme is more than 5% overfunded, a plan of action for reducing the surplus over a five-year period has to be agreed. Measures can include increasing the pensions of existing and future pensioners, agreeing a reduction or suspension of employee or employer contributions to the fund (a 'contribution holiday') or making a payment to the employer (less 35% tax). One of the most common solutions – though this tends to be unpopular with employees – is for the employer to take a contribution holiday, but a combination of measures may also be used.

Company insolvency

If a company goes bust, the insolvency practitioner winding up the business will appoint an independent trustee to look after the interests of pension scheme members. Normally the scheme will be closed down, but this procedure can take several years while the trustee checks members' records and ascertains the value of the assets.

Then, if there are sufficient resources, immediate annuities can be purchased from insurance companies to provide pensions for those members who have already retired, while deferred annuities will be bought for those retiring in the future. An alternative to a deferred annuity is for members to take transfer values and switch them to their new employers' schemes or to personal pension plans.

If the scheme is in deficit and does not have enough assets to meet the full benefits, any deficit becomes a debt of the employer. But if the company has gone into liquidation, this may not be its only debt and the pension fund will rank alongside other unsecured creditors.

However, if the employer has failed to pay in employees' contributions to the fund in the previous 12 months, a claim can be made on the government's Redundancy Fund. If fraud or theft by an employer can be proved, the Pensions Compensation Board (see Appendix 2) may make up the missing funds. But if the shortfall is due to a poor choice of investments, compensation will not be available.

Mergers and takeovers

If your employer is taken over or decides to merge with another company, you could be faced with a variety of options on the pensions front. Ideally, your new employer will offer you membership of a scheme with the same or superior benefits to your existing one. While it would normally be worthwhile for you to join such a scheme, whether you should transfer your previous scheme benefits will depend on the terms you are offered and how long you expect to continue working for the company. If in doubt, it is best to seek professional advice.

Transferring your benefits from a final salary scheme with your previous employer to a money purchase arrangement with the new company is not generally advisable. Although it is possible for a 'bulk transfer' to be made from one employer's scheme to another, these are relatively rare as an actuary would have to certify that the scheme will provide the same level of past service benefits as the old one.

Your new employer may decide to wind up the previous scheme. The trustees will then have to buy annuities to provide pensions immediately for those who have already retired and deferred annuities to guarantee the future payment of pensions at retirement age to those still working.

Complaints

If you are unhappy about any aspect of your employer's pension scheme, there are various channels through which you can complain. First, you should use your scheme's internal disputes procedure. Write a letter explaining your problem to your pension manager, or whoever has been nominated to deal with complaints (remember to keep a copy of your letter). This person must look into your problem and provide you with an answer within two months. If you are not satisfied, you can go to the trustees of your scheme (or with public sector schemes, to the appropriate Government department).

If you are still unhappy, you can turn to the Office for the Pensions Advisory Service (Opas), which has experienced advisers throughout the country. (See Appendix 2.) If Opas cannot clear up the matter and thinks you have a good case, it will pass your complaint on to the Pensions Ombudsman, who has statutory powers to enforce his decisions. If the Ombudsman investigates and decides in your favour, he can award compensation if appropriate. His decision is binding, although you or the pension scheme can appeal to the High Court on a point of law.

9

State, Stakeholder and Personal Pensions

The basic state pension is for everyone who pays a sufficient number of National Insurance contributions. For some people it is the only pension they will get if they do not have any other retirement savings. Although state pensions for employees were boosted through the creation of the State Earnings-Related Pension Scheme (Serps) in the 1970s, it was later decided that the cost to the state would be too great due to the growing number of retired people in the population.

Serps pensions were cut back in the 1980s and the government tried to encourage people to take out their own personal pensions instead. This attempt had some success, but it still left many people with potentially inadequate state pensions.

The current government is hoping to persuade more people to save for retirement. It has made reform of pensions a priority and has introduced stakeholder pensions, to help people save for their 'third age'. It is also making changes to the state pension scheme to improve the position of the low paid.

Despite these improvements, state pensions are increasingly becoming a safety net. They are unlikely to provide you with anything more than the bare minimum to live on. If you want to have enough income for an enjoyable retirement, you have to make sure you save enough through your own pension plan.

State pension provision

Men qualify for state pensions at age 65 and women at 60, but the pension age for women is being raised to bring it into line with men by the year 2020. The increase is being phased in from 2010. This means women born between April 1950 and April 1955 will receive their state pensions between the ages of 60 and 65 depending when their birthday falls, while all women born after April 1955 will have to wait until 65. For a full listing of retirement ages see booklet NP46, *A Guide to Retirement Pensions*, available from Social Security offices.

Equalising the state retirement age

When women born on selected dates between April 1950 and April 1955 will retire

Date of birth	Pensionable age	Pension date
06/04/50 to 05/05/50	60yrs to 60yrs 1mth	06/05/2010
06/10/50 to 05/11/50	60yrs 6mths to 60yrs 7mths	06/05/2011
06/04/51 to 05/05/51	61yrs to 61yrs 1mth	06/05/2012
06/10/51 to 05/11/51	61yrs 6mths to 61yrs 7mths	06/05/2013
06/04/52 to 05/05/52	62yrs to 62yrs 1mth	06/05/2014
06/10/52 to 05/11/52	62yrs 6mths to 62yrs 7mths	06/05/2015
06/04/53 to 05/05/53	63yrs to 63yrs 1mth	06/05/2016
06/10/53 to 05/11/53	63yrs 6mths to 63yrs 7mths	06/05/2017
06/04/54 to 05/05/54	64yrs to 64yrs 1mth	06/05/2018
06/10/54 to 05/11/54	64yrs 6mths to 64yrs 7mths	06/05/2019
06/04/55	65yrs	06/05/2020

Source: DSS booklet NP46, *A Guide to Retirement Pensions*

How much state pension?

The amount of state pension you get can vary. It will depend on such factors as your National Insurance contribution record and your employment status. You may only qualify for the basic retirement pension, which is a flat rate amount, or you may get benefits from the additional State Earnings-Related Pension Scheme (Serps). Some people also qualify for a graduated pension if they paid graduated contributions between April 1961 and April 1975. Each element of the pension is normally revised in line with the Retail Price Index every year.

State pension rates for the 2001-02 tax year

	Per week
Single person's basic pension	£72.50
Married couple's basic pension	£115.90
Maximum Serps pension	£125.30*
Maximum graduated pension	
Men	£7.79
Women	£6.52
***Rate for 2000-01**	

Calculating your own state pension is not easy. To find out how much you can expect from the state, you should ask for a pension forecast from the Department of Social Security (DSS). To apply for a forecast, you can contact the Retirement Pension Forecasting and Advice Unit on 0191 218 7585 and it will fill in an application for you over the phone. Alternatively, you will need to complete form BR19 available from your local DSS office or from the internet.

The forecast will show the amount of pension you are already entitled to based on your contributions to date and how much you will receive at state pension age assuming you continue paying contributions. It will also show whether you can improve your state pension by paying voluntary contributions.

Around four months before you retire you will be sent a form (BR1) so you can claim your state pension. If you do not receive this, contact your local DSS office.

The basic state retirement pension

Contrary to popular belief, the basic state retirement pension is not a universal right. You must have paid or been credited with sufficient National Insurance (NI) contributions to qualify.

As a general rule you must have paid full-rate NI contributions for 90% of your working life to get a full pension. Only full years of contributions count. These are known as qualifying years. A year for this purpose corresponds to the tax year, which runs from April 6 to the following April 5.

The DSS considers your working life to start from the beginning of the tax year in which you reach age 16 and finish at the end of the tax year before the one in which you reach state pension age. To clock up the required record, men must have contributed for at least 44 qualifying years and women for 39. By the end of the year 2020, women will also need to have contributed for 44 years.

If your contribution record is less than the amount required for a full pension, you will get a reduced benefit. However, you must normally have contributed for at least ten qualifying years to be eligible for the minimum basic pension, which is 25% of the full rate.

Not all gaps in your NI record will affect your pension. Children who remain at school until age 18 are credited with contributions (although students in higher education are not). If you are unemployed or off work due to incapacity, credits will also be provided as long as you receive Jobseekers Allowance, are registered as unemployed or receive sickness benefit.

Only men aged 60 or over who have stopped work will receive credits automatically up to age 65 (from 2010 this will be extended to women).

Home responsibilities protection

If you take time off work to care for children or look after someone who is sick or disabled, you will receive 'home responsibilities protection' (HRP), which means you will require fewer years of contributions to qualify for a full basic pension. HRP has been available for complete tax years since April 1978. It is given automatically if you are receiving child benefit for a child under 16, or are getting income support so that you can look after a sick or disabled person at home.

If you are not receiving benefits but are looking after someone for at least 35 hours a week who is getting attendance allowance or a similar benefit, you may also qualify. But in this situation you will need to apply on form CF411, *How to protect your state retirement pension if you are looking after someone at home*, available from your local DSS office. Although HRP can reduce the number of qualifying years you need for a pension, you will still require at least 20 years of ordinary contributions to receive a full basic pension.

Married women

Some married women retiring today do not receive a full pension because in the past they opted to pay a reduced rate of NI contribution, often referred to as the 'married woman's stamp'. This option has not been available since April 1977 to newly married women, or women going back to work after two years out of employment or getting divorced, but some continue to pay these reduced rate contributions.

Married women in this position can claim a pension based on their husbands' contribution records, but this entitles them to a spouse's pension only, which is less than the ordinary single person's pension. The total of the husband's single person's pension plus the spouse's pension is normally described as the married couple's pension. Married women paying reduced rate contributions do not get home responsibilities protection either.

Gaps in your contribution record

Although many people qualify for NI credits or home responsibilities protection when not working, you may still have gaps in your contribution record if you have worked abroad or had a very low paid job which did not require NI contributions.

Working abroad

If you were working abroad and domiciled there, you will normally have made social security contributions in your host country instead of the UK. If it has a reciprocal arrangement with the UK, these contributions can count towards your UK pension. If you are planning to work abroad in the future, it is best to check with the DSS Overseas Branch to find out what your situation will be before you go away. If you are working abroad for a multinational company, your employer may arrange to pay your contributions here. If you are not covered, you could consider making voluntary Class 3 contributions.

Low paid or part-time work

Anyone paid less than the primary threshold (this changes each year but is currently £87 a week) does not have to make NI contributions. However, you may still qualify for home responsibilities protection if, for example, you are working part-time while your children are young. Or you could consider making voluntary Class 3 contributions.

Boosting your basic state pension

Voluntary NI contributions

Paying voluntary Class 3 NI contributions (currently £6.75 per week) can be a useful way of filling gaps in your contribution record. They can be particularly worthwhile if you have worked for only part of a tax year. By paying voluntary contributions to top it up to a full year, it will count towards your pension. Any years of partial contributions do not count.

You have up to six years to make up for missing contributions. But voluntary contributions may not always be a good idea. If they don't help you to achieve at least ten qualifying years, you won't be eligible for a pension anyway. If you are a married or divorced woman, you may get a better pension claiming on your husband's NI contributions. For further information see DSS booklets CA07, *National Insurance – Unpaid and Late Contributions*, and CA08, *National Insurance Voluntary Contributions*.

Dorothy Miller, 58, paid full-rate National Insurance contributions for the first eight years of her working life. When she married her husband Fred, 56, she opted to pay reduced rate contributions. This means she has not got the minimum ten years' worth of full contributions to qualify for a pension in her own right. She can get one on her husband's NI contributions but she will have to wait until he is 65, by which time she will be 67.

Dorothy is considering paying voluntary contributions to ensure she gets a small pension until her husband draws his. She needs to get a pension forecast from the DSS to tell her whether this may be worthwhile.

Delaying your retirement

If you do not claim your pension at state retirement age it will be increased by 7.5% for every year you delay, with pro rata increases for shorter periods. This increase will apply to each element of your pension – basic, graduated and Serps. At present it is possible to defer for a maximum of five years. This would increase your pension by about 37.5%. From April 6, 2010 you will be able to put off receiving your pension indefinitely, and it will increase by 10.4% for each year you delay.

For further information see DSS leaflet N192, *Giving Up Your Retirement Pension to Earn Extra*. However, deferring your pension is not usually recommended. If you don't need the money because you are still working it is better to put it into a savings account.

The minimum income guarantee

If you retire on a low pension income – currently less than £92.15 a week for single pensioners and less than £140.55 a week for pensioner couples – you may be eligible for a government top-up to bring your income up to these levels. This minimum income guarantee (MIG) was introduced in April 1999. However, it is means tested, and you will only be eligible if you have less than £12,000 in savings. If you are 60 or over, you can apply for help under the MIG by calling 0800 028 1111.

Graduated pensions

You may qualify for graduated pension if you were employed between April 1961 and April 1975 and earned more than around £9 a week. However, the amounts involved are pretty small. Your entitlement will depend on how many 'units' of graduated contributions you paid at the time and the value of the units when you claim your pension. The maximum number of units is 72 for a woman and 86 for a man. Each unit is currently worth 9.06p. So the maximum amount payable to a woman is £6.52 a week, while a man could get up to £7.79. However, most people who receive a graduated pension get less than £3 a week. Once in payment the benefit is increased in line with inflation like the basic state pension.

The State Earnings-Related Pension Scheme

Serps was introduced in April 1978 to provide employees with an additional income-related state pension. Initially every employee who paid NI contributions was a member of the scheme, unless they belonged to an employer's pension scheme that had contracted out of Serps and was providing a replacement pension. Otherwise only the self-employed were excluded.

Serps relates to the band of earnings between what are known as the lower and upper earnings limits. It was originally designed to provide a pension of 25% of the best of these earnings averaged over 20 years. But the scheme was radically revised in 1988 bringing down the pension entitlement to 20% of earnings averaged over an employee's entire working life.

This reduction, which was phased in, is just starting to take effect. For people retiring between now and 2010, the percentage applied to their earnings since 1988-89 is being reduced on a sliding scale from 25% to 20%.

One of the good things about Serps is that there was no minimum membership period to qualify for benefits – unlike the basic state pension, which requires at least ten years of contributions. So even if you were only a member of the scheme for a few years you will receive some benefit. Serps will be soon be replaced by the new second state pension, but any entitlement to Serps which you have already accumulated will be calculated as before.

For more information on how your Serps pension is calculated, see DSS booklet NP46, *A Guide to Retirement Pensions*. Alternatively, if you request a pension forecast, it will include a calculation of any Serps pension you may be due. Once you start receiving a Serps pension it will increase each year in line with inflation, like the basic retirement pension.

Why you may not get a Serps pension

The self-employed were not covered by Serps and were not required to contribute to the scheme. If you are self-employed you will only qualify for a basic state retirement pension. Employees may not receive a Serps pension if they worked for an employer with a contracted-out pension scheme. Part of their company pension is designed to replace Serps.

After 1988, it became possible for employees to opt out of Serps and have part of their own and their employer's NI contributions paid into a personal pension plan instead. To encourage people to opt out, the government paid an extra bonus into their plans for the first five years after the scheme was introduced.

However, it was not a good idea for everybody to opt out, particularly people in their late 40s or early 50s, and those on low incomes, as the size of their NI contributions rebates meant it was unlikely they would get a better pension than they would get from Serps.

Opting out of Serps

People who opted out of Serps have had their contributions paid into a special type of pension plan known as an 'appropriate' or 'rebate' personal pension. The contributions build up to provide a 'protected rights' fund. The amount of pension you can get from this is not guaranteed. As with other types of personal pension plan, investment performance, management charges and annuity rates at the time you retire will determine how much pension you receive. However, you should get an annual statement from your pension company showing how much you may get in the future, based on certain growth assumptions.

Although appropriate personal pensions are very similar to personal pensions, there are certain restrictions on how the 'protected rights' fund is used at retirement:

◆ The pension cannot be taken until state retirement age.
◆ It must be taken as a pension and cannot be commuted for a tax-free lump sum.
◆ A 50% widow or widower's pension must be provided on death.
◆ The pension must increase at 3% a year for that part of the fund built up until 1997 and at 5%, or by the rise in the Retail Price Index if lower, on funds built up since then.

The state second pension

As part of its plans for improved pension provision, the government is making changes to state pensions. The basic state pension will remain as it is now. But from 2002, Serps will be replaced by the state second pension. The new pension is intended to be particularly beneficial to people on low incomes and those who are unable to stay in work because of caring responsibilities, illness or disability. As with with Serps, it will not cover the self-employed.

Anybody earning more than the lower earnings limit (the amount on which NI contributions must be paid – currently around £3,750 a year) and up to around £10,000 will be significantly better off with a state second pension than they would have been with Serps. They will be treated as though they had been earning around £10,000. The new pension will also be more generous for anyone earning up to around £22,000. For people earning more than that, it is expected to be practically the same as Serps.

Carers and people with long-term disabilities who are off work will receive credits towards their state second pension. However, the proposed conditions required to qualify for these credits will be tighter than those for the basic state pension.

To qualify, people must spend at least 35 hours a week caring for someone in receipt of relevant disability benefits, or have a child aged five or under, or be incapable of long-term work, having worked in the past. Credits will not be available when people are unemployed or receiving child benefit for a child over the age of five as they are currently for the basic state pension.

It will be possible to opt out of the state second pension in the same way as it was possible to opt out of Serps. If you decide to do this, NI rebates will be paid into your stakeholder pension instead. It will only be worth doing this if you are likely to get a higher pension from a stakeholder plan than from the state second pension. For people earning less than £10,000, this is unlikely. However, the government is hoping that anyone earning more then £10,000 will opt out and it is intending to encourage those earning between around £10,000 and £22,000 with more generous NI rebates than they would have got under Serps.

If you decide to opt out of the state second pension, the NI rebate you receive will not be considered part of the £3,600 contribution limit to a stakeholder plan.

The introduction of the second pension will mean anyone retiring after 2002 could end up with a state pension made up of four elements – the basic retirement pension, a graduated pension, Serps and the second pension.

The pension credit scheme

To ensure that people on lower earnings are not discouraged from saving into a stakeholder plan by the fact that they might be no better off than others who qualify for means-tested state benefits, such as the minimum income guarantee, the government is introducing a 'pension credit' in 2003. This will give pensioners extra cash on top of their other state benefits if they have a small amount of private pension.

The government wants people to feel they are being rewarded rather than penalised for their saving. Depending on how much they have managed to save, pensioners will receive between £1 and £23 on top of the minimum income guarantee, which by 2003 will be at least £100 for single pensioners and £154 for couples. According to the government, the pension credit will be of particular advantage to women, who tend to have much smaller occupational or private pensions than men.

In future, when someone's entitlement to the state pension is calculated, an income assessment will be made to find out how much they are entitled to under the minimum income guarantee and the credit scheme.

Stakeholder pensions

The main part of the government's plans for reforming pensions is the introduction of stakeholder pensions. It hopes to encourage – but not compel – all those who can afford it to save for their retirement. It believes one of the main reasons many people have not started a pension in the past is because existing pension arrangements have been too costly and complex.

Stakeholder pensions are intended to offer a new approach. They can be sold by existing pension companies, but the detailed rules about how they work have been set by the government to ensure they are low cost, flexible and user-friendly. Although they are aimed at people on moderate earnings (defined as between around £10,000 and £20,000) they will also be attractive to those on higher incomes. The government estimates up to five million people may join stakeholder schemes.

Stakeholder pensions went on sale in April 2001. Their main features are:

◆ They are money purchase schemes. This means you will build up a pot of money in your scheme. The amount of extra pension you get at retirement will not, therefore, be guaranteed. It will depend on how much you save, the charges deducted, how well the investments perform and annuity rates when you retire (that is the rate at which your fund is converted to a pension and depends largely on long-term interest rates at the time).

◆ Contributions of up to £3,600 a year are allowed automatically. It will not be necessary for these to come out of earned income (previously all pension savings had to be made out of earned income). This will mean people can put savings or money they have been given into their pension. It will help people to build up a pension when they are not working, which will be particularly useful for the unemployed, mature students or women staying at home to care for young children or elderly relatives.

◆ There is no minimum age limit. This means parents or other relatives will be able to pay money into a stakeholder pension plan for a child.

◆ Contributions above £3,600 a year will be permitted providing they fall within the limits for personal pension plans. These allow contributions of up to 17.5% of earnings up to age 35, increasing to 40% for ages 61 and over, subject to an earnings cap. (For details see page 153.) These contributions will also be allowed to continue for up to five years after earnings have ceased.

◆ Contributions will be eligible for tax relief. They will be paid net of basic rate tax by everyone including the self-employed. This tax will then be reclaimed from the Inland Revenue by the pension provider. Higher rate taxpayers will have to reclaim their extra relief through their self-assessment tax returns.

◆ Contributors must be UK residents. If someone ceases to be a UK resident contributions can continue for a maximum of five years.

◆ Schemes are required to meet a number of minimum standards. To keep them simple and transparent, they will be allowed to make only one type of charge, an annual fee of no more than 1% of the accumulated fund. Any additional charges for further services must be optional.

◆ 'Decision trees' will be provided to help people decide whether a stakeholder plan is right for them, highlighting if more detailed advice is required. If individual advice is needed, pension companies or financial advisers will be able to make an additional charge.

◆ No additional charges may be made by schemes if members want to transfer to another pension scheme.

◆ To encourage small savers and to allow for small one-off contributions in addition to regular payments, minimum contributions to schemes must be no higher than £20. Savers must be free to contribute when they want – providers will not be able to make you contribute regularly.

◆ A choice of investment options may be offered, but schemes must stipulate a suitable 'default' strategy for those who prefer not to make their own choice.

◆ Stakeholder pension schemes can either be run by a board of trustees or a stakeholder scheme manager, such as an insurance company, authorised by the Financial Services Authority. Trustee schemes, where at least a third of the trustees will have to be independent, will be overseen by the Occupational Pensions Regulatory Authority (Opra). (See Appendix 2.)

◆ All employers with five staff or more will be required to provide employees with access to a stakeholder scheme from October 2001, if they do not already provide an occupational pension scheme or group personal pension scheme to which they are making contributions of at least 3% of employees' earnings.

Where an occupational scheme requires employees to wait more than a year before they can join, or puts restrictions on part-timers joining, a stakeholder scheme will also have to be provided. Employers will have to designate a scheme and pass its details to each employee and deduct contributions from pay if the employee wishes.

They must offer a scheme to employees within three months of their starting work. Employees will have the right to vary the amount their employer deducts from their pay at six monthly intervals. However, employers will not be liable for the performance of the designated scheme.

◆ After you agree to join a stakeholder scheme you will have a cooling off period of 14 days during which you can change your mind and get your money back.

Getting the best out of stakeholder pensions

One of most important factors if you want to get the best out of any pension is not to delay. So if you are offered access to a stakeholder pension scheme by an employer, don't put off the decision about whether to join or not. If you are not offered a scheme because the business you work for is too small or you are self-employed, it is even more important not to procrastinate.

You can probably think of plenty of reasons to delay starting a pension – retirement seems too far away, you need to use the money for something else, and so on. However, generally speaking, you will lose more than you gain from delaying. Although you may not think it will do any harm to wait another year or two, it means you will either have to save more or make do with less pension when you reach retirement. The older you are, the more difference a delay makes, as the table shows.

The cost of delay
Assumes pension contribution before tax relief of £100 a month

Male age next b'day	Fund value at 60	Pension per year	Loss in fund	Extra premium required to achieve £12,000 pension
25	£146,000	£12,000		
Delay taking out pension to age:				
26	£136,000	£11,200	6.8%	£7
27	£126,000	£10,400	13.7%	£15
28	£118,000	£9,710	19.2%	£24
29	£109,000	£9,030	25.3%	£33
30	£101,000	£8,390	30%	£43
35	£69,600	£5,730	52%	£109
40	£46,000	£3,780	68%	£214
45	£28,700	£2,360	80%	£405
50	£16,000	£1,320	89%	£800

Based on standard PIA assumptions and mid-rate investment return of 7% a year
Source: Legal & General

Naturally, a pension is not the only way of saving for retirement but it is one of the most tax efficient. Pensions have three major tax advantages:
◆ Income tax relief is given on contributions at your highest marginal rate.
◆ Any growth in your pension fund investments is virtually tax free.
◆ At retirement you can take up to 25% of your pension savings as a tax-free lump sum.
If you want more information about stakeholder pensions, there is a stakeholder pensions helpline on 0845 601 2923 which is run by Opas, the Office for the Pensions Advisory Service.

Contribution limits

Almost everybody will be allowed to pay up to £3,600 into a stakeholder or personal pension plan from 6 April, 2001. Only members of occupational pension schemes earning more than £30,000 a year will be excluded. However, contributions above that amount will be restricted by the current personal pension limits as shown in the table. For the highly paid, there is further a limit on contributions because of the cap on the amount of earnings that can be counted. This is normally revised each year. It is £95,400 for the 2001-02 tax year.

Personal pension contribution limits
Maximum contribution for 2001-02 is the lower of:

Age at 6 April	% of earnings	Cash amount
Up to 35	17.5%	£16,695
36 to 45	20%	£19,080
46 to 50	25%	£23,850
51 to 55	30%	£28,620
56 to 60	35%	£33,390
61 or over	40%	£38,160

How much to save

Few people save as much towards their pension as they should. This is partly because many people do not know how much they should be saving. They can, on the other hand, usually say roughly how much pension they would like. Research has found that most of us would like between a half and three-quarters of our current income. There are two ways of trying to achieve this goal:
◆ **Save a set percentage of your income** If you start when you are under 25 and save 17.5% of your earnings throughout your life, there is a good chance you could achieve a pension of two-thirds your income at retirement. If you leave it until later, say, when you are in your early 30s, you will need to save around

20% to achieve that level. If you are older, the percentage would be even greater. Whatever level of savings you choose, one of the advantages of the percentage approach is that it ensures you invest more in your pension as your earnings increase.

◆ **Save a cash amount** Find out how much you would need to save to build up the pension pot required to buy the amount of pension you want. To achieve a £10,000 pension, for example, calculations by one major insurance company show a man would require a sum of around £250,000 at present, while a woman would need about £285,000. (This is because annuities for women are more expensive as they tend to live longer than men.)

The table shows how much the company calculates you would have to save at different ages to be able to buy various amounts of pension. However, as with any money purchase pension plan, the figures are based on certain assumptions about investment returns and interest rates and are not guaranteed. They assume inflation remains at current levels.

How much you need to save for your pension

Pension at 65	Monthly contribution before tax relief			
	Male		Female	
	30 at outset	40 at outset	30 at outset	40 at outset
£10,000	£180	£290	£200	£325
£15,000	£270	£430	£300	£480
£20,000	£355	£570	£400	£640
£25,000	£440	£710	£500	£795

Figures based on growth rate of 7% a year
Source: Legal & General

Bob Jackson, 39, knows he should have started a pension a long time ago but somehow never got round to it. He decides he will begin by making regular savings of £150 per month. With basic rate tax relief added, this means he will be investing £192 per month in his pension. He chooses a plan with built-in annual premium increases to make sure he saves more in the future. His financial adviser also points out that he could pay lump sums into his pension to help to make up for lost time. Bob decides to put in the £2,500 bonus he received recently. With tax relief, this will add another £3,250 to his pension plan.

Choosing a stakeholder pension

Deciding which stakeholder pension is right for you will depend on a number of factors:

◆ **Employees** If you are offered access to a stakeholder pension by your employer, you do not have to choose that scheme, but for most people it is likely to be the best option especially if your employer offers to contribute too. It will also be convenient because your employer will deal with the administrative side of things. You will probably find saving easier if your contributions are deducted from your pay at source as you won't be tempted to spend the money on other things. Charges may also be lower than with an individual plan. Although the company providing the scheme will be dictated by your employer, you will probably be offered a choice of investment funds.

◆ **Other employees and the self-employed** You will be free to choose from any of the stakeholder schemes. As their terms and conditions have been determined by the government, variations between different companies' policies are limited. Some charge less than 1%. However, the main difference is likely to lie in the type of funds they offer and the investment performance the company can achieve if you opt for one that is actively managed rather than an index tracker. Some pension fund managers will also offer other companies' investment funds. For more on funds, see below.

How stakeholder pensions work

All stakeholder plans will have to conform to the government's minimum standards. They must:

◆ Have a single annual management charge of 1% or less;
◆ Have no other charges, such as a policy fee or bid/offer spread;
◆ Have a minimum savings requirement of no more than £20;
◆ Invest 100% of your savings;
◆ Allow you to stop and start your savings without penalty;
◆ Allow you to increase or decrease your savings at any time without penalty;
◆ Allow you to transfer your savings to another provider without penalty.

Investment choices

Most stakeholder plans will offer a choice of funds. Before making a decision, savers will need to consider their attitude to risk and how close they are to retirement. As a rule of thumb, funds which hold shares have historically produced the best returns over the long term, while over the shorter term funds that invest in fixed-interest securities and cash deposits are a more secure option.

If you cannot decide which fund to choose, the pension provider is likely to put your savings into a mainstream UK stock market fund, a managed or a with-profits fund.

◆ **Stock market funds** A variety of funds which invest in shares may be available through your pension policy. UK equity funds, for example, invest purely in UK shares. Most are run by professional investment managers who choose the shares they expect will give the best returns. But their performance can vary considerably. Other funds are run as index trackers. These invest in the shares which make up a stock market index, such as the FTSE-100, so their performance matches that of the stock market in general. Both types of funds can go up and down in value as share prices fluctuate.

Overseas equity funds buy shares in foreign stock markets. This means their value will be affected by currency fluctuations as well as share price movements. They normally focus on major foreign markets such as the US, Japan and Europe. A general international fund may also be available.

Ethical funds also invest in shares either in the UK or on an international basis which conform to certain ethical criteria laid down by the pension company. Typically, this means they do not buy shares of companies involved in the production or sale of alcohol, tobacco, armaments, nuclear power or pornography, or where the company's activities involve animal testing or environmental damage. Some funds also have a positive approach of supporting companies which are doing something beneficial for the environment or for the community.

◆ **Unit-linked managed funds** These funds invest in a spread of assets – UK and overseas shares, property, fixed-interest securities and deposits – to provide a balanced portfolio for long-term growth. The value of your savings will reflect the underlying investments, which can go down as well as up in value as investment conditions vary. These funds are likely to be less risky than stock market funds, and some adopt a more cautious approach than others by investing a greater proportion of their assets in lower risk investments. However, over the longer term, they may not provide as much growth as stock market only funds.

◆ **With-profits funds** With these, your savings are invested in a mixture of UK and overseas shares, property, fixed-interest securities and deposits. Based on the returns from these investments, the insurance company calculates a regular annual bonus which is added to the value of your policy. These bonuses are designed to smooth out the fluctuations in interest rates and investment markets. To achieve steady returns, past performance and possible future returns are taken into account when bonus levels are decided. This means that after a period of particularly good returns, some profits may be held back to cushion any future fall in bonus rates when markets turn down again. These reserves can also be invested to generate extra returns.

At the end of the investment term, when your policy is due to mature, a final bonus will normally be added to make up for any growth that has not been reflected in the regular bonus additions. However, this final bonus tends to be volatile, as it will depend more closely on the state of investment markets at the time your policy matures.

A major attraction of with-profits policies is the security offered by the build up of bonuses. However, prospective policyholders should check how bonuses are affected if retirement comes earlier than expected. Insurers often retain the right to adjust the value of your policy if investment markets have slumped.

◆ **Property funds** These may invest both in physical property or the shares of property companies in the commercial sector – shops, offices and industrial properties.

◆ **Fixed-interest funds** These hold government securities and corporate bonds which pay fixed rates of interest and provide fixed repayments of capital at maturity. They generally fluctuate less in value than equity funds.

◆ **Deposit or cash funds** These invest in the money markets. They function like bank or building society accounts. They do not fall in value but do not produce any capital growth either.

◆ **Lifestyle funds** These are arrangements where your savings start off invested wholly in shares to gain from the higher growth potential of the stock market. Then, in the run up to retirement – typically over the last five to ten years – the fund is moved gradually into more secure investments, such as fixed-interest securities, to protect it from a sudden fall in the stock market.

Individual pension account

Together with stakeholder pensions, the government has launched individual pension accounts (IPAs). These are a new type of investment fund which will allow unit trusts and open-ended investment companies (Oeics) to be used more freely within stakeholder pensions. Although pension companies have offered investors access to unit trusts within pension plans in the past, it was more usual for premiums to be invested in unit-linked insurance company funds. When unit trusts were used, investors had to pay stamp duty, whereas the insurance-based funds were free of this. IPAs will be exempt from stamp duty.

They could also offer savers greater flexibility. If you want to change pension provider, it will mean you no longer have to cash in your existing plan. Instead, you should be able to transfer the IPA intact. It should also be possible to hold several different companies' IPAs within one pension.

Sue Turner, 31, considers herself a cautious investor so she is inclined to invest her pension savings in a with-profits fund which she believes will give her steady returns. However, her financial adviser points out that as she has around 30 years to go until she retires, she will probably get better returns from a stock market fund which invests wholly in shares. She can then switch her savings into a safer fund as she approaches retirement.

Investment performance

Investment performance can have a greater impact on the final value of your pension pot than any differences in charges. Surveys of past performance show there are wide variations in the results achieved by different pension companies. However, there is considerable debate about how much value should be attached to past performance information in deciding your choice of pension provider.

There is certainly no guarantee that because a company's pension plan has produced good results in the past it will do so in the future. However, most financial advisers feel more comfortable recommending companies which have a record of delivering consistently good past performance than those which have failed to do so.

Companies' performance records can be found quite easily in the surveys which are published regularly in magazines and periodicals such as *Money Management* and *Life & Pensions Moneyfacts*. However, various factors need to be borne in mind when examining these figures.

With stock market funds, the best results tend to be produced by specialist funds, but so do the worst. Don't be tempted to put any more than a small fraction of your pension into such high-risk funds. The majority of investors are better off choosing mainstream UK equity or managed funds, so it is the performance of these that is most relevant. The alternative is to choose an index-tracker fund. Then you do not have to bother about studying past performance because the returns from these depend solely on future stock market movements.

The performance of conventional with-profits funds is particularly difficult to assess because current bonuses do not necessarily reflect recent investment performance. A company which has amassed large reserves as a result of being less generous with past generations of policyholders can afford to pay larger bonuses today. Fortunately, nowadays, most insurers run other funds such as unit trusts which should enable you to gain a more up-to-date picture of how good their investment performance is. Large reserves can also be a good sign. A company with financial strength will be better able to withstand competitive pressures and market fluctuations.

The role of personal pensions

The introduction of stakeholder pensions has made many pension companies go back to the drawing board and radically change their existing plans. However, generally speaking, if you have been contributing to a personal pension for several years, there is no reason to change. Although in the past personal pensions had higher charges than those being offered today, the heaviest deductions were normally made in the first year or two. After plans have been running for a few years, charges are not normally a problem.

Still, if you are unsure about the merits of your existing pension plan or you are considering an increase in your contributions, you could ask an independent financial adviser to suggest what action you should take. If investment performance has been poor, you could consider transferring your fund to a different provider.

It is also possible to stop making contributions to your plan and make it 'paid up'. This means your money is left invested with the same pension company until your usual retirement date. However, it is important to consider carefully what the charges will be for each of these options.

If you want to increase your contributions to an existing plan, you should make sure there will be no high up-front charges deducted from these extra payments. Ask your provider for an illustration of the benefits you would get, and then ask a stakeholder pension provider for an illustration for a contribution of the same amount. You can make a comparison to see which offers the best deal.

Nowadays, all companies have to provide prospective policyholders with a key features document, which includes a table showing how their charges will affect the growth of your savings over time and how much you might get back, assuming a standard investment growth rate of 7%. This means a direct comparison can be made between the two companies.

Remember, if you want to top up your pension, you can do so with a one-off 'single premium' contribution. The cheapest option is often to add a lump sum to an existing plan, but if you want to spread your investments around, you could choose a different provider.

Self-invested personal pensions

Ordinary personal or stakeholder plans will meet most people's investment needs, at least for most of their working lives. If investment diversity is required, lump sum investments can be placed with other pension companies. An alternative option is a self-invested personal pension (Sipp). These plans are normally administered by an insurance company but they leave you free to choose your own investments. As well as being able to invest in any unit or investment trust, you can include direct investments in shares, gilts and even commercial property.

However, a full Sipp is only practical for substantial investors because of the high set-up and running costs, which may include employing an investment adviser if you do not have the time or the expertise to make the investment decisions yourself. Some schemes, known as hybrid Sipps, can be somewhat cheaper. They are a halfway house between a managed and a self-invested plan, usually requiring a minimum contribution each year to the insurance company's own funds while other money can be invested elsewhere.

Waiver of premium

Your plans for retirement could suffer a nasty blow if you contract a long-term illness. This is why it is worth considering paying a small extra charge for a benefit known as waiver of premium. This ensures contributions to your pension plan are maintained on your behalf by your provider if you are unable to work due to disability. It comes into effect normally around three to six months after you become sick or disabled and continues until you reach pension age if necessary. However, make sure you choose a company that defines disability with reference to your inability to carry out your own occupation. Avoid those which will only pay out if you are unable to do paid work of any kind.

Death

State pensions

A widow or widower who does not qualify for a basic state retirement pension on the basis of their National Insurance contributions can inherit this entitlement from their husband or wife. In the case of Serps, where a spouse has reached state pension age before 6 October, 2002, their widow or widower can inherit up to 100% of their Serps benefit when they die. Thereafter, the amount inherited is being reduced in stages, so that any widow or widower whose husband or wife was due to reach state pension age on or after 6 October, 2010 will only be able to inherit up to 50% of their Serps benefit when they die.

When the state second pension is introduced, the maximum amount a husband or wife can inherit will be 50%.

Personal and stakeholder pensions

If you die before reaching retirement, your pension may be treated in two parts. If you have used it to opt out of Serps, the part financed from National Insurance rebates will provide a 50% spouse's pension. The pension fund built up from your own contributions will normally be paid as a lump sum into your estate.

Remember that as time goes by your pension fund is likely to become a very substantial investment, so it is important to make sure that tax is not incurred unnecessarily if you die early. You can prevent this by writing your policy 'in trust'. This will ensure that the proceeds are not included in your estate for inheritance tax purposes and that your beneficiaries gain immediate access to the money. Your pension company should be able to provide the forms for this.

In the early years, the value of your pension is not likely to be great. So you should consider taking out extra life assurance to help protect your spouse or partner from financial hardship after your death. Pension term insurance can be attractive as you will receive tax relief on your premiums, but the maximum payment for life insurance is 10% of the pension contributions.

Also it is still worth checking if you can get a cheaper deal with an ordinary life insurance policy.

Divorce

As people build up more savings in personal and stakeholder pensions, it has become increasingly important that these assets should be taken into account in divorce proceedings. Where a person is a member of Serps, the extra pension can also be significant and cannot be ignored. Many women still rely on their husband for an adequate retirement income. In the past, they often lost out on pension benefits.

Nowadays, it is possible for wives to get a fairer deal. The value of a couple's pension rights must be considered in a divorce settlement and rules introduced on 1 December, 2000 mean there are now three ways of dividing them up.

◆ **Offsetting** If a couple has assets such as a house, it may be possible for a wife to receive a greater share of these instead of splitting the pension. Where, for example, a husband has a pension fund worth £100,000 and their home is also worth a clear £100,000, the husband could keep the pension, while the wife takes the house.

◆ **Earmarking** Under the Pensions Act 1995, courts can earmark part of a pension for the benefit of the ex-spouse. However, this has not been a very popular choice as divorcees have to wait until their ex-husbands retire before receiving any pension and when he dies their pension also ceases.

◆ **Sharing** The Welfare Reform and Pensions Act 1999, which came into effect on 1 December, 2000, means that couples can now divide up pension rights at the time of the divorce. Those rights can either remain in the scheme in the wife's name for her to take at retirement, or she can use them to set up her own personal or stakeholder pension plan.

If you are considering a divorce, the guide *I Want to Apply for a Financial Order* (D190), available from county courts, may be useful.

Pensions taken out before July 1988

If you took out a pension plan before 1 July, 1988, you will have what is known as a 'retirement annuity' or 'section 226' policy. Although they are very similar to today's personal pensions, there are a few key differences. One is that the contribution limits are lower for older age groups. However, the earnings cap which puts a cash limit on contributions to personal pensions does not apply. Also, the government's recent proposals to abolish the carry forward rules on personal pensions, which allow unused tax relief from past tax years to be taken up, do not apply to these policies.

Another distinction is that a pension cannot be taken from a retirement annuity until age 60 (with a personal pension it is possible to start drawing the benefits at 50) and there is also a difference in the way the tax-free lump sum is calculated at retirement. If these restrictions prove inconvenient, there is nothing to stop you converting your policy into a personal pension, although you will need to check with your pension provider whether there are any extra costs involved.

If you have a retirement annuity pension, it is also advisable to find out what it would pay out on your death before retirement. Under a personal pension contract, the death benefit is normally the full value of the fund.

However, when retirement annuities were being sold, this provision was less common. It was more usual for a return of premiums plus a modest rate of interest to be paid on death. The difference between this amount and the actual value of the pension fund can be substantial. It may be possible to switch to a 'return of fund' basis but this can be costly. Another option is to take out extra life insurance. An independent financial adviser can help you decide what action to take in this situation.

Retirement annuity contribution limits

Age at 6 April	% of earnings
50 or less	17.5%
51-55	20%
56-60	22.5%
61 or over	27.5%

Pensions mis-selling

Some people were wrongly advised to buy personal pensions during the late 1980s and early 1990s when they would have been better off in a company pension scheme. If you were one of them, you should already have been contacted by the financial adviser or pension company which sold you the personal pension so your case can be reviewed and redress offered.

However, if you have not been contacted and think you might have a case, you can get information about what to do by calling the Financial Services Authority public enquiries helpline on 020 7712 8990.

If you have any other complaints about a personal or stakeholder pension, you can take the matter to the Financial Ombudsman Service. For more details about making complaints see Chapter 15.

10

Investing your Capital

When faced with decisions about how to invest money, you will be pulled in different directions by fear and greed, the two motivations referred to in Chapter 1. Should you protect and preserve, or venture and grow?

Answering this question requires you to set aims for your capital over a period of at least five years. The long-term rates of return defined in Chapter 1 are your starting point. There is a simple trade off: the higher the rate of return you aim for, the more the value of your investments will vary on a day-to-day basis. The longer the timescale of your investment and the more robust your character in the face of adversity, the better placed you will be to withstand such fluctuations.

Putting this in more concrete terms, if you want to make a return of 10% a year on top of inflation, you will have to put almost all of your capital into equities (stocks and shares) – as you saw in Chapter 1, there is no chance of getting that return from less risky investments. Stock markets nowadays tend to move together, so even after spreading your money around you will still find the value of your investments could fall by 15% to 20% in a month or 30% to 40% in a year.

In the past, stock markets have always recovered from such falls – often quickly, but sometimes slowly. If you suffer such a fall after your investments have already risen by 100% or more, you can shrug your shoulders and will probably suffer little anxiety. But if the value of your investment falls by 30% soon after you have made it, what then?

This is why even bold aims need to be tempered with caution, and why even if your aims are ambitious, you will probably want to use the principle of diversification to reduce the risk of suffering a sudden 40% drop in the value of your capital.

The three types of investment

Most people will want to hold some assets in capital secure cash deposits, some in relatively secure fixed-rate investments and some in riskier equity investments. The higher the proportion in equities, the higher the returns you can expect over a period of ten years or more.

The table gives examples of the asset split you might use depending on the overall level of real return you are aiming for and the level of variability in the value of your portfolio you are comfortable with.

Allocating your capital to the three types of investment

Your aim for annual real returns (on top of inflation) from your capital

	2-4%	4-6%	6-10%
Proportion of your capital invested in:			
Deposits	40%	20%	10%
Fixed rate	40%	30%	20%
Equity	20%	50%	70%
Total	100%	100%	100%
Expected volatility	Low	Moderate	High

If you have only 10% of your capital in equities, even a 30% fall in their price will only lower the value of your whole portfolio by 3%. But if you have 80% of your money in equities, the day-to-day fluctuations in the portfolio's value will be far larger. This much, and the fact of higher long-term returns from equities, is certain. But there is no scientific formula for applying this. Investment is an art rather than a science, and at the end of the day you have to be comfortable with your investments.

At the height of the Wall Street boom in 1929, a small speculator cornered the great financier John Pierpont Morgan at a cocktail party. Perspiring and anxious, the investor recounted how in 1928 he had bought shares and their price had doubled. So he had borrowed money and invested more, and the shares had doubled again. He had borrowed yet more money and once again all his holdings had doubled. He explained that he was now (on paper) rich but was very worried about the level of the market, he couldn't sleep and was not sure what to do. Morgan gave him a slow and condescending look. "Sell, down to sleeping point," he pronounced before turning and walking away.

The cost of insurance

The principle of diversification is not as simple as 'not putting all your eggs in one basket', though this is its basis. Research in the past few decades has considerably increased our understanding of the trade offs between risk and return. The key thing about the right sort of diversification is that it can reduce your risk of loss by more than it reduces the rate of return you obtain – an issue covered later in this chapter.

Starting with the basic point about spreading your money across a range of investments, there is a cost associated with this. With deposits, the more you place in an account, the better the interest rate. So dividing money between accounts will cost you in terms of lower interest, but this may be worthwhile to minimise risk, especially if you use smaller and newer banks.

Collective investments, such as unit and investment trusts and others discussed below, undertake that spreading of money for you in stock market investments. Because they deal in large sums, their transaction costs are far lower than yours would be, saving you money as well as time and trouble. But they also levy initial charges which balance this out.

As the examples below show, buying and selling collective investments is slightly more expensive than buying and selling shares. And collective investments also levy annual charges. The best way to view these charges is as a form of insurance premium. If you could not insure your home against fire or flood, would you rather own your own home or own a 1/100th share in your own and 99 other homes? Clearly the latter is less risky. Likewise, owning shares in 100 companies is less risky than owning shares in one or two. So the annual charge on a collective investment is like an insurance premium you pay to reduce your risk of loss.

Just as the insurance premiums you pay over the years will reduce the overall return you make from owning a house, so the annual charges on collective investments will reduce the return you make from owning shares. In the same way that you want the best cover for your home at the lowest possible cost, you will want the best type of collective investment at the lowest possible annual charge. And just as with insurance, there will be a trade off between quality and cost.

Costs of buying and selling compared

	Shares via stockbroker	Unit trust
Buying cost		
Commission	1.65%	Nil
Stamp duty	0.5%	Nil
Initial charge	Nil	5.0%
Total	2.15%	5.0%
Selling cost		
Commission	1.65%	Nil
Price spread	2.0%	1.5%
Total	3.65%	1.5%
Total cost	5.8%	6.5%

This comparison assumes that you pay the commission charges typical for an advisory service stockbroker and the full initial charge on a unit trust. Stamp duty is contained within the unit trust price spread, as are share dealing costs. You pay the initial charge when you buy a unit trust, but when you sell you get a price some 6.5% lower than the buying price. Effectively, therefore, you pay the extra 1.5% representing this 'spread' when you sell. Likewise, there is a spread between the buying and selling price of shares on the stock market. It varies from 1% on blue-chip shares to 5% or more for small companies. Again, you effectively pay this spread when you sell.

You can lower dealing costs in both shares and unit trusts, the result being that overall costs still remain similar for a buy-and-sell transaction. (See the DIY approach on page 183.)

The collective proposition

Collective investments in general offer a five-fold proposition to investors.
◆ **Risk** Spreading investment, as collective investments do, reduces risk as compared with holding a few individual securities.
◆ **Cost** The cost of buying and selling collectives is often similar to and can be lower than the cost of buying and selling individual securities.
◆ **Professional management** Collectives entrust your money to full-time professional investors.

◆ **Convenience** Owning collectives results in considerably less paperwork and decision-making for the investor.

◆ **Regulation** Collectives are subject to well-defined legislation and prudential rules enforced by effective regulation, making fraud virtually impossible and providing adequate compensation in the event of loss caused by any breach of the rules by the fund manager.

Risk, cost, convenience and regulation are relatively uncontentious. What the reduction in risk provided by collectives is worth to you will depend on how risk-averse you are. If you are ambitious for return, you may decide the opportunities for profit in choosing your own shares outweigh any extra costs. The more you hate paperwork and making decisions, the more attractive collective investments will be. Regulation of collective investments in the UK has been extremely effective in protecting investors from any loss and providing compensation for losses resulting from breaches of the rules by investment managers.

The value of full-time professional management of your investments, however, has been increasingly questioned in recent years. Most professionally managed funds have produced worse results than funds which simply track a stock market index, something that can be done mechanically at low cost. While the facts are not in dispute, over-simplistic conclusions have been drawn from them by some commentators. There is a case for trackers but also for actively managed funds.

The types of collective investment

Collective investment funds can be categorised in two ways: by their legal structure (which also determines their tax treatment) and by the type of assets they invest in. The table covers both aspects.

The different types of UK collective investment

Legal structure	Open/ closed	Separate custodian	Single/ dual pricing	Use of gearing	Type of assets			
					Deposits	Fixed	Property	Equity
Unit trust	Open	Yes	Dual	No	Yes	Yes	Yes	Yes
Open-ended inv. co. (Oeic)	Open	Yes	Single	No	Yes	Yes	Yes	Yes
Inv. trust	Closed	No	Single	Yes	No	Yes	No	Yes
Life ins. fund	Open	No	Dual	No	Yes	Yes	Yes	Yes

Open-ended funds are those where the size of the fund expands when investors put money in and shrinks when investors take money out. Closed-ended funds have a fixed number of shares which are traded on the stock market.

Unit trusts

These are so called because their assets are held by a trustee. The trustee is part of a large financial group and must be separate and independent from the company that manages the investments, providing comprehensive investor protection.

A unit trust holds a set of investments that are valued at least once a day. The price of a unit is the value of the investments divided by the number of units in issue. To this basic valuation are added the costs that would be incurred in buying the current investments, and on top of this the manager adds an initial charge of up to 5%. This gives the 'offer price' of units, which is what you pay when you buy. The 'bid price', what you get when you sell, is usually about 6.5% below the offer price.

Unit trusts are 'forward priced': when you place an order to buy, you get units priced at the next valuation. After your purchase, you receive a contract note setting out the date and terms of the deal, and then either a certificate or a statement of your registered holding. As with shares, it is the entry on the register that provides legal title of ownership, not the certificate.

The unit trust manager handles purchases and sales of units and also the buying and selling of investments. But the investments and cash are all held by a custodian who is responsible to the trustee. The trustee is liable to investors for the safety of these assets.

Units may be bought from the manager or may be purchased through independent advisers or stockbrokers. These advisers are entitled to a commission of up to 3% on purchases. However, they may not only offer reductions in this commission but may also negotiate discounts with the managers. It is usually, therefore, better to buy units through an adviser than direct from the manager.

Unit trusts may invest in shares and fixed-rate securities listed on stock markets. They may invest a small proportion of their assets in unquoted or private shares, but very few of them do because such assets are hard to value. Unit trusts may also invest in commercial and industrial, but not residential, property.

Trusts are not permitted to borrow money to add to their pool of assets. They may use derivatives only if this results in no additional risk for investors. Trusts may not hold more than 5% of their assets in any one security, so the minimum number of companies in which a trust will hold shares is 20, though most hold far more.

There are some 20 different types of unit trust, such as those investing in the UK for growth and for income, in America, Japan or Europe, in technology or financial or health shares, in natural resources and in smaller companies.

Unit trusts pay dividends net of tax. The net dividend is not subject to any more tax if you are a basic rate taxpayer, but higher rate taxpayers will have an additional liability depending on whether the income comes from fixed-rate investments or shares (see Appendix 1). Unit trusts pay no capital gains tax on profits when they buy and sell shares. Individual investors will be liable to capital gains tax when they sell if their gains exceed their annual allowance.

Open-ended investment companies

In most of the rest of the world, collective investments take the form of companies rather than trusts. Recent UK legislation has permitted the creation of open-ended investment companies (Oeics) whose main difference from unit trusts is that they are companies, not trusts, and do not have two prices. Instead there is just one price. When you buy, a sales fee is usually added to this by the manager.

Oeics have the power to redeem their own shares at their current net asset value (Nav), which is the value of the investments divided by the number of shares in issue. Like unit trusts, they have independent custodians who hold the assets. Each unit trust is a separate legal entity, but an Oeic may be a single company with 20 or more different funds within it.

Oeics may also have different classes of share linked to the same investments. The class of shares available to institutional investors, with a minimum investment of £100,000 or more, has lower charges than that available to individual investors.

Oeics have the same investment powers and restrictions as unit trusts and a similar range of funds are available. The tax treatment is the same.

Investment trusts

These are the oldest form of collective investment, dating back to 1868. They are simply companies whose shares are listed on the London Stock Exchange. They hold a portfolio of shares in other companies, so their assets consist entirely of investments. The value of the investments divided by the number of shares in issue gives the net asset value per share. However, the share price in the marketplace may diverge substantially from this. When a share price is below the Nav, it is said to be at a discount, and if the share price is above Nav, it is at a premium.

The most important factor giving rise to discounts or premiums is supply and demand, which itself has several causes. Investment trusts do not create and redeem shares on demand. They issue a fixed number which are then traded on the stock market between investors. Depending on the type of investments a trust holds, investors may be more or less enthusiastic about their prospects. The more enthusiastic they are, the higher the demand and, therefore, the higher the share price relative to the Nav.

Investment trusts are permitted to borrow money to add to their investments. The Nav of a highly geared trust (see table on the next page) will rise and fall more in relation to the prices of the underlying investments it holds than the Nav of a trust with no borrowings. So when the price of its investments is rising the shares of a highly geared trust are likely to trade at or above Nav, while when its investments are falling, the price of the trust's shares is likely to fall to a large discount to Nav.

Investment trust managers prefer not to have their shares trading at large discounts and use several techniques to avoid this. One is to provide low-cost savings plans that bring in new investors. Another is to buy back some of their shares from investors.

Investment trusts are taxed on the same basis as unit trusts and Oeics. To qualify for these concessions, trusts must pay out almost all their income as dividends and meet certain investment criteria. Some managers run investment companies which are very similar to investment trusts but do not meet these requirements. To avoid adverse taxation of capital gains, these are usually registered in an offshore tax haven but listed on the London Stock Exchange.

Investment trusts are allowed to invest in companies whose shares are not listed on any stock market. Some trusts specialise in venture capital and place most of their money in such investments, which are naturally far riskier than companies that have attained a stock market listing. The majority of investment trusts hold only a small portion of their assets in unlisted companies.

The more recent split-capital investment trusts have a more complex structure and the different categories of share offered by these may incorporate much higher risks (see Chapter 13).

How gearing affects returns

	Trust A	Trust B
Capital subscribed by shareholders	£100m	£100m
Borrowings	Nil	£50m
Total assets	£100m	£150m
If value of assets rises 20%	£120m	£180m
Deduct borrowings	Nil	£50m
Assets for shareholders	£120m	£130m
Divided by 100 million shares in issue = Nav	120p (+20%)	130p (+30%)

If the value of assets fell 20%, Trust A's Nav would fall 20% but Trust B's would fall 30%.

Life insurance funds

Life insurance companies run many funds and offer lump sum investments linked to them. Unlike unit trusts, Oeics or investment trusts, when you buy an investment from a life insurance company you do not become legally entitled to any of the assets. You buy a policy whose claim value against the company may be defined in terms of units or in other ways.

Unlike these other investments, too, life insurance companies pay tax on their income and their capital gains. Individual policyholders do not pay capital gains tax on any gains, nor do they pay basic rate income tax on any gains or income. But higher rate taxpayers may become liable to tax on their profits or withdrawals from the policy at a rate equal to the difference between the basic rate and the higher rate of income tax.

The funds offered by life insurers fall into four categories: with-profits, unit-linked, guaranteed and high income.

◆ **With-profits** Lump sum investments in a with-profits fund earn bonuses. Usually one rate of bonus is paid annually and an extra terminal bonus is paid on encashment or death. Added together these bonuses usually give a rate of return somewhat greater than the best rates available on deposits. For more on with-profits bonds, see Chapter 13.

◆ **Unit-linked** Like unit trusts, life insurance funds invest in shares or fixed-interest securities in the UK or overseas. Insurers also offer 'managed' funds which divide their investments between equities, fixed-rate investments and property. Property funds invest in commercial, industrial and retail property. In general, the average performance of any given category of these funds has been significantly worse than that of the comparable unit trust average over most periods, a difference that is only partly explained by life funds' less advantageous tax position.

◆ **Guaranteed income and growth** As discussed in Chapter 2, some insurers offer fixed returns with capital guarantees over periods from two to ten years. The rates are usually somewhat better than the net rates available from deposits.

◆ **High income** These offer a high rate of income but only give you your capital back at maturity if a given stock market index is above a certain level. The risks involved in these bonds can be very high since the potential loss of capital at maturity can be 50% or more.

Using equity Isas

The equity Individual Savings Account (Isa) is a tax-exempt 'wrapper' that can be put around unit or investment trusts and Oeics.

The equity Isa comes in two forms, mini and maxi. A mini-Isa permits you to invest up to £3,000 each year in equities, unit or investment trusts or Oeics. A maxi-Isa raises the maximum to £7,000 in each tax year up to 5 April, 2006.

Most unit trust, investment trust and Oeic managers offer Isas which can be wrapped around their funds. With unit trusts and Oeics, there is usually no extra charge: you simply pay the same charges as you would in the relevant unit trust or Oeic. With investment trusts, there is often an additional fee.

Within an Isa offered by a manager of unit trusts or Oeics, you may invest in one or more funds and switch your money between them without losing the tax-exempt status. Almost all unit trusts and Oeics qualify for inclusion in Isas.

Both income and gains within an Isa are tax-exempt. In addition, until 2004, part of the tax deducted at source on share dividends can be reclaimed from the Inland Revenue. This means that if as a basic rate taxpayer you would normally receive a net dividend of £80, you would receive £88.90 within an Isa.

The fact that Isas are exempt from capital gains tax may not be of much benefit to you today if you have only small sums to invest, because you are unlikely to exceed the annual threshold below which you pay no CGT anyway. But if you put £5,000 into an Isa each year, by the end of ten years you would have an investment which could generate taxable gains, so the scheme may save you tax eventually.

If you invest in an Isa run by one fund manager, then want to switch your money to a fund run by a different manager, you will have to switch your Isa. Though you are allowed to do this, there may be extra costs involved. The alternative is to set up a 'self-select' Isa – for more on this, see Chapter 11.

Given the tax breaks, it is clearly worth using the Isa up to the annual limit. The maximum investment has been set at £7,000 up to April 2006.

Each year you can, if you want, set up an Isa with a different manager. If you are investing lump sums, this will make sense, but if you are using the Isa for regular savings it is probably better to stick with one fund.

What type of investment?

If you want to achieve the elusive balance of good returns and low risk, you will need to hold different types of investment. The table shows the performance of various types of investment over a number of years together with their returns over five-year periods.

How investment returns from collective funds vary year by year
Total return from an initial investment of £1,000

| | Return in calendar year | | | | Five-year return to end of | |
| | 1996 | 1997 | 1998 | 1999 | 1996 | 2000 |
Unit trusts	£	£	£	£	£	£
UK income & growth	1,073	1,158	1,063	1,082	1,775	1,713
UK smaller companies	1,108	1,019	903	1,721	1,867	2,039
Europe	1,080	1,173	1,225	1,209	1,974	2,263
Japan	828	736	1,032	2,020	1,099	992
North America	1,073	1,192	1,126	1,230	2,282	2,180
Emerging markets	951	973	737	1,574	1,639	1,033
UK fixed-interest	1,034	1,095	1,098	960	1,466	1,464
Building society account	1,036	1,040	1,046	1,036	1,261	1,162
UK Retail Price Index	1,027	1,032	1,028	1,014	1,134	1,145

Unit trusts: average performance of the sector (In 1999, UK income & growth was replaced by UK equity income and UK fixed-interest by UK other bonds). Offer to bid prices with net income reinvested.

The figure for the Retail Price Index shows how much you would have needed at the end of the period to buy what £1,000 would have bought at the start.

One problem you face as an investor is that most of the data presented to you will be up to one very recent date. The performance of all investments up to this date will be largely determined by recent market performance. As the table shows, the comparative position of different investments at different points in time can vary substantially. This is why it is worth looking for investments with different characteristics and behaviour (in City jargon, ones that have low correlation).

An ideal choice would be two fast-growing investments whose fluctuations cancel each other out so the net value of an equal investment in them rises in a straight line. Of course, this ideal pattern does not exist in real life, and even if it could be found in the past there would be virtually no likelihood of it being repeated in the future. Nevertheless, combining different asset types in your portfolio is worthwhile. Adding low-correlation investments will give it more stability without necessarily reducing the return.

Investments with historically low correlation with the UK stock market are emerging stock markets, commercial property, fixed-interest, mining and natural resources. The correlation between the developed markets of America and Europe has increased in recent years, though Japan has a lower correlation with either.

What collective investment funds do

Most collective investment funds, besides stating that they will invest in a particular geographical area or type of share, have an objective which is not written into the prospectus. It is to produce investment results that put it among the top 25% (or top quartile) of all funds of a similar type. Only funds that achieve this with some consistency will attract the support of investment advisers, and investment advisers account for over three-quarters of all the new subscriptions to collective investment funds.

Only a tiny minority of collective investment funds achieve this kind of performance year after year. The majority are more erratic: a year in which they produce better-than-average results is followed by a worse-than-average year, and so on. Studies have shown fairly convincingly that past performance on its own is not a reliable indicator of future performance.

Choosing a collective investment

Investment advisers advocate doing detailed research into the 'investment process' to try to understand how and why investment managers make their decisions. The theory is that successful managers will have common characteristics. Unfortunately, reality does not support this theory any more than the previous one that past performance proved superior talent.

The few collective investments that have demonstrated consistent long-term success have been run by individuals with widely different styles and processes, in other words, by mavericks. This is not a pejorative term. Warren Buffett, the world's most successful investor, is also a maverick. He does not conform to the norms that almost all other investment managers accept. Nor do the long-term successes among UK collective fund managers. Each is a one-off, so it is hard to identify them by conventional yardsticks.

Index trackers versus active management

The absence of a convincing theory about how to pick winners among collective funds has fuelled a trend towards 'index tracking' which is discussed below. But just because you cannot be sure a fund is going to produce the best performance does not mean you should only buy index-tracking funds.

For a start, in the UK, European and Japanese markets, there is a cycle during which shares in small and large companies respectively produce higher returns. In the UK the cycle used to last about four years and though, like most cycles, this is less dependable than it used to be, the mid-1990s saw UK small companies performing very poorly indeed compared with larger ones, a trend that appeared to reverse during 1999. Index-tracking funds miss out on the high returns produced by smaller companies during such upturns.

Index-tracking funds also produce relatively little income. This is because many of the largest companies in terms of market value pay low dividends. If you want and need an income from your investments, you will need to look at actively managed funds where the managers seek out shares paying dividends.

Finally, stock market indices work well for the American and UK markets but far less well for Japan and Europe. In Japan, there have been many periods in which the majority of UK unit trusts have produced higher returns than the most representative Japanese index. In these areas, trackers have less to offer.

The art of investment

Returning to the issue of collective fund management, quantification – of performance or processes – is part of the problem, not the solution. Investment advisers produce ever more sophisticated ways of looking at historic performance, but you should not be too impressed. Investment is an art, not a science, and it is better to think of the talented fund manager as an artist rather than as a scientist. Just as one artist prefers landscapes and another portraits, managers thrive best in particular market conditions.

Well-informed professional advisers who stay in close touch with the leading fund managers often have a feel for this and know which managers are 'on song' at any time. You may also get a sense of this from the reports and interviews with fund managers in newspapers and magazines.

You may hanker after hard evidence, but hard-nosed analysis has shown that most of this is useless. The fact that a more touchy-feely approach to selection conflicts with our ideas about money actually says more about our ideas than anything else.

Managing investments is a process that involves both reasoning and emotion, and all the evidence is that it is the emotional aspect, in terms of the fund manager's character, that is the more important. If you ask why this should be so, return to the opening question of the chapter. How would you feel if an investment you had just bought fell by 30%? Do you buy more, sell or just hold on? Turbulent emotions make it more difficult to reach the right decision. Perhaps we should eliminate feeling and let the computer choose? So far, the results of doing so have been disastrous: judgment is not a purely rational faculty and computers do not have it.

There is no alternative to accepting that investment is a tough game and that its winners will display qualities of emotional strength which rational analysis will find hard to identify.

Index-tracking funds

Index trackers invest the same proportion of their assets in the shares of each company as that company represents of the chosen index. At the time of writing, Vodafone accounted for some 12% of the FTSE-100 index (the Footsie). This means the total value of all Vodafone's outstanding shares represented 12% of the total value of all the outstanding shares in the 100 companies making up the index, at their current prices. A fund aiming to track the Footsie would, therefore, place 12% of its assets in Vodafone shares. In the case of a unit trust, if investors subscribed new money to the trust, 12% of that money would be allocated to buying shares in Vodafone and so on through the list of 100 companies.

The Footsie changes every three months. The companies nearest the bottom whose shares have fallen in price are removed, while the ones that were 101st, 102nd and so on before but whose prices have risen are promoted into the index.

An index-tracking fund, therefore, will sell investments only if they fall out of the index, and these are the ones in which it has the least amounts invested. Overall, therefore, the transaction costs incurred by index trackers are low compared to those of actively managed funds.

These low costs are the principal reason trackers on average produce better results than actively managed funds.

UK index trackers may aim to replicate either the FTSE-100 or the FTSE All-Share index, which contains over 700 companies. Whereas actively managed funds may have initial charges of up to 5% and annual charges of up to 1.5%, index trackers generally have no or minimal initial charges and annual charges of around 0.5%. They are, therefore, the cheapest way of obtaining a diversified portfolio of UK shares. As either unit trusts or Oeics, index trackers may be held tax free within Isas.

The core-and-satellite approach

There is considerable evidence suggesting the biggest handicap you can give yourself as an investor is to buy and sell frequently. The transaction costs usually outweigh any extra returns. For this reason most financial advisers recommend a buy-and-hold policy. Trackers are ideal for this because their make-up changes only gradually, in line with changes in the market.

But it does not make sense to regard all investments in the same way. If you buy into riskier areas, such as Japanese smaller companies or emerging markets, it may make more sense to try to time your investment, aiming to buy in at low levels and sell when you have made a satisfactory profit. Bear in mind that in areas like these, there have been two-year periods when unit trusts have made over 100% and others when they have lost over 50%. You do not need to buy at the very bottom or sell at the very top to do well out of such dramatic swings.

One way of formalising the difference between these two approaches is the core-and-satellite approach. This means identifying a part of your capital which you invest on a long-term basis and expect never to change. With-profits bonds, tracker funds and very broadly diversified funds, such as the large international investment trusts, are most suitable for the core of your portfolio.

The satellite portfolio or portfolios are for more volatile areas and sectors. You might have just one satellite portfolio with a few specialist unit trusts investing in smaller companies, the Far East, and so on. You might also have a satellite share portfolio – for more on shares, see Chapter 11. You would review these investments at regular intervals and aim to take profits on successful ones and reinvest in other promising areas.

Investing for growth

If your aim is growth in the value of your capital and you do not need to draw any income, you have the widest possible investment choice. You may consider investing in shares directly, which is covered in the following chapter. As far as collective investments are concerned, you should certainly think about placing a significant proportion of your capital in overseas investing funds. You can do this in three ways:

International funds

The managers generally keep a fairly high proportion (about half) in UK shares with the balance spread among other countries. The majority will go into developed markets in America, Europe and Japan, with smaller amounts in a few emerging markets. These trusts have among the most stable historical performance of all unit trusts.

Regional funds

These invest in geographic regions such as Europe, Asia or South America. The bigger the area and the more markets across which the investment is spread, the less volatile the fund is likely to be. Each year it is usually one set of regional funds that produce eye-catching and chart-topping gains.

Country funds

Some trusts and funds invest in single countries such as Thailand, Korea or Brazil. Here the risks are very much higher, and while you may double your money in a year you also risk losing half of it.

Investment portfolios for growth
Allocation of £50,000 capital

Lower risk portfolio

With-profits bond	£25,000	50%
UK tracker fund	£10,000	20%
UK smaller company fund	£5,000	10%
European fund	£5,000	10%
US fund	£2,500	5%
Far East fund	£2,500	5%
Total	£50,000	100%

Higher risk portfolio

UK tracker fund	£15,000	30%
International fixed-interest fund	£5,000	10%
International equity fund	£5,000	10%
UK smaller company fund	£5,000	10%
European smaller company fund	£5,000	10%
Japanese smaller company fund	£5,000	10%
US smaller companies fund	£5,000	10%
Technology fund	£2,500	5%
Global emerging markets fund	£2,500	5%
Total	£50,000	100%

Investing for income

Capital gains are more lightly taxed in the UK than income. If you generate more income than you need from your investments, you will also pay more tax. So assess your needs carefully and realistically and set out to generate only the income you actually require.

The more income you need from your capital (in City jargon, 'the higher your yield objective') the lower the rate of capital growth you can expect. This is because to get that income you will have to place your money either in fixed-rate investments or in higher yielding equities.

At times in the past, the average dividend yield on UK shares has exceeded 5%, but in the post-war era, high yields also coincided with high rates of inflation. So long as inflation stays at under 2% it seems unlikely dividend yields will remain at well above 3% for any length of time.

The reason is dividends normally grow at 5% a year or more, so that even if you get a low yield to start with, if you hold shares over five years or more you end up with an income that has beaten inflation by a wide margin. Typically, the fastest rates of growth in dividends have come from those companies whose shares stood on the lowest yields (2% or less) to begin with.

If you want a growing income from your investments, try to reduce the initial yield you need. This will let you put more money into lower yielding shares which have better long-term prospects for increasing both income and capital value.

Some advisers have started to recommend schemes where you draw off capital gains as income. If the income yield from a fund is 3% they may suggest you draw an income of 5%, of which 2% a year will come from encashment of units or shares. Evidence since 1980 suggests there is little risk attached to this policy, but even a low rate of capital withdrawal can be damaging if the price of the fund falls and stays low for a couple of years. It is safer to withdraw the bonuses paid on with-profits bonds, because in this case your capital is not directly affected by market movements.

Investment portfolios for income
Allocation of £50,000

Lower yield portfolio	Amount	Net yield	Net income
With-profits bond*	£20,000	4%	£800
UK fixed-interest fund	£10,000	5%	£500
UK high yield corporate bond fund	£10,000	6%	£600
UK high income equity fund	£10,000	3%	£300
Total	£50,000	4.4%	£2,200

* Withdrawing only part of the bonuses and leaving the rest to add to capital.

Higher yield portfolio			
With-profits bond*	£20,000	6%	£1,200
UK fixed-interest fund	£10,000	5%	£500
UK high yield corporate bond fund	£10,000	6%	£600
UK high income equity fund	£5,000	4%	£200
UK high income fund	£5,000	5%	£250
Total	£50,000	5.5%	£2,750

* Withdrawing all the current bonuses paid. Higher rate taxpayers need to restrict withdrawals to 5% of the original investment or they will incur some higher rate tax.

Note: these portfolios reflect conditions at the time of writing: inflation 2%, short-term interest rates 6%, long-term interest rates 6.5%, dividend yield 2.2%.

If you need a very high income, you will have to consider investments that involve erosion of your capital. These include:

◆ **Income shares** On some types of income shares issued by split-capital investment trusts, yields can be up to twice those on fixed-rate investments.

◆ **With-profits bonds** Some allow you to withdraw more than the rates of bonus currently being paid.

◆ **Annuities** You pay an insurance company a lump sum and it guarantees a set level of income for life. These are a last resort and are rarely worth considering at under the age of about 75. For more details on these investments, see Chapter 13.

Portfolio planning

History suggests there are two really serious mistakes you can make with your capital. These are:

◆ Not investing in the stock market because you fear the risk. Over the long term, shares have always produced better returns than other types of investment. Provided you are investing for a period of at least five years, you can afford to sit out any downturns in the meantime.

◆ Selling after a crash. Sometimes the stock market rebounds swiftly after a crash, as in 1994. At other times it takes longer, as in 1987. Usually you will suffer the worst loss if you succumb to panic and sell.

In the aftermath of a stock market crash, there are always companies and even whole sectors that never recover their previous peaks. If you hold widely diversified investments such as with-profits bonds and tracker funds, this need not concern you, but if you invest in specialist funds you need to be aware they are more vulnerable to such dramatic changes in market conditions.

Getting advice

There are two principal sources of investment advice focusing on collective investments: independent financial advisers and company representatives.

Independent financial advisers are free to recommend the products of any company. They may be paid by commission on the investments they place or by fees. Many IFAs handle a limited amount of investment and do not have a comprehensive knowledge of collective investments. This type of IFA will probably recommend placing the bulk of your money in insurance funds. This is unlikely to be an optimal solution. A limited number of IFAs specialise in lump sum investment and will be more able to construct a well-balanced portfolio.

Company representatives are barred by law from recommending products other than those of their employer. The range may be quite narrow, but in the case of larger companies it may be extensive. However, an essential element of diversification in a portfolio of collective investments is to have funds run by different managers, so company representatives are often handicapped in constructing optimal portfolios, though (depending on their skills and qualifications) their generic advice may be perfectly sound.

Charges and commissions are fully disclosed in the documentation you will be given. Broadly, you should expect to pay the equivalent of an hourly fee of £100 to £200 whether you pay it in fees or commissions. If the commissions work out at significantly more than this you should expect an IFA to rebate part, not in cash but as enhancements of the capital value of the investments.

See Chapter 15 for more on the topic of financial advice.

The DIY approach

If you have the time and inclination to construct your own investment portfolio, you can save substantially on costs. There are now many discount brokers who offer collective investments of most types at lower cost. They do this in two ways:

◆ **Rebating commissions** On most unit trusts and Oeics the normal initial commission is 3%. On insurance funds it can be as high as 6%. Some discount brokers will rebate all of this, in the form of enhanced capital values, because they also receive ongoing or 'trail' commission at the rate of 0.5% of the current value of holdings in unit trusts, Oeics, Isas or many insurance funds.

◆ **Negotiating discounts** Discount brokers, like other IFAs, will also negotiate deals with the managers of collective investments. Often the manager, after paying commission, would receive an initial fee of up to 2% on the normal charging basis of a unit trust or Oeic. In many cases IFAs will negotiate a reduction to 1% or less.

The net result is that if you make up your own mind about what you want, you can buy it through discount brokers at minimal cost.

Be wary, though, of assuming the information sent out by discount brokers is 'advice'. They may send you heaps of guides, brochures and newsletters, but the legal position is that they are only sending you information and not providing advice. You are transacting on an 'execution-only' basis and the broker has no responsibility for what you buy. If you do want to deal on a DIY basis, do not rely on what the broker sends out, especially in relation to new funds, where it will probably be getting special incentives from the managers to promote them. To be a successful DIY investor, you must do your own research.

11

Investing in Shares

There is a conflict between the desire for high returns and the desire to protect one's capital. It was neatly summed up by an American investor, Gerald Loeb, who said: "The greatest safety lies in putting all your eggs in one basket and watching the basket."

Loeb was in fact criticising the practice, common in his day and still prevalent today, of what he called 'the wrong kind of diversification'. Once you own shares in a large oil company, he argued, there is little point in buying shares in another. It does not significantly reduce your risk. As Loeb said, if you follow the all-eggs-in-one-basket principle, "you simply cannot afford to be careless or wrong. Hence, you will act with much more deliberation."

This is only one among many aspects of investing on the stock market on which experts and successful individual investors disagree. Peter Lynch, for example, who managed the giant Fidelity Magellan Fund in the US for a decade with outstanding results, held shares in an enormous number of companies and was always ready to buy into a new one if he liked its story. Lynch instead criticised the 'diworseification' that led companies to buy or merge with others outside their field of competence.

Probably the single most telling statement about the stock market, and one you should consider deeply before you venture into buying shares in individual companies, is: "If you don't know who you are, this is an expensive place to find out."

Penned in light-hearted mood by Jerry Goodman back in the 1960s, this points at the hardest part of stock market investing: your own psychology. If you do not understand your own motivations you will be far more vulnerable.

Goodman cites some amusing examples, including a woman who regarded her stock selections as her babies, and a man who looked upon successful share selections in the same light as successful seductions. Goodman's ultimate metaphor for the stock market is a game. Projecting your own emotions onto the market may make the game more interesting but it also makes it far more dangerous.

These are deep waters and though the rest of this chapter is largely about facts and techniques, some of the books listed in Appendix 2 explore many more dimensions of stock market investing.

What's in it for you?

Collective investments provide most of the benefits of the stock market without the pain of personal effort. So why invest in shares of individual companies? The principal answer is that you can achieve higher returns.

Successful companies, if you trace them back to their earliest beginnings on the stock market, have often shown returns on an original investment of several thousand percent, converting £1,000 into £100,000 or even more over a decade. You do not need to pick many shares that perform like this to become wealthy. The challenge is to do it without incurring huge risks to your capital.

The starting point has to be deciding what proportion of your capital you want to invest in individual shares. For many people, tracker funds and other collectives form the bedrock of an investment portfolio. And the costs of such investments can be significantly lower than buying and selling individual shares.

As an individual investor in shares, costs are your biggest handicap. You may pay commission of about 1% to buy or sell a share if you deal on an 'execution-only' basis. That is about eight times what a large institution will pay – simply because it is dealing in much larger amounts.

For most people, it will therefore make sense to have a significant proportion of capital in collective investments. If these provide the safety net of diversification, there is no point in repeating this with a share portfolio. Instead you need to define realistic objectives, types of share you will and will not invest in, the extent to which you will 'trade' or speculate rather than invest, how much you will normally invest in each company, and so forth. Essentially, you need to do for yourself what a large institution does when it sets its investment policy and defines how it will set about achieving it.

Your investment policy checklist

◆ What is your primary objective?
◆ Over approximately what period do you expect to keep your capital invested?
◆ What proportion of your capital do you plan to invest in company shares?
◆ What types of company do you plan to invest in? Large blue chips, medium-sized or smaller companies. Types of company such as: innovative, stable,

recovery. Sectors such as: banking, utilities, retailing, pharmaceuticals, information technology and so on. Why?

◆ What types of company will you definitely not invest in? (For example: arms manufacturers, tobacco, gambling). Why?

◆ Roughly how much will you invest in each company?

◆ Roughly how many companies do you expect to end up owning shares in?

◆ Will you only make long-term investments or will you also speculate?

◆ If so, what is the maximum proportion of your total investment you will put into speculative shares?

◆ What will you do if a share price falls after you have invested?

Today's stock market

The boundaries of the old national stock markets have been eroding for decades. Many British companies now have share listings in New York as well as London. The major European stock exchanges are discussing merger plans. New all-electronic exchanges threaten the older established exchanges both in Europe and America.

As far as small and mainly domestically focused UK companies are concerned, the choice is between a listing on the London Stock Exchange (LSE), a listing on the Alternative Investment Market (Aim), or making arrangements for the shares to be traded privately, as they are through Ofex (see below).

The LSE is more demanding than Aim in terms of its listing requirements and charges higher fees. Companies without track records cannot list on it, for example. The level of 'due diligence' applied to checking the facts and figures is higher for the LSE than for an Aim listing.

In both cases the process affords some investor protection. You can be sure that no director of a company listing on either exchange will have a criminal record, for instance. If a company seeking a listing has entered any agreements or contracts with companies controlled by its directors, these will be fully disclosed. In these and many other areas, the structure of limited companies provides ample opportunity for insiders to cheat incoming investors, so the policing of listing requirements is an important feature of stock exchanges.

Naturally, promoters of new all-electronic exchanges focus more on the cheapness of dealing costs. It is in their interests to relax listing requirements to attract companies to them.

Ofex is not a market at all. It is simply a facility for trading shares in privately owned companies that have not been subject to any exchange's listing rules. Just because a firm is a Plc (public limited company) does not mean it is listed on a stock exchange. It only means it has more than five shareholders and pays slightly more in audit fees for its annual report than a limited company.

Individuals are not allowed to trade directly on stock exchanges. They must transact their deals through stockbrokers who are accredited members of the exchange. The brokers themselves are responsible for settling transactions, which means collecting and paying over the money. The security and dependability of settlement is another defining feature of developed stock markets, but this is notably absent from many emerging stock markets.

When you buy or sell shares, the stockbroker deals with a market-maker. The market-maker buys and sells shares, like a wholesale greengrocer, aiming to make tiny profits on most trades. He risks his own capital in doing this, whereas the broker simply acts as your agent in fulfilling orders you have given. Confusingly, big banks own both market-making and stockbroking companies, though they are supposedly kept separate by 'Chinese walls' designed by regulators to prevent companies exploiting information to profit at customers' expense.

Shareholders are last in line

Shareholders in a business are the last in line when it comes to entitlement to take money out. A company has a legal responsibility to pay the following:

◆ Any taxes due to the government including income tax, capital gains tax, VAT, or customs duties.
◆ Any taxes due to the local authority (business rates).
◆ Wages due to its employees.
◆ Money owed to its bankers.
◆ Payments due to its suppliers.
◆ Money owed to other lenders including bondholders.

All these rank ahead of shareholders. Only when they have been paid what they are due is a company entitled to make payments to its shareholders. Thus, shareholders bear the most risk. But since they are entitled to everything that is left after meeting these obligations, they also obtain very high returns when a company prospers.

Companies can make themselves more or less risky for shareholders. The principal factor is debt. The more debt a company has, the more profits it must make to pay the interest before shareholders get anything. The ratio of debt to equity is therefore one of the most important features of a company's financing.

The value of debt is simply all the debts of whatever kind added together. The value of equity is the amount shown in the balance sheet as attributable to shareholders. This is the total of all the amounts subscribed for shares plus the company's retained profits and reserves created from them over the years.

Analysing companies' accounts used to be a matter of combing through reports and calculating figures. But today a huge amount of this is done by providers of databases which can be accessed through the internet. This has removed a lot of the drudgery, but you should still read one of the basic books on valuing companies so you understand the principles.

The valuation basics

◆ **Equity** A company's equity is owned by its shareholders. The equity is the value of the business net of all its liabilities. This is only partially reflected in the company's balance sheet, its statement of total assets and liabilities. The balance sheet will include all tangible assets, but may not include the market value of brand names, patents, intellectual property and key personnel.

◆ **Net asset value** The net asset value (Nav) per share is the balance sheet figure for assets attributable to shareholders divided by the number of shares in issue. It may be close to the market value of the business in the case of, say, a property company that has recently revalued its assets. Most businesses have a market value far higher than their Nav.

◆ **Market capitalisation** The capitalisation (or market value) of a business is the number of shares in issue multiplied by the share price. Several valuation measures relate this market value to other factors.

◆ **Price to sales** A company's market value may be less than the value of its annual sales if it consistently makes a low profit margin on those sales. But in the case of a fast-growing, hi-tech company the market value can be as much as 100 times its sales.

◆ **Price to book** A company's market value may be equal to its book value – as in the case of the property company referred to above. In most cases it will be far higher.

◆ **Earnings** The company's profits, after tax and permitted adjustments, are its earnings. Earnings divided by the number of shares in issue give earnings per share.

◆ **Price/earnings ratio** The price/earnings ratio is the share price divided by earnings per share. If the share price is 250p and the earnings per share are 15p, the ratio is 16.7.

◆ **Dividend yield** Companies pay dividends per share. The latest total annual dividend per share divided by the share price and multiplied by 100 gives the dividend yield. This tells you the return you get in the form of income when buying a share. If the share price is 250p and the dividend 8.75p, the yield is 3.5%. UK companies' dividend yields are now usually quoted net of 20% tax.

◆ **EBITDA** This refers to earnings before interest, taxation, depreciation and amortisation. The rate at which companies depreciate their assets varies. Many analysts now use EBITDA to compare companies. Value investors do not, because they consider it misleading to ignore depreciation.

◆ **Profit margins** Profits before tax as a percentage of sales or turnover.

◆ **Interest cover** The extent to which annual interest payments on debt are covered by gross profits.

◆ **Return on capital employed (ROCE)** Profits before tax, interest and dividends (but after deducting depreciation and amortisation) expressed as a percentage of capital employed, defined as equity plus long-term debt.

Fundamental and technical analysis

Fundamental analysis is the study of a company's business and prospects using tools such as those described above. The basic tenet of fundamental analysts is that the more you know and understand about a business, the better placed you are to assess its value relative to its peers, helping you make better buying and selling decisions.

Technical analysis is the study of market-related data such as movements in share prices, the volume of shares traded, the ratio of rising to falling share prices each day or week, and so on.

Technical analysis used to be mainly a matter of looking at price charts and trying to identify predictable trends. Computers have led to a huge array of extremely complex calculations all of which can be cross-related and monitored. A fashion for computer-driven share trading in the 1980s was temporarily halted by the 1987 crash, but today 'hedge funds'– often speculative funds trading with borrowed money – use similar methods on a large scale.

Many investors use both fundamental and technical analysis to make their decisions.

What is a good business?

Defining a successful company is difficult. Think of two of Britain's best-known brand names, both of which were, until the mid-90s, long-term successes: Marks & Spencer and Sainsbury's. Both were regarded as blue-chip investments, with huge financial strength and powerful brand names. Yet both lost the plot in terms of meeting their customers' needs.

Sainsbury's undercut its 'quality' image by embarking on a price-focused battle with Tesco – which it lost. Marks & Spencer's styling of its clothing range was perceived as so dull that its customers went elsewhere. Both companies' share prices crashed by over a third while their rivals' share prices bounded ahead.

These cases provide two important morals for investors:
◆ **Nothing is forever** However good you think a company is, you must keep an eye on its performance. If its standards look as if they are starting to slip, investigate quickly and, unless you find good reasons to expect a downturn to be only short term, sell.
◆ **You saw it first** Good or bad news on the high street is visible in the stores long before the City analysts can measure it in sales or profit figures. Empty M&S clothing departments gave the clue to the story months before the shares

crashed. Busy Tesco car parks pointed to its success in winning customers from Sainsbury's.

Trust your experience

There are many areas in which professional, full-time investors enjoy advantages over individual investors. It is no good thinking that because you can access lots of information on the internet you can compete with them. For a start, the professional fund managers often have first-class honours degrees, they spend all day thinking about investment and have access to far more information than you do.

The real advantage you have as an individual is your own experience. First, you have your own general experience of buying goods and services. Companies with clearly better deals for consumers are going to win business from rivals. Look for evidence of this around you, not just in the shops but in services and utilities.

Second, you have your own particular skills and contacts. Perhaps you work in the packaging industry – in which case you should know something about the big packaging companies and which are doing well. Perhaps you work in the civil service – which companies are winning contracts to install computers, develop software, subcontract services?

Use your network of friends and acquaintances to research and test ideas. If a store is busy in your town, is it doing as well elsewhere? If your local cable company's service is terrible, is this just a local flaw? Is the new hotel going up on the edge of town part of a chain? And watch for local press reports on locally based listed companies – you will often get far more detail in these reports than in brief national press comments.

Warren Buffett, the world's most successful investor, defines a successful business as one with a franchise that is hard for someone to invade. Local newspapers are a good example. So long as you turn out a decent product, the advertising revenue will keep it rolling along. It is almost as good as a monopoly.

Fund manager Peter Lynch saw quarries as having similar attractive qualities. No quarry owner tries to sell his gravel to people living on the edge of a competitor's quarry, but he is content to take a near-monopoly profit on all sales within a radius of his own hole in the ground.

Buffett sees global brands in the same light: he has been a long-term investor in Coca-Cola and American Express, for example, which must be two of his country's best-known exports. But with a brand, you still have to check that it is secure from competition or erosion of its profit margins by cheaper rivals.

Successful businesses are easy to identify with hindsight. But very few investors climb on board a company such as Microsoft or Glaxo near the start of the journey. Still, the encouraging thing is that you do not need to.

As Buffett remarks, it is far better to pay a fair price for a great company than a great price for a fair company. He confessed in one of his shareholder reports that he only bought shares in Coca-Cola after 20 years of admiring it and consuming its products. He still made a fortune. Big winners usually go on rolling ahead for many years, so if you find one you believe has the potential, do not be put off by the fact that the price has already risen a lot.

New issues

When a company makes its stock market debut it offers shares to investors. The American term for public issue is initial public offering, or IPO, and it is gradually coming into use in the UK.

The company has to satisfy the listing requirements of the relevant stock exchange. This will require a report from its auditors as well as its directors. A prospectus will be issued giving the company's history, latest profit and loss account and balance sheet, and usually an indication of likely profits for the current financial year. You apply for shares, which are normally on offer at a fixed price, by filling in an application form and sending it in with your cheque.

When the stock market is especially buoyant, new issues usually get off to a flying start. Optimism is widespread, so people apply for more shares than they want, expecting to be able to sell them at a premium when dealings start. Over-subscription may mean that investors receive fewer shares than they applied for, possibly resulting in even greater demand when dealings begin. So when trading does start, new issues can soar to a premium of 50% or, in the case of internet stocks in 1999, 200% on the first day.

If that all seems enticing, not to say intoxicating, sobriety is just around the corner. Detailed research in the US has shown that, on average, investors get worse returns by buying IPOs than they would by buying an index-tracker fund. This was not true for 1998 and 1999, years in which the internet and technology craze drove new issues to gigantic premiums, but the long-term evidence should make you wary of expecting instant riches from new issues.

Most of the most brilliant long-term winners on the stock market could have been bought at any time in a period of two or three years and still have returned gigantic profits. Sponsors of IPOs like to create an air of excitement and pay heavily to public relations consultancies to achieve this. The reality is that an untried business needs a few years to prove itself. Even if the shares rise a lot, they will still offer huge upside in a couple of years' time and they will be a much less risky investment.

Penny shares

Many investors believe that shares priced in pennies offer greater profit potential than those priced in pounds. This is simply not true. The upside potential of a share relates to the profitability of the business, not to how its shares are priced.

Many penny shares are in small companies, and often in small companies that have fallen on hard times. Very few companies issue shares in pennies, and for a share to get from a typical issue price of 50p or 100p down to 5p, the business must have done something wrong. There may be recovery prospects. Or there may be hopes of a deal whereby entrepreneurs inject new assets into the company in exchange for shares. Such developments can result in huge gains but they are rare.

Moreover, dealing spreads in penny shares can be enormous. A company whose total capitalisation is £5m with 50 million shares in issue at a price of 10p as quoted in the newspapers can have a dealing spread of 11p to buy and 9p to sell. That is 20%, which means the first 20% of any gains will go not to you but to the market-maker in the shares.

Dealing frequently in penny shares may or may not make you rich, but it will certainly help the stockbroker and market-maker extend their country mansions.

Choosing an investing style

There are many different styles of investing. The word style is used because this is not just about deciding on a method but about how you apply it. It also suggests that, as with fashion, the one you adopt has to suit your character or you risk making yourself appear ridiculous – or, in the case of investing, poor.

The three styles described here are well-defined and have been applied by many investors over long periods. But they are only applications of a set of rules within given boundaries. There is really no limit to the number of investment styles, each of which will be differently applied by every investor. So you do not have to adopt one of these styles. But the evidence does suggest it is hard to be a contrarian part of the time and a growth investor the rest of the time. You may succeed in applying two styles if you use separate pots of money. But on the whole, you are probably better off deciding on one approach and then trying to refine it.

Value is biggest and best

Value investing is the approach that has been in use for longest and with the most consistent results. It was invented by Benjamin Graham, author of a tome on security valuation, and applied by him from the 1920s to the 1950s. Warren Buffett, whose Berkshire Hathaway has produced annual returns far in excess of the average investment fund, is a Graham disciple, as have been many other successful investors.

The key features of Graham's approach are:

◆ **The business** Know and understand the business, its history, its strengths and weaknesses, its opportunities, its management, its products.

◆ **The numbers** Value investing is very analytical. In particular, look at trends in terms of sales, profits and earnings, and at the ratios of stock to turnover, short-term debtors to creditors and debt to equity, and at the return on the capital employed in the business, adjusting for any accounting measures which may produce a falsely rosy picture.

The two areas in which reported numbers can, according to Buffett, give investors misleading impressions are earnings and return on capital.

Accounting standards do not treat the issue of share options to employees as a cost, even though those extra shares will rank alongside existing ones and will, therefore, dilute the company's future earnings. The more shares a company issues in this way, the greater the growth in profits it will need to achieve a similar rate of earnings growth. Buffett argues that the issue of such share options should be treated as a direct cost to the company, though this is not current accounting practice in the US or the UK.

If, for example, Microsoft's issue of share options to employees was treated as a cost, the company would have made losses in 1999 instead of its reported profits. Value investors take such dilution of existing shareholders' interests into account when valuing a company.

Return on capital shows how efficient a company is: the higher the better. But companies may adjust the figures. They may 'write down' the value of assets, especially after a takeover. Such a reduction in the 'book' value of the assets may make it look as if the company is earning a high return on its capital. Value investors want to know what the company is earning on what it actually spent and what its assets are actually worth. This may require significant adjustments to the reported figures.

◆ **The margin of safety** This was Benjamin Graham's key contribution. He wanted to buy a dollar for sixty cents. In the 1930s, 1940s and the early 1950s it was easy to do so. If you analysed the numbers, many companies' shares were selling at sixty cents when the assets of the company were clearly worth a dollar. Buying such a share gave the margin of safety that Graham always wanted.

In more recent times, very few shares have been available on terms like that. This is partly because tangible assets such as land and buildings, important in Graham's day, now make up a small proportion of companies' assets. Nowadays, the value of a company's brands, patents and key personnel is often more important than its tangible assets. Measuring these intangibles is not as easy. The margin of safety may still be there, but it is harder to quantify.

Buffett has progressively moved from a strict interpretation of Graham's methods to one in which the value of a brand or 'franchise' provides the margin of safety.

Working with Mr Market

Value investors buy and hold. Buffett has held many shares for ten years or more. He claims to pay no attention to market prices, and he is fond of citing Graham's 'Mr Market' analogy. It goes like this. When you buy a share, think of yourself as becoming a partner in a business with Mr Market. Mr Market is very accommodating. Every day he turns up and states a price at which he will buy your share of the business, or sell his share to you.

But though the business may be stable, Mr Market's quotations will be anything but stable. "For, sad to say, the poor fellow suffers from incurable emotional problems. At times he feels euphoric and can see only the favourable factors affecting the business. When in this mood, he names a very high buy-sell price because he fears that you will snap up his interest and rob him of imminent gains. At other times he is depressed and can see nothing but trouble ahead both for the business and the world. On these occasions he will name a very low price, since he is terrified you will unload your interest onto him."

Buffett points out that under these conditions, the more manic depressive Mr Market's behaviour is, the better for you. But this is on one condition: Mr Market is there to serve you and not to guide you. It will be disastrous if you fall under his influence. "Indeed, if you aren't certain that you understand and can value your business far better than Mr Market, you don't belong in the game."

Value investing is austere, analytical and a touch arrogant. Yet the evidence is clear: its practitioners have included more of the most successful investors than any other style.

Growth investing

When the number of companies whose shares qualified as value investments shrank in the 1950s and 1960s, analysts cast about for other methods. One that was highly successful was the growth investing style of T Rowe Price, an American stockbroker. He argued that it was worth paying an apparently high price for shares in companies capable of rapid growth in profits and earnings, and the boom of the 1950s and 1960s proved him spectacularly right.

The market crash in 1969-70 saw many growth company shares fall by 50% or more, and for a while growth investing was marginalised. But it returned in spectacular style in the late 1990s as technology-related stocks soared to unprecedentedly high valuations on the basis of their supposed ability to produce very high rates of growth in earnings for many years.

◆ **The life cycle** T Rowe Price believed that companies went through a life cycle. In their earliest and latest stages they were most risky. But the least risky time to own them was when they had established themselves and sales and profits were growing strongly. The aim was to own them until they entered the period of maturity and to sell them before they entered the period of decadence. Most analysts are sceptical of this notion of the life cycle of companies, but the idea of them as living organisms does have some credible supporters.

◆ **Cyclical and secular** The ideal growth stock is one capable of secular growth in earnings, which means that it will continue to grow through several business cycles during which its sector and the whole economy expands and contracts. Shares in such a company will still fall along with those of its peers in a cyclical downturn, but will recover much more strongly in the next upturn.

◆ **Moving on** When a company reaches a plateau, or when external conditions erode its ability to grow, its shares should be sold. Unlike value investing, growth investing is active in disposing of previously successful companies and replacing them with new hopefuls.

The high valuations sometimes attained by growth stocks lead to widespread scepticism. As so often in the stock market, rationality and emotion conflict.

Here is how another insightful American investor, Walter K Gutman, sees them reaching a resolution: "Because no wealth you will ever have – even if you are the richest man in the world – will equal your dreams, stocks go to particularly high levels when a lot of people think they might equal their dreams. Those stocks that are called growth stocks might better be called dream stocks. But dreams are real – we have them every day. It's a big mistake to think that dreams are unreal and what is called real life is real. If dreams were unreal, it would be possible for you to feel richer than your dreams if you were the richest man in the world. When the dream of a new industry comes true, then the dream ends and the stocks sell more conservatively, relating to what is real rather than to what was dreamed."

They're all wrong

Contrarianism is the investment style based on the view that if a great majority of investors are doing the same thing, it is usually wrong. Its application is more limited than the other styles and may best be thought of as a kind of medicine.

Edward C Johnson II, founder of the giant US mutual fund manager Fidelity, pointed out that contrary opinion was of little use in matters of fact. If the vast majority of analysts who have visited a company think it is reasonably well run, there is no merit in thinking the opposite. If most analysts think a company is going to make 10% more profits this year, it is probably not worth arguing with that, either.

Where contrarianism comes into its own is as a defence against crowd psychology.

◆ **Evidence in favour** Study of transactions by small investors on the New York Stock Exchange over many years showed that when the vast majority were buying, you would be better off selling, and vice versa. In the second half of 1974, sellers consistently outnumbered buyers in the UK market, and share prices doubled in the first few months of 1975. In summer 1987, buyers hugely outnumbered sellers and along came a 30% crash in October.

◆ **Greater fool**   The greater fool theory of investment is that it does not matter if you buy at a foolish price so long as there is a bigger fool willing to pay an even more foolish price. For this to work there must be an adequate supply of bigger fools, and if this is to happen, crowd psychology must be at work. As Johnson observed: "Crowds, when they carry often sound ideas to foolish extremes, tend to commit suicide." And as a successful old-time speculator in cotton, Dickson Watts, advised: "Against the crowd, act boldly. With the crowd, act cautiously. It may at any time turn and rend you."

◆ **You too**   For contrarianism to work you have to apply it to your own pet ideas as well as to those of others. Why do you believe X? What would you do if you did not believe X? Used in this way, contrarianism is an attempt to undertake a very difficult task: to listen to what the market is saying, not what people (you included) are thinking and saying about the market.

Fads and fashions

Finding and holding onto a great investment for years while it makes you rich is one possible investment objective, and there is plenty of evidence to prove it is attainable. But this is not what the majority of professional investors do, and since the professional investors own the bulk of the shares, they are the ones who determine short-term and even medium-term market movements.

The problem with these professional investors is that they are accountable to investors, advisers and trustees on a short-term basis. This motivates them to attain short-term results. Generally, they will be considered successful if they have done better than the average of their competitors. So, in broad terms, they pile into sectors and shares they believe will go up in the short term and out of those they believe will go down in the short term. Their timescale is three to six months or at most a year and almost never more.

As long ago as 1935 J M Keynes, who was not only a great economist but a great investor and speculator, spotted this.

He wrote: "It might have been supposed that competition between expert professionals, possessing judgment and knowledge beyond that of the individual investor, would correct the vagaries of the ignorant individual left to himself. It happens, however, that the energies and skills of the professional investor and speculator are mainly occupied otherwise. For most of these persons are, in fact, largely concerned, not with making superior long-term forecasts of the probable yield of an investment over its whole life, but with foreseeing changes in the conventional basis of valuation a short time ahead of the general public."

Keynes equally acutely explained why professional investors would not, by and large, be long-term investors: "It is the long-term investor, he who most promotes the public interest, who will in practice come in for most criticism, wherever funds are managed by committees or boards or banks. For it is in the essence of his behaviour that he should be eccentric, unconventional and rash in the eyes of average opinion. If he is successful, that will only confirm the general belief in his rashness; and if in the short run he is unsuccessful, which is very likely, he will not receive much mercy. Worldly wisdom teaches that it is better for reputation to fail conventionally than succeed unconventionally."

For a recent example of this truth, consider the fate of Phillips & Drew Fund Management, part of the Swiss banking giant UBS. PDFM is principally a value investor, and it disliked the hi-tech stocks that started to perform so well from 1998 onwards, considering them overpriced and in many cases over-borrowed.

As a result, the portfolios it managed for clients contained none of these soaring tech stocks and, therefore, performed well below the average of their competitors for the following two years. PDFM was certainly ridiculed by rivals who had, as the saying goes, 'filled their boots' with hi-tech stocks, and probably lost a significant number of clients because of it. But look now at the value of many of these stocks.

Sector rotation

The fads and fashions of the stock market are ever-changing, but 'sector rotation' is the old perennial. A few months of gloom from the high street, a couple of companies reporting profits not as good as expected, and suddenly all retailers' shares are heading down, the good along with the bad, only to rise again six months later when reports of 'equity withdrawal' from housing spark expectations of a spending boom. In the meantime, the money goes into utilities because they are cheap on a yield valuation, so up go the utilities' shares. A slightly tougher-than-expected statement from a utility regulator – and down go water or electricity shares, only to rise again in six months when the companies announce exactly the same dividend increases that had previously been forecast.

Almost all the research and opinions cited in newspapers and magazines will reflect the current professional consensus. You have a simple choice: try and find out what the consensus is as quickly as possible, so you can join in and keep up with it; or be aware of it but use it simply as another piece of information in your attempt to select long-term investments.

If you do want to play alongside the professionals, you must recognise your dealing handicap – the fact that trading costs you eight times what it costs them – is far heavier in the world of short-term trading than it is in long-term investing.

Stockbroker services

Stockbrokers offer two types of dealing service to individual investors: advisory and execution-only.

Advisory

With an advisory service, you may ask your broker for advice. The broker may also provide research material and newsletters. Dealing costs are typically 1.5% to 1.9% on the value of each trade. You will usually deal with the same individual or small group who will get to know you and your account.

Execution-only

With an execution-only service, the broker offers no advice and takes no responsibility for your investment choices. He simply provides a dealing and settlement service. The cost is usually under 1% of the value of a trade. When you call you will usually talk to one of a group of order-takers who can summon up details of your account on-screen.

Normally when you call a broker with an order you will not know until some time later whether you actually got the shares or sold them at a specific price. With newer internet services, you can in many cases deal in real time. Effectively, you get access to the same dealing systems the brokers use, and can confirm your purchase of a number of shares at a specific price with a click of the mouse.

Price competition has already reduced execution-only dealing costs significantly in the last few years and is likely to cut them further. In the US they were up to 50% lower than in the UK at the end of 2000.

Until recently, when you bought shares you received a share certificate. This was not legal title of ownership. Legally, it is the entry on the company's share register that represents title to shares, but it was traditional to issue certificates.

Now all trading and settlement is handled electronically, registration of ownership has also gone electronic with large companies and will progressively do so with smaller ones. Stockbrokers prefer you to hold your shares in a nominee account, which means the broker operates one electronic account through which all clients' shareholdings are held. You can open your own account with the Stock Exchange clearing system (Crest), but the charges may be as much as £100 a year with many brokers.

There are two problems with nominee accounts. One is that you do not receive communications from companies, because these go to the nominee. Some brokers allow you to have information redirected, but they usually charge for this.

The second problem is security. Legally, you are the owner and if the nominee company went bust you would still be the owner. But in the past, people who were in the process of settling transactions found that if a nominee company did go bust it took many months to sort out their entitlement. Brokers have two answers to this problem: insurance and use of third parties. If a broker runs its own nominee company, it should have a very large sum of insurance to cover any potential client losses and should be happy to tell you what cover it has. Or the broker may use an independent nominee company which is much larger and part of a financial group with much more capital.

Brokers who hold your shares in nominee accounts are obliged to send you periodic statements showing exactly what you hold.

Self-select Isas

Many stockbrokers offer self-select Individual Savings Accounts. This means you set up a plan with the broker, subscribe cash to it and then buy shares within the Isa.

Dealing costs are normally the same as advisory or execution-only services, but there are usually extra charges to watch out for. These are generally in one of two forms. Brokers either charge on a per item basis for collecting dividends and paying money out to you, or they levy an annual charge, typically at 0.5% or 1% a year on the value of your investments, and make no extra charges for these services.

You will need to examine the small print carefully to work out the effect of these charges. But do think about the long term. A 1% charge on a £5,000 investment is only £50 a year, but suppose you achieve your aims and treble your money in the next three years. Now the charge is £150 a year. Wherever possible, select plans with the lowest annual charges – and consider those with no annual charges so long as the per item charges are not too high.

Unlike their Pep predecessors, Isas allow you to buy shares in overseas as well as in UK companies. Watch out for higher costs here since commission rates of 2.5% or even more may be charged on purchases and sales of non-UK companies' shares.

Cutting losses

Most professional investors agree that individual investors do worse than they could because they do not dump their losers but hold them all the way to the bottom. This is largely a matter of psychology. If you over-identify with your investments, the failure of one becomes a personal failure. This is a hard trap to avoid. Also, when you buy a share you can only be wrong once: if it goes down. If you hold a share that has already gone down, you can be wrong twice. First, so long as you do not sell you can tell yourself it is only a paper loss. When you do sell and the loss becomes real, you crystallise a wrong decision. Second, once you have sold there is a possibility that the share will quickly go up again, in which case you will have missed the recovery.

These obstacles should not blind you to the reality. This test is the one proposed by several professional investors. Regardless of what you paid for it and when you bought it, and knowing what you now know about the company, would you buy its shares at the present price? If not, sell.

Successful investors are divided on the use of automatic 'stop-losses'. Some investors when they buy a share set a stop-loss, a price at which they will sell if it falls. They argue that strict adherence to this policy may result in some disappointments, when a share bounces quickly back after falling through the stop-loss level, but it saves you from far worse losses on the shares that just keep on going down.

It's all there

Doing your own research on companies is much easier in the internet age. An increasing number of Plcs have their own websites from which you can download annual reports and other investor information. Stockbrokers are starting to offer free research reports. Many offer access to charts of share prices. Independent sites tell you how many shares are rising and falling, which companies' directors are buying and selling, which shares are being bought or sold by private investors, and many sites let you record your own portfolio and set alerts so you get e-mailed when prices hit specified levels. All this and far more is available provided you are prepared to spend the time trawling through the ever increasing number of websites.

Old-fashioned paper magazines and newsletters still exist, too, offering information, analysis, opinion and share tips. As with the websites, the best policy is to sample their wares, then pick a few reliable sources and make them your basic sources while keeping an open mind and an open eye.

Investment clubs

One way of learning about investing while having fun is to join an investment club. Members meet regularly, trade ideas, argue and choose shares in which their pooled money (quite small amounts, usually) is invested. An organisation called Proshare (see Appendix 2) provides guidance on setting up or joining a club.

You need time

It is no accident that many of the most active individual investors are retired people. Finding and studying all that material, chatting on internet bulletin boards, even going to companies' annual meetings, simply takes up too much time for someone who has a full-time job and perhaps a young family.

Share investing can be a part-time hobby if you stick to a few simple trading rules and do not over-commit yourself. But if you want to put a lot of your money into shares, be realistic about the amount of time you need to do this effectively. If you do not have the time, it may be better to use collectives for the bulk of your capital and to restrict your involvement with shares.

Out and out speculation

If you are attracted by the idea of high-risk, short-term trading, or speculating, you can also consider spread betting through one of several specialist bookmakers. The costs of betting on the movement of a share price can be less than those of buying and selling the shares themselves, and while bookmakers may ask for a 'margin' this will usually be small by comparison with the capital you would need to invest to have the same profit potential as the bet. Since betting gains are tax free, the package can look attractive. But the important point to remember with spread betting is that you can lose as well as make huge amounts of money. On a scale with a low risk being one and high risk ten, spread betting would rate 11.

12

Pre-retirement Planning

A century ago, retirement was something for the lucky few – and if you did make it, you probably enjoyed only four or five years' worth. Today, retirement can span a period almost as long as our working lives. So planning for our retirement finances is immensely important. How can we make sure we will have enough income to enjoy a retirement that could last for 30 years – and maybe even longer?

As the population as a whole gets older, there is much debate on the subject, and politicians are already talking of the need to raise the formal date of retirement, possibly to 70. A depressing thought, maybe, but it's unlikely to be a simple matter of continuing to sit behind the same old desk for a decade longer. Instead, people will take on different jobs, perhaps part-time, not just to keep the income flowing in but to use their energy and talents to good purpose.

This is not to say pre-retirement planning will become superfluous – far from it. People will still need to plan and to save, to provide the extra income that will give them greater freedom in deciding how they spend their later years.

Most people's thoughts start to turn to retirement perhaps ten years before the big day, and increasingly so as they come within five years of it. It might seem a little early to start serious planning five years ahead of retirement – until you remember what you were doing five years ago, which, of course, seems like yesterday.

Even with five years in hand, it is already too late to remedy serious defects in your pension, but you can certainly put some useful icing on the cake.

Finding out your pension entitlement

The first step in pre-retirement planning is to find out how much income you can expect in retirement. It is likely to come from at least two sources: state benefits and occupational or personal pension schemes – and quite possibly a combination of all three. The following is a summary of what you can expect to get on retirement; further details are given in Chapters 8 and 9.

State benefits

There are three main types of state pension you may be eligible for: the basic old-age pension, the State Earnings-Related Pension Scheme (Serps) and graduated retirement benefit (which is paid to people who paid certain National Insurance contributions between 1961 and 1975).

The basic old-age pension

This is payable (currently) to women at 60 and men at 65. The retirement age for women is to be raised, eventually, to 65, but this is being phased in over a number of years and does not affect anyone born before 6 April, 1950.

If you are still working, you can delay taking the basic pension for up to five years after the state retirement age. If you do, your entitlement will be increased by around 7.5% for each year you put it off (with pro-rata increases for shorter terms), except when you are receiving some other state benefit. Even if you don't need it, it probably makes sense to take the pension and invest it. However, if you currently pay income tax at 40% and expect to drop down to the basic rate once you retire, you could consider deferring the state pension until your tax rate falls.

The full pension is currently £3,770 for a single person and £6,026.80 for a married couple, but the amount you actually receive depends on the length of time you have been paying National Insurance contributions. If you have less than a full record, the amount is scaled down. The are two useful booklets: FB6, *Retiring? Your Pension and Other Benefits*, and NP46, *A Guide to Retirement Pensions*, which give full details; you should be able to find them in post offices, local Social Security offices and Citizens' Advice Bureaux.

The system works by establishing the number of years of your working life, defined as 49 for a man and 44 for a woman. The pension you get depends on the number of qualifying years for which you have paid or been credited with NI contributions. A contribution record of 90% or more provides a full pension, with scaled down amounts for shorter periods, as the table shows.

Although working life notionally starts at 16, children at school up to age 18 automatically qualify for those two years, and people who take time off work to bring up children or look after someone who is sick or disabled may receive home responsibilities protection which cuts the number of qualifying years required to receive a full pension.

If you retire before the formal state pension age, it may be worth paying voluntary contributions to safeguard your entitlement. However, men who retire after 60 will have contributions automatically credited on their behalf.

How much of the basic pension will you qualify for?

Women Number of qualifying years	% of pension	Men Number of qualifying years	% of pension
0-9	Nil	0-10	Nil
10	26%	11	25%
15	39%	15	35%
20	52%	20	46%
25	65%	25	57%
30	77%	30	69%
35	90%	35	80%
39 and upwards	100%	40	91%
		44 and upwards	100%

Getting a pension forecast

To save you working through the details yourself, you can get a pension forecast from the Benefits Agency, which provides details of the amount due to you, based on your contribution record. You need form BR19, available from local Social Security offices or by telephoning 0191 218 7585. It can be requested any time up to four months before state retirement age.

If your contributions record is patchy, the local office will tell you if it is possible to make voluntary contributions now, and if so, how much. These can be backdated, but only up to six years.

The pension forecast will also include pensions due under the other two state schemes: graduated retirement benefit and the State Earnings-Related Pension Scheme (Serps).

Graduated retirement benefit

If you paid National Insurance contributions between 1961 and 1975, and were earning over £9 a week at the time, you may also get a small pension based on these contributions. The maximum pension payable is just over £7.50 a week.

The State Earnings-Related Pension Scheme

Many employees are 'contracted out' of Serps through their company pension schemes, and the self-employed are also excluded. For others, the maximum Serps pension is about £125 a week, depending on the number of years for which qualifying National Insurance contributions were paid.

All state pensions are linked to increases in the Retail Price Index; they are always paid gross, but are taxable.

Getting the pensions forecast is the first step to working out your income in retirement. Next you need to establish your pension entitlement from company or personal schemes.

Final salary company pension schemes

If you have worked for the same employer all your life, finding out your expected pension on retirement is relatively easy. Final salary schemes pay a proportion of your final salary as pension for each year you have been a member. A good final salary scheme pays 1/60th of final salary for each year of service; if you have worked for the company for 40 years, you can expect a pension of two-thirds of your final salary. (This is, in fact, the maximum allowed under Inland Revenue rules.)

Contact your personnel or pensions department to find out your exact entitlement if you are not sure. Remember to check whether the pension will increase in line with inflation. Most good company schemes pay some increases, though few go as far as guaranteeing to match inflation at all times. The main exception is civil service pensions where inflation-linking is guaranteed.

While this is relatively plain sailing, complications can set in under the following circumstances:
◆ If you are taking early retirement;
◆ If you want to take a tax-free cash sum on retirement;
◆ If your earnings are above the pensions 'cap';
◆ If you have pension entitlements from previous employers.

Early retirement

Retiring even a few years early can have a significant impact on your pension. Within the overall Inland Revenue rules on maximum pension benefits, companies have considerable leeway in deciding how generous to be. But unless the company has an early retirement policy in force (perhaps because it is engaged in a downsizing exercise) it is unlikely it will be over-generous. Pensions paid early will be scaled down by between 4% and 6% for each year an employee retires early, to take account of the fact that fewer contributions are being made and the pension will be payable for longer.

John Elliot decides to retire five years early at age 60 rather than 65, and after 25 years' service rather than 30, on a final salary of £40,000. If he had stayed until he was 65 (assuming his salary did not rise in the meantime), he would be due a pension of 30/60ths of final salary – £20,000. As it is, before the scaling down, he would be entitled to a pension of 25/60ths or £16,666. Five years' worth of scaling down at 6% equals 30%, so his pension will in fact be £11,666.

Taking a cash sum on retirement

Employees are allowed to take a tax-free cash sum on retirement of up to one-and-a-half times their final year's salary, depending on their length of service. But this is deducted from the eventual pension, and to assess the effect this will have on your own pension, you need to ask your company what its 'commutation factor' is. The answer is likely to be in the region of 12 for someone retiring at age 65 and 16 for someone retiring at age 60.

This is how it works: if the factor is 12, you take the cash sum and divide that by 12. The resulting figure is the amount by which your pension will be reduced.

Jim Scott is entitled to a cash sum on his retirement at age 65 of £36,000. His company uses a commutation factor of 12. He divides the £36,000 by 12, which equals £3,000. This is the amount by which his pension will be reduced.

Companies do alter their commutation factors from time to time, but they tend to stick with the same one for several years, so it should at least be a useful indication.

Note that, once again, civil service and other government pensions are different in this regard. These pension schemes provide, typically, for a pension based on 1/80th of final salary for each year of service, plus a cash sum.

Earnings above the pensions cap

Anyone who joined a company pension scheme after June 1989 (or a new scheme set up after 14 March, 1989) is subject to the pensions cap, which means they are not allowed an ordinary pension in respect of earnings above this. The level of the cap is raised each year in line with prices: for the tax year 2001-02 it stands at £95,400. Any pension savings made by either employee or employer in respect of salaries above that level get none of the tax reliefs associated with pension schemes.

The arrangements companies make for high earning employees vary widely and you will have to consult your own pensions department. If you joined your scheme before the dates above, you are not affected by the cap.

Pension entitlements from previous employers

Many companies continue sending pensions information to ex-employees, but if you have lost touch, contact the Pension Schemes Registry (see Appendix 2). It has details of around 200,000 schemes on its register and should be able to tell you their current whereabouts.

Company money purchase schemes

An increasing number of company pension schemes are run on a money purchase basis. Instead of promising a pension based on final salary, the company only promises to save a certain percentage of your current salary in a pension fund.

You will probably be told the value of your pension pot at least once a year. This must eventually be used to buy an annuity which will provide your pension. To turn this value into an estimated figure for your pension, you need to make two guesses: one about how much the fund will grow between now and retirement, and the other about the level of annuity rates.

Broadly speaking, at current interest rates an annuity will provide a level pension of between £700 and £900 a year for each £10,000 in the fund at retirement, depending on whether you are a man or woman, and retiring at 60 or 65. Men get higher annuity rates than women, because their average life expectancy is lower; the younger you are, the lower the rate will be.

Even a few years before retirement, all you can do is make a semi-educated guess on the amount of pension you are likely to end up with. It will not be surprising if annuity rates fall further in the next few years, as average life expectancy is increasing all the time. On the other hand, your pension fund might grow faster than expected if the investment performance is good.

If you are, say, five years from retirement, here is a rough and ready approach to work out how much pension your fund will buy. Take the fund's current value and assume the annuity rate will be 9% or 10% (in other words, each £10,000 of pension will provide an annuity worth £900 to £1,000). Make no allowance for any future growth in the pension fund.

If you are planning to retire well before age 65, or if you plan to get a joint life pension and your partner is much younger than yourself, it might be as well to assume an annuity rate of 7% or 8% to be on the safe side.

Saving extra for your pension

Whichever type of company scheme you have, you can probably make additional contributions, to make good any pension shortfall you have identified (Chapter 8 gives full details). Because there are Inland Revenue rules on the maximum pension allowed, you should check with your pensions department first that saving extra will not leave you 'overfunded'.

All company schemes must offer an additional voluntary contribution scheme (AVC) facility for their members. Many offer a choice of at least two, with one being invested mainly in equities, and the other a deposit-type scheme. If you start saving just a few years before retirement, it may be sensible to opt for the deposit-based scheme, where there are no risks that your capital could fall. Because AVC savings, like savings into the main company scheme, attract full income tax relief, it can be worth doing even if you only have a year or two to go before retirement.

If it turns out that you have overfunded for the maximum pension allowed, the Inland Revenue insists contributions are returned to you, less a tax charge of 33% for basic rate taxpayers and a total of 50% for higher rate taxpayers.

Personal pensions

Personal pensions cater for people who do not belong to a company scheme, including the self-employed. They work on the same principles as company money purchase schemes: your savings are invested and the size of pension you get at retirement will depend on the size of your fund and annuity rates at the time.

If you are within a few years of retirement and want to know how much your pension is likely to be, you must be content with making only a rough estimate. As with company schemes, you can use a percentage figure of between 7% and 10% of the total current fund value.

Last-minute saving into a personal pension

Personal pension planholders are allowed to put a certain percentage of their earnings each year into their pension. The precise figure varies with age, and also depends on whether you have the newer personal pension (available since 1988) or the older 'Section 226' or 'Self-employed' pension plan which preceded it.

Age on 6 April	Proportion of earnings that can go into:	
	Section 226	Personal pension
35 or less	17.5%	17.5%
36-45	17.5%	20.0%
46-50	17.5%	25.0%
51-55	20.0%	30.0%
56-60	22.5%	35.0%
61-74	27.5%	40.0%

Most people will obviously be able to make bigger contributions into a personal pension plan, but if they are earning more than £100,000 a year, it is worth checking first. Personal pensions are subject to an earnings cap, which means savings can only be made in respect of earnings up to £95,400 for the tax year 2001-02. If you are earning well over this figure, you might be able to save more by using the lower percentages available under the Section 226 plan, because there is no cap on the income level.

Stakeholder pensions: a new option

In April 2001, a new form of personal pension, the stakeholder pension, became available. This works just like a personal pension, but the rules are slightly different. Almost everyone is eligible to save money into a stakeholder pension: the upper age limit is 75, there is no lower age limit and, unlike other pension plans, you do not have to be earning – you can still make contributions after you have stopped working.

You can save up to £3,600 a year gross – although if you are earning, you can use the percentage of earnings limits shown in the table above, which may result in higher contributions. The only people barred from using a stakeholder plan are employees who are already in a company scheme and are earning more than £30,000 a year.

If you are coming up to retirement, taking out a stakeholder plan could help you to increase your post-retirement income. Unlike personal pension plans, they have a government imposed cap on their charges of 1% a year. They may be especially useful for non-earning wives, for instance, or women with a broken employment record and little pension entitlement in their own right. They can use a capital sum to invest in a stakeholder plan – and obtain automatic basic rate tax relief on the contributions – and thus get their own pension. In effect, it is a way of converting capital into a guaranteed income for life. With the tax relief on contributions, this can be a worthwhile exercise.

On retirement: the annuity choice

Anyone with a personal or self-employed pension plan, as well as employees with money purchase company pensions, faces a major decision at retirement: what sort of annuity to buy. People in final salary schemes do not have this decision in respect of their main pension, which is paid directly by the scheme, but they may have a money purchase AVC scheme which also requires an annuity to be bought. The main options are:

◆ a fixed-rate annuity, which pays a level income every year until death, or one increasing at a set rate, or

◆ a with-profits or unit-linked annuity, where rates depend, in part, on the performance of an underlying investment fund.

In addition, people with personal pensions and many of those with company money purchase schemes have a further choice. Instead of buying an annuity straight away, they can choose:

◆ an income drawdown plan, or

◆ a staggered pension arrangement.

The place for advice in choosing an annuity

Independent advice can bring in immediate benefits when you are deciding what annuity to buy. Although the pension company you have been saving with will automatically offer you its own annuity, you are entitled to take the fund at retirement and go to any other company in the marketplace. It is a competitive market, but there are still big differences between the best and worst annuity rates. Picking the best could result in an increase in your immediate income of 10% or more – and this difference will continue for the rest of your life.

It is, in effect, a no-lose situation: if it turns out the annuity quotation you received from your original company is the best of the lot, you can stick with it. Most advisers do not charge a fee for this initial work, expecting to make money from the commission on selling a different annuity to you. However, if you are happier paying a fee, you should be able to negotiate this at the outset, in which case any commission will be returned to you. Paying fees is likely to be cheaper overall if your pension fund is very large: anything over, say, £200,000.

The one point you have to be certain of is that any competitive quotations are prepared on a 'like-for-like' basis. For example, if your pension company has provided a quote for a joint life annuity, payable until the second death, and your partner is five years younger than you, this should not be compared to a single life annuity from another company, based only on your own life.

While most people will be considering a straightforward fixed-rate annuity on retirement, those with larger pension funds may well opt for the income drawdown option or a staggered arrangement (see pages 215 to 219). In this case, too, it is sensible to take advice on the best course of action.

Fixed-rate annuities

Even if you decide to go for a straightforward fixed-rate annuity, there are still a number of options. The principal ones are:

◆ **Fixed or escalating** As noted above, you can choose an annuity that is payable at a fixed level throughout life, or one which is increased by a set percentage each year. It is also possible to choose one where increases will be guaranteed to match the Retail Price Index. The right choice depends on your own circumstances.

A level annuity pays a higher sum initially, as the table on the next page shows, but over the years its purchasing power will decrease. Even if the rate of inflation stays at around 2% a year, after ten years you would need £1.22 to buy £1-worth of goods in today's terms, and after 20 years, nearly £1.50. So taking a level annuity, however attractive initially, has significant risks attached.

On the other hand, you may have other sources of income which are index-linked, such as the state pensions. Company share dividends should also increase at least in line with inflation. If you are prepared to save part of the annuity payments initially, rather than spending them all, taking the level option may be best all round.

◆ **Joint or single life** Clearly, if you are married or have a partner, a joint life pension is the most sensible choice. With a single life pension the annuity payments stop when you die.

There might be circumstances in which it is sensible to take a single life pension: for instance, if one of your pension policies offers guaranteed annuity rates available only on a single life basis. If it only forms a relatively small part of your retirement funds, it could be worth taking – as long as you are in reasonable health.

◆ **With or without a guaranteed period** All annuity payments are guaranteed to last as long as you live – but if you (and your partner) died tomorrow, that is a lot of money down the drain as no capital is returned after death. An annuity with a guaranteed period promises to continue paying the income, whether you live or die, for a set number of years after it is purchased.

As a rule of thumb, it is often worth choosing an annuity with a five-year guaranteed period as it can cost very little (in fact, it can sometimes produce marginally better rates than an annuity with no guarantee at all). A ten-year guarantee is more expensive, and not so attractive. Remember that as long as you live beyond the period stipulated, the guarantee is effectively worthless.

◆ **Payable monthly, quarterly, half-yearly or yearly** You can choose the frequency of annuity payments from monthly in advance at one extreme, to annually in arrears at the other. The longer the delay, the higher the income will be. Opting for payments made quarterly in arrears rather than monthly in advance will result in an increase in annual income of perhaps 1.5% or 2%.

◆ **With or without proportion** This relates only to annuities paid in arrears. If you die just before a payment is due, an annuity without proportion makes no balancing payment. An annuity payable with proportion will make a part-payment of the amount due at the date of your death. If you choose an annuity payable yearly in arrears, it may be worth choosing one with proportion, although this means the rates are slightly lower overall.

Typical annuity rates for a capital sum of £10,000

Income	Single man aged 65				Single woman aged 60		
	No guarantee	Guaranteed 5 yrs	10 yrs		No guarantee	Guaranteed 5 yrs	10 yrs
Level	£876	£867	£842	Level	£728	£725	£719
3% rise	£674	£668	£650	3% rise	£520	£518	£514
5% rise	£553	£549	£535	5% rise	£400	£399	£396
RPI	£647	£642	£624	RPI	£495	£494	£490

Joint lives, man aged 65, wife aged 62. Payments guaranteed for five years

Income	Level of spouse's pension after first death		
	50%	67%	100%
Level	£774	£747	£669
3%	£572	£545	£500
5%	£453	£428	£386
RPI	£546	£520	£476

Payments in these examples are made monthly in advance
Source: The Annuity Bureau

Annuities for people in bad health and smokers

If you do not enjoy good health, you may be able to get higher annuity rates than those shown above, and it is worth getting advice before buying. Each case is underwritten individually and higher rates may be available for people with diabetes, liver impairment, heart conditions or who have had any type of cancer.

Regular smokers may also get better rates. If you have smoked at least ten cigarettes a day for the last ten years you may qualify for enhanced rates – and if you give up smoking once the annuity has been set up, the rates will not be cut.

If you are looking for a joint life pension rather than a single life one, your partner's state of health will also influence the rates available.

Other special rate annuities

Manual workers living in certain areas may also benefit from higher annuity rates, as statistics have shown they have a lower than average life expectancy.

Guaranteed annuity rates

Ten or 20 years ago, a number of pension companies offered guaranteed annuity rates to their policyholders. These were well below those actually available at the time, but as interest rates have come down, the guaranteed option has in some cases become very valuable.

If you had such a guaranteed option on your policies, it will almost certainly be worth taking. However, many pensions companies only offered the guarantees on a single life pension, so on the face of it, they are not much use to married couples. But there are options worth exploring. For example, you could take the single life pension and, at the same time, take out a life insurance policy to pay a cash sum on your death. This could then be used to provide an income for your partner, if you are the first to die.

Investment-linked annuities

The amount paid out by these annuities depends partly on the level of interest rates and your life expectancy, but also partly on the performance of an underlying investment fund. If this performs well, payments should rise over the years, but they could also fall if investment returns are low. At the outset, the holder must specify the level of income required, which in turn depends on a target investment return being achieved.

Investment-linked annuities are not suitable for people retiring on a tight budget because of the risks involved. But they can be very useful in other contexts, especially for people retiring at younger ages, or those looking to buy an annuity with their AVC fund when they already have a secure pension from their main employer's pension scheme.

Most of these annuities are linked to with-profits funds, while others are unit linked. The with-profits option is the less risky.

One annuity or several?

If you have several pension plans – as many self-employed people do – there is no need to choose a single annuity. You might, for example, choose a fixed-rate annuity for the bulk of your retirement income, but have an investment-linked policy as a top-up.

Should you take the tax-free cash?

Every type of pension plan allows members to take a certain proportion of their fund as a cash lump sum on retirement. The rules differ between schemes.

◆ With personal and stakeholder pension plans, you can take up to a quarter of the total fund as a lump sum.
◆ With Section 226 schemes, you can take cash equal to three times the remaining pension. Depending on annuity rates at the time you retire, this is likely to be equivalent to between 20% and 25% of the total fund.
◆ With company schemes, you can take up to one-and-a-half times final salary as cash, depending on your length of service.

Most people decide to take the cash sum – perhaps to finance that round-the-world cruise they have been dreaming of. But this, of course, means your pension is reduced. So if you are operating on a tight budget, and need all the income you can get, should you go without the cash sum?

In fact, there can still be circumstances where it makes sense to take the cash, and invest it in an ordinary life annuity instead of a pension annuity. It will depend on your circumstances. The rates on ordinary life annuities are generally lower than those for pension annuities (this is because they tend to be bought only by people in good health, whose life expectancy is greater than average) but they are taxed less heavily. As long as you expect to be paying income tax on your retirement income, taking the cash sum and investing it in an ordinary annuity can provide a higher after-tax income.

Robert Wilson has a pension fund of £40,000. He is 65 and single. The £40,000 would buy him a pension annuity paying £2,950 a year after basic rate tax. However, if he chooses to take a £10,000 in cash sum, his pension annuity will only pay £2,210 after tax. But if he uses the £10,000 to buy an ordinary life annuity, this will buy an additional income of £835 after tax.

In total, therefore, his income will be £3,045 net of tax if he takes the cash sum and uses it to buy an ordinary annuity, compared to £2,950 if he simply took the full pension.

Alternatives to annuities

Some people hate the very idea of annuities, for one simple reason: once you buy one, you have lost access to your capital for ever, in return for a regular income.

But before considering the alternatives, it is worth saying a word in their defence. Annuities provide an income that is guaranteed to last for the rest of your life. True, if you died tomorrow, that is a very bad bargain. But suppose you live to 100? The risk of your living longer than expected is taken on wholly by the annuity company, so there is no prospect of the income running out before you do.

As matters stand, there is, in any case, little choice. You can put off buying an annuity but only until age 75. At that stage, an annuity of some sort must be bought. There has been much lobbying in recent years to abolish this requirement, or at least to extend the age to, say, 80. To date, the rules have not been changed, but it will not be surprising if they are at some time in the future.

At least until age 75, there is a choice. There are two possibilities for people who do not want to buy an annuity straight away on retirement: to go for a staggered pension arrangement, or an income drawdown plan.

These choices are open to anyone with a personal pension or Section 226 plan, and to many of those in company money purchase schemes.

Phased retirement

This scheme is in effect something that many self-employed people have been doing, in an informal way, for years. Instead of retiring overnight, and drawing all their pension in one go, they wind down gradually from work, and phase in their various pension policies over a period of years, turning some into annuities immediately, and keeping others going for a few years longer. As their working income decreases, they can gradually build up their pension income.

This, of course, assumes people have more than one pension policy. In fact, you probably do have, whether you are aware of it or not. Most personal pension plans are automatically segmented into hundreds of tiny parts, so you can fine tune the phasing.

The advantages

There are several benefits to the phased approach to retirement. Retiring overnight and turning all your pension fund into an annuity on a single day means taking a big risk on the level of annuity rates, and the value of your fund, on that day. If you have the bad luck to retire on a day when annuity rates have just dropped, at the same time as the stock market has taken a tumble, you will be penalised twice over: the value of the fund will have fallen, and the amount of income it buys will have fallen too.

Phasing means you spread this risk across several years. It should also mean at least part of your pension fund can benefit from a few extra years' of investment growth. And because annuity rates rise the older you are, it should also mean that each year, your money will buy that bit more income.

Meanwhile, should you die before the full pension fund has been turned into annuities, the balance can be left to your heirs. Once it has been turned into an annuity, there is no such option.

The table shows how phasing might work in practice, with fresh policies being cashed in each year from the age of 60 right through to the upper age limit of 75. It assumes that each time a pension policy is turned into an annuity, the maximum 25% cash sum is taken, to form part of the income for that year. It also assumes the funds remaining invested grow at 7% a year.

The disadvantages

Investment growth cannot, of course, be guaranteed. Investments might grow faster, more slowly, or indeed fall in value from one year to the next. So phasing is not sensible for people who want to rely absolutely on a fixed level of income.

In addition, a strict phasing programme requires you to use the lump sum available each time a pension policy is cashed in, as part of your income for that year. This means you can never get your hands on one big capital sum, so you might have to forego that round-the-world cruise.

Phased retirement in practice

Pension fund: £300,000. Target yearly income: £20,000

Age	Starting fund	Amount encashed	Tax-free cash	Annuity payment	Total income	Remaining fund
60	£300,000	£65,400	£16,350	£3,650	£20,000	£235,000
61	£235,000	£52,100	£13,000	£7,000	£20,000	£192,000
62	£192,000	£41,600	£10,400	£9,600	£20,000	£160,000
63	£160,000	£32,900	£8,230	£11,770	£20,000	£135,000
64	£135,000	£25,700	£6,440	£13,560	£20,000	£116,000

and so on until...

Age	Starting fund	Amount encashed	Tax-free cash	Annuity payment	Total income	Remaining fund
73	£81,700	£2,510	£628	£19,370	£19,998	£84,300
74	£84,300	£1,330	£334	£19,600	£19,934	£88,300
75	£88,300*					

*This will provide tax-free cash of £22,000 plus an additional pension of £8,650 a year alongside the continuing pension of £19,600.

The table assumes level annuity payments and annual growth at 7% on investments remaining within the fund. If they grew more slowly, income would diminish with age. Remember, each year's annuity payments are added to those being made from the annuities started up in earlier years. Income payments are shown before tax.

Note this particular scheme involves a big leap in income from age 75.
It would be possible, by cashing in more segments in the earlier years, to have a smoother progression, but the thinking behind it is to build in a bit of a safety net in case investments do not grow steadily at the 7% forecast. This is a very sensible precaution, because there can be no guarantees.
Source: Clerical Medical

Income drawdown plans

Income drawdown plans allow people to delay turning any of their pension fund into an annuity until age 75. Instead, they can draw an income directly from the fund, in amounts more or less to suit themselves, although there are minimums and maximums that can be taken, laid down by the government. If you want to take the cash sum available on retirement, you must do so at the same time as you start the income drawdown.

Minimum and maximum income

The maximum amount you can draw down in any year is equivalent to that produced by a straightforward fixed-rate annuity for someone of your age. The minimum is 35% of the maximum.

The advantages

There are two main advantages. First, there is the possibility of future investment growth in the fund which remains invested. Second, is the fact that if you die before age 75 most of the capital remaining can be returned to your heirs (less a tax charge of 34%). If there is a surviving widow or widower, the income withdrawal can continue until the survivor reaches 75 (or the planholder would have been 75, if this is earlier) or it can be turned into an annuity straight away.

The disadvantages

As with phased retirement, the main disadvantage is that you continue to take an investment risk with the pension fund. If it falls in value, your income may do so, too, especially if you decided to withdraw the maximum possible. And if the fund falls below a certain level at any age, there is a requirement that it is immediately turned into an annuity, even if it happens before you reach age 75.

Many experts suggest that people set up a self-invested pension plan when they start a drawdown scheme. This involves paying a fee to a pension company, which will set up a 'shell' scheme, and thereafter you (or your adviser) will be able to pick and choose between different investment managers, to split it between several, or even to manage it yourself. This may well turn out a cheaper option in the long run than taking out a full scheme run by an insurance company, but probably only for those with substantial sums – say, £200,000 or more – to invest.

It is simple to set up such a scheme if you originally had a personal pension, but there may be complications for those whose scheme was a company one, and you will need to take advice.

A final choice

If you want extra flexibility in planning your pension income, you can operate a combination of phasing and drawdown, which means you can draw a very low level of income to begin with, building it up gradually over a number of years. This approach might suit you if you continue to work part-time for many years after your formal retirement date and need some additional income, but do not want to go without the possibility of investment growth on your fund by turning it into an annuity.

Pre-retirement planning courses

A number of colleges and adult education centres run courses on pre-retirement planning and preparation. There are also a number of commercial operations in this field, and many large companies provide places on such courses for their employees (and, often, their spouses as well). Such courses can last for an evening or a few days, and will cover many aspects of retirement, not just financial matters.

The Pre-Retirement Association, a registered charity, exists to raise standards in the education and training of pre-retirement advisers. It publishes an annual directory of course providers, which is available (price £10.50) from the address shown in Appendix 2. It also runs pre-retirement courses which are open to both individuals and companies which have a few employees approaching retirement.

Individuals can join the association, entitling them to discounts on its publications and seminars, and copies of *Saga Magazine* (ten times a year) and *Your Retirement* (annually).

13

Post-retirement Planning

Investment planning after retirement will, for most people, involve a big about-turn in their thinking. Until now, planning has probably been concentrated on building up capital; now, you will be far more concerned with the income it produces.

Planning at any time is usually an exercise in achieving the best possible compromise between conflicting aims. We all want an investment that combines a high and rising income, good capital growth, no risk and is tax free. But that is having your cake and eating it: it cannot be done.

Stocktaking for inflation

The first step is to assess your current sources of income. Inflation may have been largely conquered, and it may seem old-fashioned to continue preaching its dangers. Nevertheless, it is worth bearing in mind that even at rates as low as 2% a year, inflation will continually whittle away at the purchasing power of money. After ten years, it will have lost around a fifth of its real value; in 20 years, it is more like a half.

A woman retiring at 60 today can expect to live, on average, another 22 years; a man, nearly 18 years. And if life expectancies continue their trend of constant improvement, the odds are you will be surviving well into your 80s. So it is only sensible to consider, first, what proportion of your retirement income is capable of growth in the future, and how much is fixed for all time, before deciding how to invest your overall portfolio.

The various state pensions are all guaranteed to rise in line with prices. With other pensions, the situation varies. Good final salary schemes are likely to pay inflation-linked increases. With other types of scheme, it depends on the annuity you have chosen.

If the majority of your pension income is inflation linked, you do not need to be so concerned that income from other parts of your portfolio is not. On the other hand, if you have a level payment pension annuity, it would be wise to have at least some of your other investments capable of producing growth.

Choosing your investments

It is tempting to think, in retirement, that your principal aim must be preservation of capital at all costs: but this could be a mistake.

The big dilemma for the income seeking investor is that investments with absolute capital security do not provide growth in capital or income, while those that grow cannot provide security.

With 20 years or more of retirement in prospect, some potential for growth is important. One way of looking at it is to think of your capital as a machine to produce income. It does not matter whether the value of that machine fluctuates, as long as its income producing capacity is undiminished.

Despite the plethora of investment products available, they boil down to three basic asset classes: equities or company shares, fixed-interest securities, and cash. These three classes can also be characterised as, respectively, high, medium and low risk. The main investment principle of spreading risk applies just as much to life after retirement as before. Thus it is sensible to have part of your investment portfolio in each class, with the actual proportion dictated by your particular circumstances and attitude to risk.

The following is a whistle-stop tour of the types of investment that are likely to be most interesting to people in retirement.

Low-risk investments with total capital security

Cash deposits

Cash provides absolute security of capital, and either a fixed or variable rate of interest. It is the obvious home for short-term money. With most current accounts paying interest of little more than 0.2%, the aim should be to keep your current account as lean as possible, with anything extra going into a deposit account.

Under this heading come all building society and bank deposit accounts, many National Savings products, and Individual Savings Accounts (Isas) invested in cash. Some of the products pay a set rate of interest for a fixed term, with others it varies.

Variable rate deposits

Checking the rates on variable accounts could be a full-time job if you were so minded. Banks and building societies are constantly fine-tuning and scarcely a week goes by without some new account being launched. Most newspapers carry tables of top interest rates in their money or personal finance sections every week. To avoid losing out, it is worth checking on a regular basis, say at least twice a year. The top-rated accounts these days are almost invariably operated by the internet, telephone or post.

Some of the highest paying variable rate accounts

Investment	Amount	Interest rate (gross)
Bank/building society		
No-notice account	£1,000	5.5%-6.3%
Monthly interest account	£5,000	5.7%-6.6%
60-day notice	£50,000	6.2%
Mini cash Isa	£3,000	7.0%
National Savings Income Bond	up to £25,000	5.45%*
	£25,000-£250,000	5.7%*

*3 months' notice required for withdrawals

Fixed-rate deposits

National Savings has a number of fixed-rate offerings. The current issue of five-year, fixed-rate certificates is the 57th, paying 3.55% tax free over five years, while the current 7th issue of two-year certificates pays 3.65% tax free. In both cases, the return is paid not as an annual income but as an enhanced capital sum at the end of the term.

If you cash them in before the term is up, the rate of interest is significantly lower, so this is not the place for emergency funds. At the end of their term, the certificates go on to the 'general extension rate' – a variable interest rate which is also tax free. The general extension rate is always below the rate for a new issue (currently it is just 2.85%) so there is little point keeping the money there. If you want to continue with the investment, reinvest in the latest issue.

National Savings also provides index-linked certificates, where the capital is guaranteed to rise in line with inflation. They pay an interest supplement in addition. The 19th issue of five-year certificates pays a supplement of 1.65%, and the 7th issue of two-year certificates pays 2.15% plus inflation. As with fixed-rate certificates, returns are tax-free and there are penalties for early encashment.

These products are best suited to people who pay 40% tax on their other income and should be avoided by non-taxpayers who can get better rates elsewhere. National Savings also has a range of Pensioners Bonds (open to anyone over the age of 60), which offer fixed rates for one, two or five years where the interest is gross but taxable. Rates on the current issues are from 4.75% to 4.9%, depending on the term. And finally, there are one and two-year fixed-rate bonds, open to all comers, with current issues paying between 4.75% and 5.15% where, again, the interest is gross but taxable.

Bank and building society accounts

These also offer fixed-rate deposit accounts for varying terms, though they are less common than variable rate accounts. Terms range from one month to five years and interest is taxable.

Guaranteed income bonds

These bonds are issued by life insurance companies. Interest is paid net of basic rate tax which cannot be reclaimed by non-taxpayers, but 40% taxpayers do relatively well because the bonds are taxed more lightly than straightforward deposit accounts. The bonds are always limited offers; most newspapers carry details of the best available at any one time. They generally pay out interest once a year, or investors can choose a growth option where the full return is paid at the end of the term.

Before buying, it is a good idea to check what happens if you die during the fixed term. Some pay out income pro-rata, others make no such payment.

Gilts held to maturity

Gilts, or government securities, are a two-faced sort of investment. If you buy a gilt and hold it until its maturity date, you know exactly where you stand and the amount of capital you will get back. Held in this way, they provide absolute capital security. However, gilts are also 'negotiable securities' which means it is possible to buy and sell them during their term, via the stock market. If you sell before the end of the term the price you receive will depend on the general level of interest rates.

Gilts are classified for convenience by the length of time they have to run to maturity. 'Shorts' have less than five years to go, 'medium-dated gilts' run for between five and 15 years, and 'long-dated' gilts run beyond that. They are also classified by the size of their 'coupon' or interest yield. 'Low-coupon' gilts pay low interest, but are issued at a price well below the amount they promise to pay back on maturity. Thus, investors get capital growth in exchange for the relatively low interest. 'High-coupon' gilts pay high interest, but offer no capital growth.

Gilts may sound like an ideal constituent for a retirement portfolio, but as matters stand at present, they do not look terribly attractive. There are two reasons for this. The first is that the government has not been making many new issues in recent years. At the same time, large institutional investors – pension funds and the like – have been big buyers of gilts in the recent past. As with any other commodity, the combination of strong demand and restricted supply has increased gilt prices, and as the price of a gilt rises, so its yield falls.

In fact, it is hard to find a medium or high-coupon gilt whose price is at or below 'par value' (the price at which it will be redeemed by the government on maturity). Most are well above par, meaning there is an in-built capital loss at maturity. To safeguard your capital, you would need to put aside and reinvest some of the income produced each year – a cumbersome and not very efficient process.

Finally, there are index-linked gilts, which provide guaranteed index linking of both capital and interest. The initial income is very low, perhaps around 2% gross.

Gilts can be bought through stockbrokers or direct from the Bank of England which is a cheaper, though slower, route. The Bank publishes an explanatory booklet on gilts, available by calling 0800 818614.

Other bonds held to maturity

Corporate bonds have become popular because they can be held in Individual Savings Accounts (Isas). If held to maturity, their capital, too, is secure, with the important caveat that the issuing company does not go bust in the meantime. With gilts, of course, the government's guarantee to repay is as copper-bottomed as you can get. With commercial companies, the situation is inevitably less secure. Bonds have different ratings, from AAA (reckoned to be top-class security risks) down through AA, A, and so on to BBB and below.

If you are considering buying such a bond, it is important to take professional advice. The lower-rated bonds pay higher interest which makes them superficially more attractive, but there is a straightforward pay-off between risk and reward. It is rare for a company to be unable to pay back its debt, but it has happened in the past, and investors have been left with worthless bits of paper.

Other investments offering capital security

Guaranteed equity bonds are a hybrid investment. They provide security of capital, plus performance linked to the stock market. Typically, they may last for five years, and investors will be guaranteed a return equal to the performance of a named stock market index – such as the FTSE All-Share – over the time concerned. If the index falls, investors are still guaranteed their money back.

These bonds are extremely complex, making use of various financial derivatives. The price for this seemingly attractive combination of reward and limited risk is that they pay no income, unlike a straightforward investment in the stock market, where you get dividends as well (hopefully) as capital growth.

These bonds are limited issues, and there are any number of variations on the theme. Some guarantee a minimum return of, perhaps, 140% of capital at the end of their five-year term, but provide only half the growth in the index.

It is hard to issue blanket recommendations either for or against these bonds, because so much depends on the precise nature of the offering. On balance, though, they are probably worth considering only if security of capital is so important to you, that you would not countenance any stock market investment without it. But do bear in mind that guarantees are never cheap, however well or attractively they are presented.

Tax on interest

All interest producing investments, including deposit accounts, gilts and corporate bonds, are liable to tax at a special rate of 20%. Basic rate taxpayers have no more tax to pay; higher rate taxpayers must pay the full difference between 20% and 40% tax. Non-taxpayers can in certain instances get the full amount of gross interest paid directly. With bank and building society accounts, for example, a non-taxpayer can fill in form IR85 (available from your bank or building society) to get interest paid gross. With other investments such as gilts and corporate bonds, the interest is usually paid net of basic rate tax, which non-taxpayers must then reclaim from the Inland Revenue.

People whose marginal income tax rate is 10% can reclaim the extra 10% taken in tax from the Revenue.

The role of Tessas and Isas

The less tax you pay on your savings interest, clearly, the better off you will be. Tax-Exempt Special Savings Accounts (Tessas) are no longer on sale, but many investors will still have one running through its five-year term. Once it reaches the end, the capital can be reinvested in a special Tessa-only Individual Savings Account (Isa), where the money can be protected, once again, from tax.

Note that when your current Tessa reaches its maturity, the regulations allow the capital to be transferred to another bank or building society (although some refuse to accept such transfers-in). It is definitely worth shopping around at this point. At time of writing, for example, rates on Tessa-only Isas ranged from 5% to about 7%.

Isas are the tax-free savings plans which replaced Tessas and Peps. You can invest up to £3,000 in a cash Isa and up to £4,000 in other types of investment in 2001-02. As the rules stand, if you take out the mini cash Isa, you can invest a further £3,000 into a mini equity (stocks and shares) Isa and £1,000 into a mini insurance-linked Isa. If you forego the cash and insurance options, you can instead put the full £7,000 into a maxi equity Isa.

This rule can lead to a tricky decision. People with large equity investments may wish to use the full £7,000 allowance for an equity Isa, which means they cannot use the cash Isa. As so often in investment matters, there is no single right answer as to what you should do: it must depend on your circumstances.

Medium-risk investments

Into this category come gilts and corporate bonds once again, with-profits bonds and permanent interest bearing shares (Pibs).

Gilts and corporate bonds

As noted above, gilts or bonds not held to maturity should be classified as medium risk, because they do not guarantee security of capital. While most investors are unlikely to deal actively in gilts or corporate bonds, they may well be attracted by an actively managed bond fund, which may include gilts as well as corporate bonds and possibly convertibles.

These funds have been especially popular since Isas arrived as they can be held within this tax-free wrapper. But while the advertisements may look tempting, it is important to remember they are not the same as a deposit account. Bond funds are subject to two types of risks: the credit risk and the interest rate risk.

The credit risk is that one or more of the issuing companies goes bust, in which case, the capital is lost. This can be minimised in two ways: by research on the part of the managers into the companies themselves, and by spreading the investment among a wide range of companies, so only a small percentage of your money is exposed to any single company's bonds.

The interest rate risk is harder to control. If rates in general rise, the capital value of a bond falls, as the level of interest it is paying is no longer so attractive. So while the interest yield on a bond fund may look good, there is a price to be paid: the capital value is not secure.

When choosing a bond fund, there are three main things to look out for:

◆ **Charges** There is usually both an initial fee and an on-going annual management charge. Sometimes the annual charge is deducted from the income before it is paid out; in other cases, it is taken from the capital.

◆ **Running yield** At present, bond funds are yielding between about 5% and 9% gross. The higher the yield, the lower the average credit rating of the issuing company will be. Many fund managers run two bond funds: a standard one, and an 'extra yield' or 'high income' fund, which specialises in bonds from the lower rated companies. It is hard to quantify the extra risk involved in going for one of these funds, but it does exist. While they may seem the more attractive option, it would be unwise to put all your eggs into this particular basket.

◆ **Redemption yield** Whereas the running yield shows simply the amount of income the fund produces, the redemption yield also takes into account the capital loss or gain that would ensue if all the bonds in the underlying portfolio were held until maturity. The managers do not necessarily hold them all until then; they are more likely to be dealing fairly actively, both buying and selling. So in one sense, the redemption yield is a notional figure. But if it is much below the level of the running yield, this is an indication that, if investors drew out all the income, they would probably be eating into their capital.

Permanent interest bearing shares

Pibs are similar to corporate bonds, except that they have no redemption date – they are, as their name says, 'permanent'. They are issued by building societies, although these days many of the issues in existence are actually from former societies such as the Halifax. They are traded on the Stock Exchange. This means that if you want to sell, you must take the price being offered at the time, which may be higher or lower than that at which you bought, or at which they were originally issued. Their big attraction for investors in retirement is the level of income they pay: a good 2% more than the yield obtainable on gilts.

The interest on Pibs is paid net of basic rate tax, which non-taxpayers can reclaim, but unlike corporate bonds, they cannot be put into an Isa. They can provide a high income, but it is important to remember there is no capital security.

With-profits bonds

With-profits bonds are very popular with investors as a sort of halfway house between deposit accounts and stock market investments. They are a single premium version of the with-profits endowment policy, which many investors will be familiar with. With-profits policies invest in a mixture of property, equities and fixed-interest investments. Typically, the breakdown will be 60% or 70% in equities, perhaps 10% in commercial property and the rest in fixed-interest securities, including gilts, and cash.

With-profits funds are managed in two ways. First, like any other fund, they are handled by professional investment managers who try to maximise returns by picking the right stocks and getting a good balance between the various asset classes. But unlike other funds, the aim of the with-profits fund manager is to smooth out returns from one year to the next by making use of reserves. In good years, the company will not pay out all the money it makes, keeping some back for reserves; in bad years, it will dip into these to keep up payments.

This makes them a comfortable sort of investment, as long as the managers get it right, and as long as they have been prudent enough in the past to build up sizeable reserves. In good years, investors will not do as well as those invested directly in the stock market or through an equity unit trust, but they should be protected to some extent in the bad years. Over the long run, they will probably lag behind equity investments, but that is the price to be paid for comfort.

Returns on with-profits funds are allocated in two ways. An annual bonus, reflecting both the income earned by the fund each year and, usually, some element of anticipated capital growth, is paid into the policy each year. There may also be a terminal bonus, reflecting the rest of the growth on the underlying investments, which is paid when the policy is cashed in.

Annual bonuses, once declared, cannot be taken away, and the managers will, if necessary, use their reserves to keep them at a reasonably steady rate. Terminal bonuses are never guaranteed and can vary significantly – in some years there may be none at all, if the company has had to dip into its reserves to maintain the annual bonus.

With-profits bonds allow investors to make withdrawals each year as 'income'. The amount is left up to you – advisers suggest that if you want to preserve your capital, it should be less than the annual bonus rate.

There is no simple way to spot which companies offer the most attractive bonds. All quote their current annual bonus rate, which at present varies from about 4.25% to 5.25%. But it is not a simple matter of the higher rate being better. Companies differ in the amount of anticipated capital growth they use in their annual bonuses. All other things being equal, those paying a high annual bonus will pay a lower terminal bonus.

The past performance of the fund is also important, as is the strength of the company's reserves.

Finally, there is the matter of the 'market value adjustment factor'. This is a device by which the managers reserve the right to cut down on the value of the bond when you encash it, if investment performance has not been as good as anticipated.

Companies are, in general, reluctant to apply such a factor but, again, attitudes vary. Some guarantee that at certain points – say, at the 10th anniversary of the bond – they will not apply this factor. So if you cash in at this point, you will never get back less than the original capital. Others make no such guarantees.

Tax on bonds

The underlying investments in a with-profits bond are liable to both basic rate income tax and capital gains tax, both paid by the life company. This means that, for basic rate taxpayers, there is no extra tax to pay, but non-taxpayers cannot reclaim any of the tax paid on their behalf. Higher rate taxpayers may have to pay extra, but they are allowed to withdraw up to 5% a year free of tax for 20 years.

Higher-risk investments

Company shares or equities are the main investment for anyone who wants growth in both capital and income over the years. Company dividends generally increase at least in line with inflation and, in the past, shares have proved the most rewarding of all investments.

Elsewhere in the book (specifically Chapters 10 and 11) the topic is dealt with in detail. Here it need only be said as you approach retirement, it is likely that your equity portfolio will need an overhaul, away from purely growth oriented shares towards those that produce an income. However, there is no rush. A wholesale clear-out of your investments could lead to paying capital gains tax (CGT) at up to 40% on much of the profit, and the calculation of it can be time consuming – or expensive, if you decide to pay an accountant to do it for you. Further details on CGT are given at the end of this chapter.

Equity income funds

There are hundreds of unit trusts and open-ended investment company (Oeic) funds which aim to provide a growing income, and these may well form a part of a retirement portfolio. Unlike cash deposits or fixed-interest securities, being invested in company shares, they hold out the reasonable promise of an income that should grow over time as fast as, and probably faster than, inflation.

The drawback is that the initial level of income can be very low. Even so-called 'high income' funds tend to yield no more than 3% or 3.5% gross. Most pay out twice a year, though a few make monthly payments. Some advisers will organise a portfolio of five or six income unit trusts with different dividend payment dates to produce a regular income throughout the year.

There are a number of investment trusts with the same aim of producing a growing income. And, of course, there is no reason why you should not hold shares directly and manage your own portfolio.

Choosing income investments

Picking a good portfolio of shares that will produce a growing income is not that easy. The overall yield on the stock market is low: at time of writing, the average yield on the FTSE-100 index was just below 2.2%. It is always possible to find shares that yield a good bit more, but these are unlikely to be the companies that will produce a growing dividend income over the years – which is the main point of investing in equities.

Sometimes, income investors can have it all ways. Some companies have a high current yield purely because their price has fallen – which may be because they are temporarily out of favour with the stock market. If the company then recovers, its price will rise, leaving its original investors with a healthy capital gain as well. On the other hand, if the stock market's judgment was right in the first place, the dividends could stay flat, or even fall, and the price of the shares decline further.

Managers of equity income funds tend to aim for a healthy total return, by combining growth and income, rather than concentrating purely on income. They will include some high yielding companies in their portfolio, which they hope will eventually recover in price, but also some 'growth stocks', which, while they may not produce much in the way of income at present, should provide capital growth.

Taking an income from an equity portfolio

You may need to adapt your thinking when it comes to taking an income from equity investments. Instead of simply using the dividends from your fund each year, you should consider also realising a portion of the capital gain, to treat as income. This may go against the grain – no-one likes the idea of eating into their capital. But most experts believe it can be a sensible way of getting an 'income' from an equity portfolio and could actually be safer, in the long run, than putting all your money in very high yielding shares or fixed-interest securities.

Added to this, there is the bonus that realising small amounts of capital gain each year is tax-efficient, as there is no tax to pay so long as the profits do not exceed your CGT annual exemption.

Some fund management groups organise automatic 'withdrawal' schemes allowing investors to realise 5% of their investment each year, made up partly of income and partly of capital. A more flexible approach is probably better: if the stock market has fallen over the year, it would be wise to delay taking out any capital until it has recovered.

Split-capital investment trusts

These are a specialist form of investment trust which divide up the total returns achieved by an underlying portfolio to suit different categories of investor. The simplest form of split-capital trust has two classes of share: income and capital. The income shareholders get all the income from the underlying portfolio, but none of the growth, while the capital shareholders get all the growth, but none of the income. All split-capital trusts have a redemption date – typically, five to ten years from launch – when the underlying portfolio will be sold and the various classes of shareholder will get back whatever they are entitled to.

They can be very useful investments, but they are without doubt complicated. Trusts can have three, four or even more classes of share – in an extreme case a few years ago, one trust actually had 13 share classes. Working out their varying degrees of risk and likely reward is a matter for the professionals. If you are interested in investing in such shares, it is best to go to a specialist stockbroker or adviser who genuinely knows the market.

Within this group of investments there are a number of share classes that might find a useful home within a retirement portfolio. Their characteristics are sketched below – but each trust will be slightly different, so approach with caution. There are three broad types of split-capital income share. They all offer a relatively high income from an underlying portfolio of equities, but at the expense of capital growth.

◆ **Annuity income shares** Some trusts offer annuity income shares. These have the highest immediate income, and because this comes from share dividends, it can be expected to grow over the life of the trust. But there is a big price to pay: on redemption, annuity income shareholders stand to get back nothing – or more likely, a nominal 1p per share. They may still (sometimes) be good investments, so long as investors realise what is happening, and reinvest part of their income as they go.

◆ **Traditional income shares** Here, investors stand in line to get back the original issue price of their shares on redemption. So if the shares were originally issued at 50p, this is the sum they will get back. But, of course, they may have bought the shares part way through the trust's life, when they were standing at a higher level, in which case they will make a capital loss on redemption.

◆ **Ordinary income shares** Ordinary income shares, once again, pay out a high income to investors, but what they get back on redemption depends partly on the performance of the stock market in the meantime. It also depends on the overall makeup of the trust's share capital. The trust will have other classes of share, some of which stand in front of the income shareholders in the queue for getting assets back. Their requirements have to be satisfied first, with whatever is left going to the ordinary income shareholder. With these shares, therefore, you may or may not get back what you invested.

Stockbrokers routinely work out the different levels of risk associated with each type of share: you will need access to this type of research to choose sensibly.

◆ **Zero dividend preference shares** These are another type of share issued by some split-capital investment trusts, but a very different animal from any of the income shares. Zeros, as their name implies, pay no income whatsoever to shareholders during the life of the trust. Instead, investors are promised a fixed capital gain on redemption.

That promise falls short of a guarantee, but it is usually a reasonably firm one. It depends on the performance of the trust's underlying assets: if the portfolio performed disastrously, there would be little to pay back to anyone, even the zero-holders, although they are generally first in the queue, before the capital and income shareholders. Most zeros currently have 'negative hurdle rates'. This means the value of the trust's overall portfolio could actually fall by perhaps 2% or 3% a year yet still have enough in the kitty to pay back to the zero shareholders.

Because they pay no income, zeros might seem an odd choice for a retirement portfolio. But they can be useful if, for example, you want to put part of your lump sum on retirement into a reasonably safe and tax-efficient home for a few years, to turn into an income producing investment later. Their overall returns are likely to be a good bit higher than, say, low-coupon gilts, for only a little extra risk. Because the return is all in the form of capital gain, it may, with a bit of planning, all be tax free, as you can use your annual CGT exemption.

Investments for the later years of retirement

Most of us would like to leave a healthy sum to our children, but in a long retirement, there may come a time when you need to provide more income for yourself – particularly if you chose a level pension annuity which pays no increases.

That can mean shifting part of your money out of low-yielding equities into bonds or cash. You may decide to switch some of your Peps and Isas from equity funds into corporate bond funds, for instance. This will result in a big jump in income – from perhaps 2.5% to 6%, though it does mean there is little scope for future growth.

But once you have hit age 80 or thereabouts, it could be about time you started thinking in terms of immediate rewards rather than long-term potential. In any case, it should be remembered that inheritance tax will bite into whatever is left to your children, so spending now could actually be seen as tax efficient.

There are two investment schemes in particular worth considering if you need an immediate increase in income. The first is an ordinary annuity; the second is a home income plan where you exchange part of the value of your home in return for a lifetime income.

Ordinary annuities

An annuity pays out a guaranteed income for life, in return for a capital sum. Die tomorrow, and it's a bad bargain; but if you live well beyond the average for your age, it will be a very good one.

An annuity is a way of guaranteeing an immediate high income which is also relatively lightly taxed. With pension annuities, the whole payment is subject to income tax. But with ordinary life annuities, the system is different – and better for the taxpayer. Part of each annuity payment counts for tax purposes as a return of capital and this is not taxed. The amount received depends on your age at outset and your sex – the older you are, the higher the payment will be.

It is definitely worth going to a specialist adviser, as rates can vary significantly from company to company. The table on the next page shows some typical annuity rates at the time of writing. Because annuity rates depend largely on the yield from gilts, they will vary over time.

Annuities can make sense if you have to meet residential or nursing home fees. They can also be useful in planning for inheritance tax.

Annual annuity payments, net of basic rate tax for a purchase price of £10,000

Annuitant	Payment	Annuitant	Payment
Man 75	£1,124	Woman 75	£1,037
Man 80	£1,423	Woman 80	£1,327
Man 85	£1,934	Woman 85	£1,775
Joint 75/70	£771		

The joint annuity lasts until the second death. Payments are made monthly in arrears, with no guaranteed period.
Source: Annuity Direct

Home reversion schemes

Under a home reversion scheme, you sell a portion of your home to an insurance company (retaining the right to live there for the rest of your life) in return for an immediate capital sum or a lifetime income. The amount you will be offered will depend in part on the value of the property, in part on your age. The older you are, the higher it will be, but in all cases it is unlikely to be more than half the open-market value. You can then sell a further portion at a later date, if you choose.

The schemes are generally open to single people aged 65 or over, or couples where at least one partner is aged 69 or more. Most companies providing such schemes are members of the Safe Home Income Plans (Ship) organisation which operates a code of conduct.

As an example, a woman of 70 selling three-quarters of a property worth £100,000 can currently expect a capital sum of about £33,000 or an income for life after basic rate tax of £2,780. A single man of 80 in that situation could get cash of £42,600 or a net income of £6,850. A couple both aged 75 would receive around £33,000 as cash or £2,840 as income.

Equity release mortgages

A number of mortgage lenders offer special fixed-rate mortgages to retired people. Interest is charged, but rolled up and not repayable until after death. This means you can realise a cash sum without having to make any interest payments. The schemes include a guarantee that the total of the loan plus rolled-up interest will not exceed the market value of the home on death.

The maximum loan available depends on age: once again, the older you are, the higher it will be. Depending on the scheme chosen and your age, the maximum is likely to be between 20% and 50% of the current value of the property.

The charity Age Concern publishes a booklet explaining these schemes in detail, as does Ship. (See Appendix 2.)

Reorganising your portfolio: a note on tax

With luck (and planning) much of your portfolio will be safely tucked away in Personal Equity Plans (Peps) and Individual Savings Accounts (Isas), which means you can start taking the income tax free. It also means that you can rearrange your holdings without having to face paying capital gains tax (CGT) at up to 40%, nor the nightmare of having to calculate it.

If you hold investments outside Peps or Isas, approach any large-scale reorganisation with care. Everyone is entitled to an annual exempt allowance from CGT, which generally rises each year in line with inflation. For the tax year 2001-02 this allowance is £7,500. Almost as important is the limit on the overall amount you can sell before being obliged to declare the capital gains you have made. This stands at twice the amount of the exempt allowance, so for the current tax year, it is £15,000. In other words, you can sell £15,000 worth of investments, and as long as they have not produced a taxable profit in excess of £7,500, this does not have to be declared on your tax return.

The rate at which capital gains tax is charged is determined by adding the taxable gain to your income for the year and charging it at the appropriate income tax rates.

Higher rate taxpayers pay tax at 40% on all gains. For basic rate taxpayers, the rate payable will depend on individual circumstances. Where your income plus the realised gain come to less than the higher rate threshold, you will pay CGT at 20% on all the gain. If the gain pushes you over the threshold, you must pay 40% on the amount over the limit.

Before working out your tax, however, you must first work out your 'taxable gain', which may be very different from the actual monetary gain. Anyone whose investments pre-date April 1998 must grapple with two separate systems for calculating gains. Gains achieved before then benefit from indexation, allowing inflation-only gains to be stripped out. Gains made on investments after that get no indexation, but a system of taper relief cuts the amount of tax due according to the length of time the investment has been held.

Taper relief on ordinary investments (as opposed to business assets) only comes into play once they have been held for three complete years. If you sell after three years, the taxable gain is reduced by 5%; after four years, by a further 5%, and so on up to ten years when the maximum relief of 40% is reached.

Investments bought before 17 March, 1998 (the date the new system was introduced) were awarded a 'bonus' year. For these, the first 5% of taper relief is reached two years after 6 April, 1998, and it will only take nine years in total to reach the maximum 40% relief.

There is a detailed and somewhat daunting booklet available from the Inland Revenue, CGT1, *Capital Gains Tax: An Introduction*, which sets out the full details of how to calculate the tax.

But even with the aid of this booklet, the conclusion must be that unless you thoroughly enjoy arithmetical challenges, or are prepared to pay an accountant who does, it is preferable to avoid CGT if at all possible.

Unless your portfolio is very large, this need not be too difficult. If you spread out any reorganisation over a number of years, both before and after retirement, you may well be able to make full use of the annual exempt allowance each year.

A further option is to consider gifting some of your investments to your wife or husband. For CGT purposes, they 'inherit' from you the original purchase date and price, so the amount of potentially taxable profit on a sale remains the same. However, it means that they, too, can make use of their annual allowance, so a couple can, between them, realise profits of £15,000 in each tax year before paying any tax.

Income tax in retirement

Everyone is entitled to a certain level of income free of tax. These personal allowances are generally increased each year in line with inflation; the levels for the tax year 2001-02 are shown in Appendix 1.

People aged 65 or over at the start of a new tax year (6 April) are entitled to a higher personal allowance, known as the age allowance, and it is higher still for those aged 75 or over.

In addition, there is a small married couple's allowance, but this is only available to couples where at least one partner was aged 65 or more on or before 5 April, 2000.

These extra allowances are withdrawn progressively once your income exceeds a certain level, and will eventually be withdrawn in total, leaving you with the same basic personal allowance as those under 65.

The level at which age allowance starts to be withdrawn changes each year, as allowances in general increase, but the 'danger level' is currently between £17,600 and about £27,000.

If your income falls between these levels, the extra age allowance will be withdrawn at the rate of £1 for every £2 of extra income received. In effect, this means you suffer a high marginal tax rate on your top slice of income.

If you are in this position, there may be scope for some re-arrangement of your investments to escape 'the age allowance trap'. If you are married, for example, remember that both partners are entitled to the personal allowance. It could, therefore, be a good idea to give some of your income producing assets to your partner if their income is much lower than yours, so they can use their allowance in full.

14

Inheritance and Wills

At least half the adults in the UK have not yet made a will, and many never do: they die intestate. If you are one of them, your assets will be divided up according to the intestacy rules. These aim to be 'fair' to all potential beneficiaries, but it is unlikely they would exactly mirror your own wishes. It could also mean your heirs pay a great deal more inheritance tax than would otherwise have been necessary.

Although the image of the Victorian spinster aunt who changes her will every fortnight depending on which nephew is currently in favour is more comic than anything else, a will is not necessarily something you make once, for all time. Obvious life-changing events such as having children or grandchildren or getting divorced should prompt you to review the terms of your will, and there are many other circumstances as well.

For example, before retirement, you may have significant life insurance benefits under your pension plan – many company schemes will pay out four times salary on death before retirement – but after retirement this cover lapses, so you may wish to re-arrange the disposal of your other assets.

In England and Wales (but not in Scotland), getting married automatically revokes any will you have made previously, unless the will expressly states that it is being made in contemplation of marriage.

The intestacy rules in England and Wales

The full intestacy provisions run to around six closely printed pages, but the basic rules are as follows. They are summarised in the chart on the next page.

◆ **If you are married with children** Your spouse gets your personal belongings, the first £125,000 absolutely, and a 'life interest' (the income but not the capital) in half of the rest. The children, assuming they survive to age 18, get the balance (in equal shares), and the remainder of the estate when your spouse dies. If your children died before you, their children step up into their shoes.

◆ **If you are married without children** Your spouse gets the personal belongings, the first £200,000 absolutely and half the balance absolutely. The rest goes to relatives in a pecking order which starts with your parents. If they are dead, it goes to your brothers and sisters or, if they are dead, to their children – your nephews and nieces (and if they are dead, to their children, and so on). If your parents are dead and you have no brothers or sisters, your spouse receives everything absolutely.

◆ **If you are single** The estate goes to your children. If you have none, it goes to your parents. If they are dead, it goes to your brothers or sisters, or, if they are dead, to their children. If you have no brothers or sisters, it goes to grandparents, if alive; and if not, finally, to uncles and aunts (or their children or children's children). If you have no living relatives within these definitions, the whole estate goes to the Crown.

◆ **If you are living with someone, but not married** Your partner has no rights under the intestacy laws, no matter how long you might have lived together. However, under the Inheritance Act, such people have similar rights to spouses, as long as they have lived with their partner as common law man or wife for at least two years prior to death.

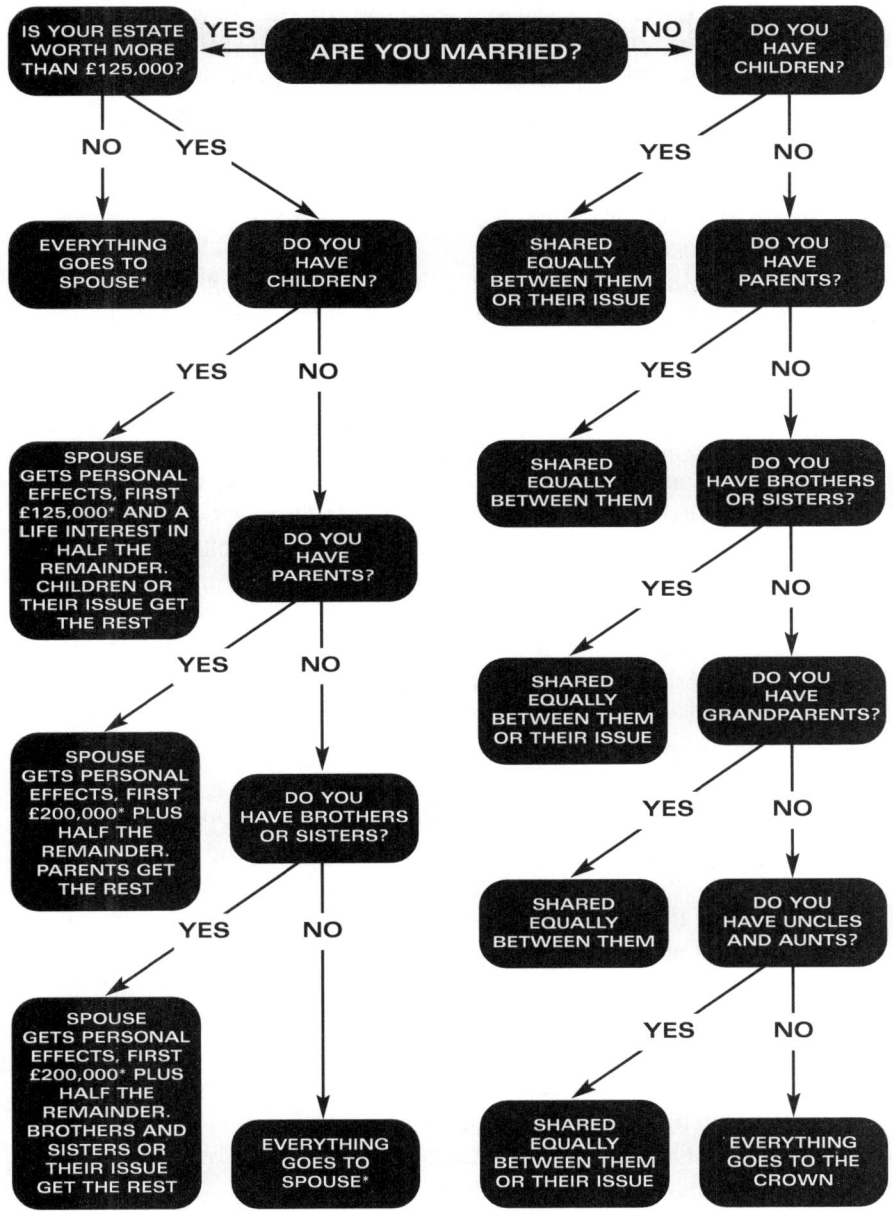

* The spouse will benefit only if he or she survives the intestate by 28 days. Where the spouse does not survive, the intestate estate will be dealt with as if there had been no spouse.

Issue means children (including illegitimate and adopted), grandchildren, great grandchildren, etc.

Brothers and sisters of whole blood come before brothers and sisters of half blood. Uncles and aunts of whole blood come before uncles and aunts of half blood.

The intestacy rules in Scotland

In Scotland, the law is different and a great deal more complex, in that if you leave a widow/widower, there is a distinction between 'prior rights' and 'legal rights'. Getting married or divorced does not make any previous will invalid. Note that the Inheritance Act does not apply to Scotland.

The following is an outline only of the situation:

◆ **Prior rights** If you are married when you die, your surviving spouse is entitled to the first £130,000 worth of the family home and is also entitled to the first £22,000 worth of fixtures and fittings in it. If you have no children, your spouse is also entitled to the first £58,000 worth of other assets such as shares or money in a bank or building society. If you do have children who survive you this right is restricted to the first £35,000 of other assets.

◆ **Legal rights** Legal rights apply whether or not you leave a will. You cannot completely disinherit your spouse or children. If you have no children, your spouse is entitled to half of your moveable estate, irrespective of the terms of the will. Moveable estate is everything except land and buildings.

If you have children but no spouse, your children are entitled to half of the moveable estate between them. If both children and your spouse survive you, your spouse's legal rights are one-third of the moveable estate and your children's legal rights are also one-third, shared between them. Your spouse or any of your children are entitled to make this claim – it is their option. If a claim is not made where you have left a will, then the estate will be divided in accordance with your will.

◆ **Marriage and living together** In Scotland it is possible to be declared married by the courts if you have lived together as man and wife and were both free to marry. This is known as marriage 'by habit and repute' and needs to be established by the court. Evidence would include, for example, sharing the same surname and being known as Mr and Mrs by family and friends, and having those names on bills and on the Electoral Register. If you live together but are not known as Mr and Mrs, your partner has no rights of inheritance unless you leave a will.

◆ **If you are single without children** The estate passes to your brothers and sisters, or their children; if none, to parents or grandparents, and if none to great-uncles and aunts and their descendants, until some relative is found to inherit. If there are none, it goes to the Crown.

How to make a will

Whether you live in England, Wales or Scotland, it would be surprising if the intestacy provisions reflected your wishes exactly. Even if they did, it still makes more sense to write a will because it should make the business of clearing up your estate that much quicker. In any case, if you want to leave personal bequests – either particular items or monetary gifts to friends, godchildren or charities, for example – the only way of doing so is to make a will.

There are three options: doing it yourself, going to a solicitor or using a specialist will-writing agency.

There are a number of specialist agencies, some of which are run by the larger charities. If you want to do it yourself, you can buy will forms for a few pounds from stationers. Given the difference in the law, it is very important that people living in Scotland do not use will forms designed for England and Wales or vice versa.

Going to a solicitor would seem the obvious choice for most people, and is recommended especially if your affairs are other than extremely simple. The cost will vary according to the amount of time a solicitor spends on your case, so make sure you are clear in your own mind what you want the will to say.

The first requirement is that the will should state that it revokes all others (even if you have not made one before), otherwise your heirs may wonder if you have left other instructions elsewhere.

Executors

You must then decide who is to be your executor – the person named in the will to deal with your affairs. Most people appoint a relative, and it may be sensible to name two people, in case one dies before you, or simply to share the burden. Executors can also be beneficiaries.

It is also possible to appoint a professional executor, such as a solicitor, accountant or bank, though this will involve a charge usually paid out of your estate.

Wording your will

The usual form of will is to choose someone as the main beneficiary of your estate, who will receive the residue of the estate after any other gifts have been made.

It may also include specific gifts to individuals or to charities – either sums of money or items such as jewellery, which should be described clearly so there is no doubt what you mean. Shakespeare, you may remember, decided to leave his wife his 'second-best bed' – if you follow his example, you had better make sure it is quite clear exactly which one is second best.

Before you get carried away, remember that if your total estate, including your house or your share of it, comes to more than the nil-rate band for inheritance tax (currently £242,000), there could be tax to pay at a flat rate of 40% on the balance. So do not leave so much in specific bequests that the main beneficiary does not end up with enough once these, and the tax, have been paid.

Signing the will and storing it

You need two people to witness your signature. They must not be beneficiaries and neither must their spouses benefit. They do not need to see the contents of the will to witness it. You must then decide where to store it – for example, with your bank or your solicitor – and keep a copy yourself.

It would be helpful to leave a note with your executors telling them where the will is stored, together with a summary of your investments and savings, and where important documents such as life insurance policies or building society pass books are to be found.

Revising the will

In England and Wales (but not in Scotland) a will automatically becomes invalid if you marry (or re-marry), unless it is expressly made in contemplation of marriage to a named person, so you will need to make a new will at this point. Otherwise, minor revisions can be achieved by adding a codicil (supplement), which must itself be witnessed – they do not need to be the same witnesses as for the original. If the changes are substantial, it is best to make a completely new will.

Deeds of variation

A will is not necessarily the final word on the matter of how your assets are distributed. It is possible for a 'deed of variation' to be executed after your death, which alters the distribution. The deed must be signed by those beneficiaries under the will who will be disadvantaged by the new arrangement (although in practice, it is often signed by all beneficiaries, including those who benefit from the variation), and it must be completed within two years of your death. One of the most common reasons for using such a deed is to avoid or reduce inheritance tax.

Inheritance tax

One of the effects of making a will may well be to realise just how much you have to leave – and, consequently, how much inheritance tax (IHT) could be payable by your estate. So, if you have not done so before, this should be the time to give some thought to ways you can cut down on the tax.

How the tax works

Inheritance tax is potentially payable both on gifts made during your life and also on assets passing at death. The big exception is assets passing between husband and wife, whether during life or after death. These are exempt from the tax. This exemption, however, will only defer, rather than cancel, an eventual tax bill.

Everyone is entitled to give away a certain amount of assets free of inheritance tax. This is called the nil-rate band and it generally rises each year in line with inflation. In the 2001-02 tax year this figure is £242,000. Any assets above this limit attract tax at a flat rate of 40%.

Lifetime gifts

If you give away assets during your lifetime, these do not immediately attract tax. Depending on how much they are, and to whom they are made, they may be immediately exempt, or they may be what is called a 'potentially exempt transfer' (Pet for short).

Immediately exempt gifts:

◆ Up to £3,000 per year, to anyone. If unused, this allowance can be carried forward, but only for one year and the current year's exemption must be used up first.

◆ Gifts of no more than £250 to each recipient per year – as many recipients as you like. But if the recipient receives more than this sum from you, you cannot claim exemption on the first £250.

◆ Gifts which form 'part of your normal expenditure out of income'. This is not strictly defined in the legislation, but broadly it means the gifts must come from your income rather than capital, and they should not be so great as to diminish your ordinary standard of living.

◆ Gifts made on marriage. Parents are allowed to give £5,000 to their children (each parent has this allowance); grandparents can give £2,500 each, and any other relative or friend can give £1,000.

◆ Gifts of any amount made from husband to wife or vice versa, as long as both are domiciled in this country. If your spouse is not, the maximum exempt gift is £55,000.

◆ Gifts of any amount to charities, recognised political parties, and certain institutions such as the British Museum.

◆ Gifts for the maintenance of your family including, for example, to children under 18 or still in full-time education.

Any other gifts during lifetime are 'potentially exempt transfers'. If you live for seven years after making the gift, they become wholly exempt, and fall out of the reckoning.

If you die in the meantime, these gifts are set against your nil-rate band. If the total of your lifetime gifts exceeds the nil-rate band, there is some taper relief available on the excess, depending on how long you lived after making the gift, as the table on the next page shows.

Years between gift and death	% of full IHT rate payable
0-3	100%
3-4	80%
4-5	60%
5-6	40%
6-7	20%

If, for example, you made a Pet of £10,000 (having already used up your nil-rate band in previous gifts) and died just over four years later, the IHT tax bill would be £2,400. The tax rate applicable is 60% of 40%, which works out at 24%.

In practice, taper relief is rarely used, because most people don't give away such huge gifts during their lifetimes as would use up the nil-rate band and more. But if you are in such a situation, the best advice is to ensure you make your gifts early enough to be sure of living the full seven years afterwards.

IHT and the family business

The rules are complex, but broadly speaking, there is 100% relief from IHT for the transfer of shares in qualifying unquoted companies – the typical family business.

How the tax is paid

If IHT is due on a Pet (because you did not live the full seven years after making the gift) it must be paid by the recipient. When you leave assets on death, the tax must come out of your estate. It usually has to be paid first before any other assets can be distributed to beneficiaries – and that could mean, for example, that the family home has to be sold first, to realise the cash to do so.

Sometimes, where the estate is largely in the form of land or buildings, the Inland Revenue will allow it to be paid in instalments over a period of up to ten years, or earlier if the property is sold.

Inheritance tax planning

One of the big misconceptions about inheritance tax is that only the very rich pay it. Far from it: last year, 21,000 families paid more than £2bn in inheritance tax.

The value of the family home is enough on its own to push many people into the IHT bracket. Any investments or savings they hoped to leave would, if no action were taken, be immediately cut down by 40%. All investments fall into the IHT melting pot, including Peps, Tessas and Isas. These may have been tax free during your lifetime, but they are not immune from IHT on death. The one saving grace is that no capital gains tax is payable on death – the Inland Revenue is content to leave it to inheritance tax to sweep up its share.

Attitudes to the tax vary widely. Some people might be quite content knowing there will be an IHT bill to pay after they die, on the basis that their children are going to benefit substantially in any case. Others are much less happy, and will do as much as they can to minimise it.

How to calculate your likely tax bill

You need to add up the value of everything you own, using the current market value of any securities and an up-to-date value for your property. Most people probably want to leave their home to their wife or husband, along with the lion's share of their estate, with perhaps small bequests to children or grandchildren. At first sight, this may seem reassuring, but you need to look ahead, as the example shows.

> Simon Brown decides to leave his share of his home (valued in total at £350,000) to his wife Vicky, together with its contents and the car. He has a company pension which will fall to two-thirds of its current level when he dies, so he also leaves most of his investments, including Peps and Isas, which total £100,000, to Vicky as well. He leaves £10,000 to each of his three children, and small bequests to a couple of charities.
>
> Result: no inheritance tax is payable because everything left to his wife is free of IHT and his other bequests total only £35,000, well within the nil-rate band.
>
> The snag comes when his wife dies. Vicky Brown's estate is worth £450,000 (assuming the value of her house and investments have not increased since her husband died). She leaves £20,000 in total to her four grandchildren and the rest in equal shares to her three children.
>
> Result: the first £242,000 falls within the nil-rate band, but the balance – £208,000 – is liable to inheritance tax at 40%, making a total tax bill of £83,200. Unless the children have large cash resources of their own, they will have to sell the family home to meet it. That may be quite acceptable, but it is awkward if they had hoped to keep it.

How to reduce the IHT tax burden

Planning for IHT can be broadly divided into two sorts: simple and complex. There is a sort of on-going guerrilla warfare conducted between the Inland Revenue and the cohorts of tax planners and accountants. The latter think up new ways to minimise IHT bills, and the former chase after them, trying to plug each loophole as quickly as possible after it has appeared.

This makes life difficult for individuals. Sometimes a scheme will last for a few years until the Revenue catches up with what is happening. Eventually it does, and unless you have died in the meantime, you could suddenly find your carefully constructed plans are worthless, and you will have to start all over again. For this reason, it may be advisable to stick with 'simple' planning, and reconcile yourself to the fact that some tax may have to be paid.

There are three possibilities:

◆ Give away as much as possible during your lifetime, either by using the annual exemptions or by making potentially exempt transfers.
◆ Try to use up at least part of your nil-rate band on death – which means leaving some money to someone other than your spouse.
◆ Consider starting a whole-of-life or term insurance policy, which will pay out on your death – the money can be used to meet the eventual IHT bill.

As far as gifts are concerned, it is more tax efficient to 'skip' a generation and leave assets to grandchildren rather than children – thus avoiding the future IHT bill on your children's estates.

Gifts with reservation

The Inland Revenue insists that gifts are genuinely 'gifts'. It has a special category of 'gifts with reservation' – where you effectively pretend to give something away but keep rights over it. For example, if you 'give' your home to your children but retain the right to live in it rent free for the rest of your life, as far as the Inland Revenue is concerned, this is not a gift at all.

Life insurance

Paying into a life insurance policy is a simple way not of avoiding the tax but of providing your heirs with the means to meet it. It has the added advantage that because premiums are payable on a regular basis, they usually fall into the category of exempt lifetime gifts which form part of your normal expenditure out of income.

A whole-of-life policy pays out on death, whenever that occurs. An alternative is a term insurance policy, which pays out only if you die within a stated period. For married couples, the most appropriate policy is one based on joint lives, which pays out on the second death (as this is likely to be when the biggest IHT bill comes in, assuming the first to die has left the bulk of their estate to their widow or widower). The policy itself will be written in trust to ensure its proceeds are not subject to IHT.

In theory, the amount the policy guarantees to pay out on death (the sum assured) should equal 40% of the total value of your assets (less the nil-rate band), so as to pay the IHT bill in full. In practice, this is difficult to achieve, because your assets may well rise in value between taking the policy out and dying. In any case, you may balk at the cost. You could always take out a smaller policy, knowing that it will at least help to meet the IHT bill, even if it doesn't provide the full amount.

IHT and your home

One of the most intractable problems with IHT planning is the home. It is the reason many otherwise modest estates fall into the IHT bracket, but there is no simple way it can escape.

As mentioned above, if you give away your home while retaining the right to live there, the Revenue simply says this does not count as a gift. If you gave your children your home and then paid them the full commercial rent on it for the rest of your life, this would probably count as a genuine gift, but it is understandably not very appealing.

One possibility is to change the form of ownership under which you hold the property. Most couples own their home under a joint tenancy, which means each person's half automatically passes to the other when the first dies. It is also possible, however, to hold it as 'tenants in common' which means each person owns a discrete 50% share, which they can pass on as they wish on death. For example, you could bequeath half of your half share to the children. This means your widow or widower would still have undisputed rights to live there for the rest of their life, but it means that at least part of the nil-rate band for IHT would be used on the first death.

You need to think carefully before going ahead with such a scheme. It's unlikely, but possible, that relations with your children might deteriorate after the first death. In these days a more likely snag is that the subsequent divorce of one of your children could mean their share of the property is counted in any divorce settlement. Also, practical problems could arise, if the survivor wants to sell up to move into a smaller and more convenient (but not necessarily much less expensive) property.

IHT and trusts

There are a number of ways in which assets can be put into trust for the benefit of future generations, either bypassing or at least minimising IHT. This is a highly complex area, and one which the Revenue has shown a propensity to attack, time after time. If you are interested in using a trust, you will need professional advice, not just at the time it is set up, but on an on-going basis, to ensure it remains a successful way of avoiding IHT.

IHT-friendly investments

The catch-22 of most inheritance tax planning is that although we could escape it if we gave our possessions away during our lifetimes, most of us cannot afford to do so, because we need the income they produce.

There are some types of investment which can be useful in this respect, such as an annuity. With an annuity, you give up a capital sum in return for a guaranteed lifetime income. It means there is less capital to leave to your heirs, but at the same time, there could be less tax to pay.

Elizabeth Hall is a widow aged 75 with two children, living in a bungalow whose value exactly matches the IHT nil-rate band. She has pension income of around £8,000 a year and other assets, mainly money in building society savings accounts, totalling £100,000. These produce an after-tax income of £5,000 a year, which she needs to live on. Much as she would like to give cash away during her lifetime, she cannot afford to do so.

As things stand, assuming the value of her house will increase in line with inflation (and with the nil-rate band) her heirs will have to pay IHT at 40% on £100,000 – in other words, £40,000.

She decides to buy an annuity with half her capital. At current annuity rates, this will give her an income of £5,185 after tax, guaranteed for life. She then earmarks a further £30,000 of her capital to give away: her two grandchildren are both getting married this year, so she gives them £2,500 each; she uses the £3,000 annual exemption for both this year and last year to give each of her children £3,000 each, and plans to use the same exemption for making annual gifts of £3,000 for each year in the future until her £30,000 is used up.

When she dies, at age 83, her financial assets total just £20,000, meaning an IHT bill of £8,000. So not only have her heirs saved £32,000 in inheritance tax, they have benefited from the money earlier – and she, not least, has had the pleasure of giving it while she was alive. Meanwhile, she has also enjoyed nearly £1,200 a year extra in income – £5,185 from her annuity and £1,000 in interest on her remaining £20,000 in her building society.

IHT: the final word

There comes a point at which tax planning can be taken too far. It may not be particularly welcome to think part of your estate will be subject to 40% tax after you die, but it is important to keep a sense of perspective. It is far more important for your widow or widower to have enough to manage on comfortably, than to use the whole of your nil-rate band for gifting assets to children.

A little bit of planning – trying to use the annual exemptions, and so on – will certainly save some tax, and for many people, this is as far as they should be prepared to go.

15

Financial Advice

It is becoming increasingly easy to buy financial products direct nowadays either by telephone or over the internet. This is convenient if all you are looking for is the cheapest car insurance or credit card. However, many aspects of our financial life are growing more complicated. Seeking professional advice in these situations is often essential if you want to avoid problems later on.

The advantage of using financial advisers is not only that you can benefit from their knowledge and expertise, but it will also give you extra protection if things go wrong. If you buy a product direct, this is known as 'execution-only' business. If problems develop you may only be able to get redress if you have been given incorrect or misleading information. If you have simply bought the wrong product or made the wrong decision, you will have no-one to blame but yourself. If a financial adviser gives you poor advice, on the other hand, you may be able to claim compensation.

The first step towards finding a good adviser is considering which type is likely to provide the service you need. Some have more expertise in certain areas than others. Finding out if they are properly authorised is another important factor. Fortunately, regulation of financial advisers has become much more rigorous in recent years. Nowadays, advisers and the companies they work for must be authorised by the financial services watchdog, the Financial Services Authority (FSA). But to be on the safe side you should always check with the FSA. You can check too what type of business the adviser is authorised to do. These details are held on the FSA's register. Its public enquiries helpline is on 0845 606 1234.

If you are a user of the internet you will also find advisers offering their services there. Here you need to be even more vigilant as they may be working from other countries where regulations are not so strict. If their website address ends in .com it is impossible to tell where they are based. But even if they have .co.uk in their address, you should still check with the FSA. Take special care also if you are offered alternative 'investment' schemes, such as ones involving stamps, old coins, wine, race horses and the like, as the providers do not have to be authorised even in the UK. Always remember the old adage that if the returns look too good to be true, they probably are.

Even if an adviser is authorised, it does not guarantee you will get good advice. It is important to be aware of the distinctions between different types of advisers, the services they are likely to provide, and how they are likely to be paid, before narrowing your choices down.

Types of advisers

Until recently financial advisers were divided into two clear groups – tied and independent. The distinction has been blurred by the introduction of 'multi-tied' advisers to sell stakeholder pensions. Whichever you deal with, they must disclose which category they fall into before you do any business with them.

Tied

These work for a particular company and can only sell you the products offered by that company. Employees of banks and insurance companies fall into this category. However, many small firms of self-employed financial consultants have the same status.

There is nothing wrong with buying financial products this way. In fact, some of the lowest cost products are sold by such advisers, often over the telephone. But some of the poorest value products are also sold by tied agents. If you use a tied agent, it will be up to you to find out how competitive their products are in terms of charges and performance.

Multi-tied

This type of adviser is relatively new. Although they work for one company, they can also sell certain other companies' products. This enables them to offer you a choice of several stakeholder pension plans. But these will not necessarily be the best ones available. The company which employs the adviser does not have to apply any particular criteria when deciding which other companies' products to sell. It is under no obligation to sell you the best pension product on the market.

Independent

These advisers can advise you on any company's products. They are required to make their recommendations based on the principles of 'best advice' and 'best execution'. This means they should advise you which products are the best to meet your particular needs, and if there are a number of providers of these they should shop around to find which offers the best value. They do not have to recommend the cheapest product on the market if there are other good reasons why another one might be more suitable.

Qualifications and regulation

All financial advisers must have some basic qualifications. To be registered, they must have passed the three levels of the Financial Planning Certificate (FPC) exam (or equivalent). The next stage is for them to take various levels of the Advanced Financial Planning Certificate (AFPC). Advisers who have passed ten subjects at AFPC level are regarded as among the best qualified.

Specialist advisers may have other relevant qualifications or be members of various professional bodies which require them to take exams and adhere to codes of practice. Though membership of such a body does not guarantee you will get good advice either, it can indicate the adviser is serious about improving his or her professional standing.

Companies and advisers who are registered with the FSA must report regularly to the regulator and their affairs are also inspected at intervals by the regulator's representatives. If a company or an adviser does not come up to scratch, a fine may be imposed, a company's salesforce told to retrain or an adviser's authorisation removed.

Commission or fees

Advice does not come free unless you are dealing with a charitable or governmental organisation. Clearly financial advisers must be paid for their services. However, there is considerable debate over whether it is better to pay a fee or accept the commission-based approach.

Commission

Traditionally, most advisers have received commission for selling packaged financial products, such as insurance policies, pensions and savings plans. Although this is paid by the financial institutions concerned, the payments come out of your money. The main advantage of this approach is that customers who do not have any ready cash can still obtain advice.

However, it has had some very negative effects. It has led unscrupulous advisers to recommend products because they paid high levels of commission rather than because they were the best option for the investor.

Another disadvantage with regular savings products, such as endowments, was that the main part of the commission was often paid to the adviser as soon as the product was sold. As the amount of commission is often based on the term of the product, this meant large deductions were made initially, sometimes absorbing most of the first year or two's contributions. Although by the end of the term, the effect could be smoothed out, problems arose if the saver had to stop paying into the contract for some reason. Many consumers were shocked to discover that their policies were worth less than they had paid into them.

Increasing regulation and transparency is helping to put an end to these practices. Nowadays advisers have to provide key features documents when they sell investment products. These show just how much commission they will receive and what effect it will have on customers' money. Also, many companies are now spreading commission payments over the whole term of their policies in fairness to customers who cannot stay the course.

Fees

Some professional advisers, such as stockbrokers, accountants and solicitors, have always charged fees. The advantage of this is that an adviser is under no pressure to sell you any product at all and may be more prepared to advise you about products which do not pay commission.

For larger investors, paying fees can actually save money. Even though fee-based advisers may charge £100 an hour or more, the final bill may still be less than commission which is based on a percentage of the amount invested. For smaller savers, it can appear to be the other way round. In the long term, though, you may also end up better off if you are steered towards lower cost, better quality products.

Joe Robinson, 55, and his son Peter, 26, both need some financial advice and are wondering about the best way to get it. Joe has just inherited some money from his own father and wants to find out how to invest it. He feels now may also be a good time to sort out his will and see if there are ways of minimising a potential inheritance tax bill.

He decides to contact a couple of local independent financial advisers to see what services they offer and also to talk to a solicitor. During a talk, one of the IFAs points out that Joe could also get his life insurance cheaper elsewhere. Joe's son, Peter, on the other hand, knows he wants a stakeholder pension. His main concern is to find out how much he should be saving for his retirement. He also decides to talk to the IFAs his father is visiting, as well as ringing one or two direct providers so he can make some comparisons.

Who offers what?

Accountants

Accountants are usually the best source of advice on tax matters. Some can also advise on investments providing they are authorised by a recognised professional body, such as the Institute of Chartered Accountants. Some of the larger accountancy firms have specialist independent financial advice departments to provide a full planning service. You will have to pay a fee if you ask an accountant for advice, but any commission generated as a result of products being purchased can be offset against your fees. For names of local accountants contact the Institute of Chartered Accountants, the Association of Chartered Certified Accountants or the Chartered Institute of Taxation and Association of Tax Technicians. (See Appendix 2.)

Actuaries

Actuaries are normally employed by insurance companies but there are also firms of independent consultants who can be approached for specialist advice on insurance related matters such as pension transfers. They work on a fee basis. The Association of Consulting Actuaries (see Appendix 2) can provide you with the name of a firm in your area.

Banks and building societies

Most larger banks and building societies have their own trained 'financial consultants'(sales staff) but they are usually tied agents and are only qualified to advise on in-house products. Still, they may be a useful starting point if you are considering your options. If no-one is immediately available at your local branch, an appointment can be made or someone may be able to come to see you at your home or office if this is more convenient. They are normally paid a basic salary but performance bonuses may be given to encourage them to generate certain types of business. Don't sign up for anything until you have shopped around.

Some banks also have private banking arms designed for wealthier customers (with, say, £100,000 or more to invest) which provide independent financial advice. There is normally an annual charge for these services. Other services traditionally offered by banks include safe deposit facilities and trustee services.

Company representatives

Many insurance companies have their own sales forces to promote their products and services. Traditional insurers such as Legal & General and the Co-operative still employ hundreds of representatives who often visit people in their own homes to discuss their financial needs. Companies selling direct by telephone also use their own representatives. By their nature, however, these staff are only qualified to advise on that company's products. So if the company does not offer certain products, the advice you can get will be limited. They normally receive a basic salary plus bonuses.

Independent financial advisers

One thing that all independent financial advisers (IFAs) have in common is that they can sell you the products of any financial company in the market. But there are considerable variations in the services they can offer. Some are one-man operations, some belong to national networks, some are nationwide companies. Many are 'general practitioners' dealing mainly with packaged products, such as life insurance, pension products and unit trusts. Others offer more extensive financial planning services. Some specialise in particular areas, such as investments, pensions or mortgages.

Although most IFAs are still paid commission, many offer a choice nowadays and will work on a fee basis if customers prefer. Some work only on a fee basis.

For the names of three local independent advisers, you can contact IFA Promotion. For fee-based independent advisers, contact the National Directory of Fee-based Advisers. Organisations which promote professional development among their members are the Society of Financial Advisers (Sofa) and the Institute of Financial Planning. Sofa is the financial services arm of the Chartered Insurance Institute. It has three categories of membership depending on how many levels of the Advanced Financial Planning Certificate (AFPC) advisers have under their belts.

If the ethical dimension of your investments is important to you, a list of specialist IFAs is also available from the Ethical Investment Research Service (EIRS). See Appendix 2 for contact details.

Solicitors

If there are legal matters on which you need advice, such as powers of attorney or drawing up a will, you should consult a firm of solicitors. They may also be able to provide financial planning and investment advice on a fee basis. There are two organisations that represent solicitors offering these services. They are the Association of Solicitor Investment Managers (ASIM) and Solicitors for Independent Financial Advice. If you have a legal problem relating to a pension, you could contact the Association of Pension Lawyers. See Appendix 2 for contact details.

Stockbrokers

Stockbrokers have become increasingly accessible in recent years. Many of the newer telephone-based services cater mainly for investors who know which shares they want to buy and sell, and they do not provide advice other than general information bulletins. However, plenty of firms still offer advisory and discretionary management services. For smaller investors, a unit or investment trust management service may be offered.

To find out which stockbrokers offer these services to private clients, contact the Association of Private Client Investment Managers and Stockbrokers (APCIMS). It has a free directory of member firms, many of which provide a full financial planning service. See Appendix 2 for contact details.

Tied agents

Also known as 'appointed representatives', these are self-employed consultants or companies, which have a contract to sell one or more of an insurance company's products for commission. The agent may operate independently in respect of other business. For example, many building societies are tied agents and will sell the investment and pension products of one life insurance company. They must make this status clear on all their stationery.

Finding an adviser

Contact some of the organisations mentioned above to get details of advisers who may be able to help you. Local advisers may be easier to deal with but many larger firms will be happy to take you on even if you live some distance away. They may be willing to send a representative to see you. A few telephone calls should help you make an initial shortlist. It will give you a feel for the type of company. You will need to ask:

◆ Whether the adviser offers the type of help you need – be it specialist or more general financial planning;
◆ Whether you are the sort of client the adviser would normally deal with – some may be oriented more towards businesses or very wealthy individuals;
◆ Whether the adviser is independent or tied;
◆ Whether the adviser works on a commission basis or charges a fee.

You should then arrange to visit two or three suitable advisers so you can learn more about them. Even a fee-based adviser should be prepared to give you an initial, half-hour or hour interview free. This discussion will give you an opportunity to see whether you get on on a personal level. It is important to feel comfortable with the adviser you choose. Before you make your visit, check that he or she is FSA authorised.

You should also use the interview to:

◆ Find out more about the type of service they offer – if it is all-round financial planning, ask which areas are covered;
◆ Ask advisers to explain their professional qualifications and what they are doing to keep abreast of the latest developments;
◆ Find out what they base their recommendations on – if they have access to a computer database or other research;

◆ Take along details of your own circumstances and requirements so the adviser can give you an idea of how he or she would tackle your affairs, but don't be persuaded to make any decisions there and then;
◆ Ask about on-going services such as annual reviews;
◆ If the adviser is fee based, ask for an estimate of initial and annual charges, find out if there will be any charge if you decide to take your business elsewhere;
◆ Ask if you can speak to two or three customers so you can find out how satisfied they are with the service.

What to expect

Once you have decided to seek the help of a particular adviser, expect to be quizzed in considerable detail about your financial affairs. It is a legal requirement for advisers to carry out a 'fact find' so they know all about your circumstances. They should ask about all aspects of your finances such as your income, pension, mortgage, debts, insurance, savings and so on, as well as discussing your present needs and what you want to achieve in the future. Only then will they be in a proper position to tell you what action they would recommend.

An adviser may be able to give you some immediate ideas on how you should proceed and discuss them with you, so it is a good idea to make notes. However, a good adviser will follow up the meeting with a letter explaining your options and setting out recommendations. This is referred to as a 'reason why' letter. You can then decide if you want to go ahead. If you don't understand, ask for a further explanation and if you are still unsure seek a second opinion.

Don't agree to anything on the spot or sign any documents, especially not if they are blank forms that an adviser offers to fill in on your behalf later. Steer clear if you are told that an immediate decision is necessary or a special offer will be missed. Be wary if an adviser suggests selling all your existing investments and buying new ones. This may generate plenty of extra commission but could be a costly exercise for you and it may take some time for investments to make up the lost ground.

Other sources of advice

Bear in mind you may be able to get help and advice from elsewhere. On pensions, for example, your own company's pensions department, your trade union, trade association or professional body could be good sources of information. If you have problems with debts or other general money matters, your local Citizens' Advice Bureau, independent advice centre or legal advice centre may be able to help.

Complaints

If you are unhappy with a financial product or service, don't suffer in silence. Although you must give the company concerned a chance to put things right, don't give up if you feel you are being fobbed off. Take your complaint to the Financial Ombudsman Service.

However, before the ombudsman will take up your complaint you must be able to show that you have exhausted the company's complaints procedure. Don't assume he will decide in your favour either. For example, if poor stock market conditions have resulted in you losing money or an insurance claim has been rejected because you did not give an insurer some relevant information, your complaint may not be upheld. However, an ombudsman may still rule in your favour, if he finds the investment risks were not properly explained to you or the form you had to complete did not make clear what information you should provide.

Making a complaint – a step-by-step guide

◆ Contact the body concerned, preferably by letter, to explain your problem.
◆ If the firm is no longer in existence, phone the Financial Services Authority public enquiries helpline on 0845 606 1234 for advice.
◆ Send the letter to the person you originally dealt with, or if that individual is no longer working there, to the head of the relevant department. You can phone, providing you keep a note of the conversation including the full name of the person you spoke to, but you will probably have to follow your call up with a letter anyway.
◆ Write 'complaint' at the top of your letter, include any reference or account numbers, explain your case as clearly and as briefly as you can and what you would like the company to do about it. You might want an apology, matters to be put right or compensation. Remember to keep a copy of the letter.
◆ If you are not happy about the reply, ask for details of the company's formal complaints procedure. If it does not have one, write to the chief executive, stating your case again and why you are still unhappy.
◆ If your complaint is still unresolved, you can take it to an independent complaints scheme. If you are not sure which scheme to contact, call the FSA public enquiries helpline for advice.
◆ Ask for a copy of the scheme's guide to making a complaint. This will explain exactly what you have to do and may provide a special form on which you can give the details of your case.
◆ The scheme will then examine both sides of the case, decide whether your complaint should be upheld and tell the firm to sort the matter out. The firm may also be told to compensate you. Some schemes can make financial awards of up to £100,000.

Fiona Jones is a member of the teachers' pension scheme. She complained to the ombudsman because some years ago she was approached by the representative of a life insurance company who suggested she could improve her pension prospects by making free-standing additional voluntary contributions (FSAVCs) through a scheme offered by his company. She later discovered she would have paid lower charges by taking out an AVC with her own pension scheme. The representative had not made her aware that this might be the case as he should have done. The ombudsman awarded her compensation.

Complaints schemes

◆ **The Financial Ombudsman Service** This provides a single complaints scheme divided into three specialist divisions for banking and loans, insurance and investments. It covers the following types of companies and organisations:
Banks
Building societies
Financial advisers
Firms dealing in futures and options
Friendly societies
Fund managers
Life insurance companies
Pension providers
Stockbrokers

◆ **The Office for the Pensions Advisory Service** Opas provides initial advice and conciliation for complaints about employers' pension schemes.

◆ **The Pensions Ombudsman** This ombudsman decides on complaints relating to employers' pension schemes not resolved by Opas.

◆ **The Mortgage Code Arbitration Scheme** This deals with complaints about mortgage intermediaries such as brokers and estate agents.

◆ **The General Insurance Standards Council** This is a voluntary scheme handling complaints about general insurance brokers such as those selling motor and household cover.

◆ **The Ombudsman for Estate Agents** This is a voluntary scheme dealing with complaints about estate agents from both buyers and sellers. About a third of agencies are members.

Protection

If you lose money due to mis-selling or maladministration, an ombudsman may be able to ensure your fortunes are restored by the company concerned. However, if the firm goes bust or fraud occurs, this may not be possible. Fortunately, tighter regulation nowadays means potential problems are usually discovered before the situation becomes that serious. If the worst comes to the worst, there are compensation schemes which cover most financial services companies. Most of them are due to come under the Financial Services Compensation Scheme sometime in 2001. The amounts of compensation available will depend on the type of business. Under the new scheme, depositions with banks and building societies will get a better deal, with compensation rising to a maximum of £31,700 compared to the previous limit of £18,000.

The Financial Services Compensation Scheme

The maximum amounts of compensation are as follows:

◆ **Deposits** 100% of the first £2,000 and 90% of the next £33,000 per individual (maximum £31,700).
◆ **General Insurance** Compulsory claims – 100%. Non-compulsory claims – 100% of first £2,000 and 90% of the rest.
◆ **Long-term insurance** 90% of the value of the policy, including future benefits.
◆ **Investments** 100% of the first £30,000 and 90% of the next £20,000 (maximum £48,000).

Pensions Compensation Board

This covers member liabilities of occupational pension schemes in full.

Offshore compensation

Investors should bear in mind that these schemes do not apply to firms based outside the UK. Although some offshore investment centres, such as the Isle of Man, may have their own compensation schemes, others, such as Jersey and Guernsey, do not. Unless you are dealing with the offshore branch of a reputable UK organisation, great caution must, therefore, be exercised before considering investment outside the UK.

Appendix 1

Facts and figures for the financial year 2001-02

Personal allowances

Personal allowance (basic)	£4,535
Personal allowance (age 65-74)	£5,990
Personal allowance (age 75 & over)	£6,260
Married couple's allowance (age 65-74)*	£5,365
Married couple's allowance (age 75 & over)*	£5,435
Married couple's allowance (minimum amount)*	£2,070
Income limit for age-related allowances	£17,600
Blind person's allowance	£1,450
Rent-a-room tax-free income	£4,250
Enterprise Investment Scheme at 20%**	£150,000
Venture capital trust at 20%**	£100,000

*Relief is restricted to 10%. Only available where at least one partner was born on or before 5 April, 1935.
**Income tax relief is only available if investments are held for at least five years. For shares issued after 6 April, 2000, the holding period is cut to three years.

Tax on earned income

Rate	Taxable income
10% on	first £1,880
22% on	next £27,520
40% on	the balance

Savings income

◆ **Interest** Taxpayers below the 40% threshold pay 20% on interest. Taxpayers whose marginal rate is 10% can reclaim 10%.
◆ **Dividends** Share dividends are paid net of a 10% tax credit which satisfies basic rate taxpayers' liability in full. Non-taxpayers and 10% taxpayers cannot reclaim the tax, while 40% taxpayers must pay extra, equivalent to a total charge of 32.5%

Capital gains tax

Tax rate

The rate at which capital gains tax is paid on chargeable gains depends on your taxable income for the year. The gains are added to your income. If the total is:

◆ below the basic rate (22%) starting limit, you are charged at 10%;
◆ between the basic rate starting and top limits, you are charged at 20%;
◆ above the higher rate (40%) starting limit, you are charged at 40%.

Annual exemptions

Personal	£7,500
Trusts	£3,750

Tax-free gains

There is no capital gains tax payable on gains made on the following assets:

◆ Your principal private residence.
◆ Private cars.
◆ Personal belongings (known as chattels – such as paintings or furniture) if sold for £6,000 or less.
◆ Foreign currency bought for personal spending abroad.
◆ British government stock, known as gilts.
◆ Peps, Isas, National Savings Certificates, most pension plans.
◆ Shares in qualifying venture capital trusts, Enterprise Investment Schemes and Business Expansion scheme shares bought after 18 March, 1986.

Taxable gains

Indexation relief is available on assets bought on or before 5 April, 1998.
Taper relief may be available on assets sold after April 1998. The percentage of the gain that is taxable is based on the number of complete years an asset is owned after 5 April, 1998.

Years owned after 5 April, 1998	% of gain that is taxable	
	Business assets	**Other assets***
1	87.5%	100%
2	75%	100%
3	50%	95%
4	25%	90%
5	25%	85%
6	25%	80%
7	25%	75%
8	25%	70%
9	25%	65%
10	25%	60%

*Assets held before 17 March, 1998 qualify for one year's extra taper relief.

Stamp duty

Stocks and marketable securities

The stamp duty rate is 0.5%.

Property

Value	Rate
Up to £60,000	Nil
£60,001-£250,000	1%
£250,001-£500,000	3%
£500,001+	4%

Inheritance tax

Nil-rate band	£242,000
Rate of tax on excess	40%

Taper relief on gifts made within seven years of death, if nil-rate band has already been used up:

Years between gift and death	% of full IHT rate payable
0-3	100%
3-4	80%
4-5	60%
5-6	40%
6-7	20%

Paying inheritance tax

Payable on death, normally within six months.

Main deadline dates for self-assessment

Filing tax returns

◆ **30 September** Deadline for filing completed tax return for previous year, if you want the Inland Revenue to calculate your tax for you.

◆ **30 September** Deadline for filing completed tax return for previous year if you want any tax you owe (up to £1,000) included in next year's tax code (applies to employees only).

◆ **5 October** Deadline for letting the Inland Revenue know if you need a tax return for previous year and have not been sent one.

◆ **31 January** Deadline for returning completed tax return for previous year, if you make the tax calculation yourself.

Fine for late filing: £100.
Additional fine if return not received by following 31 July: £100.

Paying tax

◆ **31 January** In current tax year: 50% of previous year's income tax, less tax deducted at source.

◆ **Following 31 July** 50% of income tax, less tax deducted at source.

◆ **Following 31 January** Balancing payment of income tax, and all capital gains tax.

Fines for late payment

8.5% interest from due date.
Plus surcharges on balancing payment as follows:

◆ **28 February** If payment still not received, a 5% surcharge on any amount outstanding.

◆ **31 July** If payment still not received, a further 5% surcharge on any amount outstanding.

Appendix 2

Useful names, addresses and websites

Financial Services Authority
25 The North Colonnade
Canary Wharf
London E14 5HS
Public enquiries helpline: 0845 606 1234
Website: www.fsa.gov.uk
Consumer helpline email: consumerhelp@fsa.gov.uk

Ombudsmen

The Financial Ombudsman Service will shortly be taking over all the functions
of seven separate ombudsmen or complaints schemes – see the list below.
Although the formal amalgamation has not yet taken place, your best initial
point of contact is the address and phone number listed below. You will then, if
necessary, be passed on to the appropriate scheme.

Financial Ombudsman Service
South Quay Plaza
183 Marsh Wall
London E14 9SR
Tel: 020 7964 1000

This will take over the functions of:
The Personal Investment Authority Ombudsman Bureau
The SFA Complaints Bureau and Arbitration Service
The Investment Ombudsman
The Insurance Ombudsman
Office of the Banking Ombudsman
Office of the Building Societies Ombudsman
The Personal Insurance Arbitration Service (PIAS)

Other ombudsmen, complaints and advisory schemes

The Pensions Ombudsman
11 Belgrave Road
London SW1V 1RB
Tel: 020 7834 9144

The Office for the Pensions Advisory Service (Opas)
11 Belgrave Road
London SW1V 1RB
Tel: 020 7233 8080
Website: www.opas.org.uk

The Occupational Pensions Regulatory Authority (Opra)
Invicta House
Trafalgar Place
Brighton BN1 4DW
Tel: 01273 627600
Websites: www.opra.gov.uk
            www.stakeholder.opra.gov.uk

Office for the Supervision of Solicitors
Victoria Court
8 Dormer Place
Leamington Spa
Warks CV32 5AE
Tel: 01926 822007/8/9

Ombudsman for Estate Agents
Beckett House
4 Bridge Street
Salisbury
Wilts SP1 2LX
Tel: 01722 333306

Mortgage Code Arbitration Scheme
24 Angel Gate
City Road
London EC1V 2RS
Tel: 020 7837 4483

General Insurance Standards Council
110 Cannon Street
London EC4N 6EU
Tel: 0845 601 2857

Pensions and retirement

Pension Schemes Registry
PO Box 1NN
Newcastle upon Tyne
NE99 1NN
Tel: 0191 225 6393

Pre-Retirement Association
9 Chesham Road
Guildford
Surrey GU1 3LS
Tel: 01483 301170
Website: www.pra.uk.com

Pensions Compensation Board
11 Belgrave Road
London SW1V 1RB
Tel: 020 7828 9794

Specialist annuity advisers

The Annuity Bureau
Enterprise House
59-65 Upper Ground
London SE1 9PQ
Tel: 020 7620 4090
Website: www.annuity-bureau.co.uk

Annuity Direct
32 Scrutton Street
London EC2A 4RQ
Tel: 020 7684 5000
Website: www.annuitydirect.co.uk

Wentworth Rose
Central House
75-79 Park Street
Camberley
Surrey GU15 3PE
Tel: 0127 626111
Website: www.retirement-advice.co.uk

Home income plans

Safe Home Income Plans (Ship)
c/o Hinton & Wild Home Plans
1st floor
Parker Court
Knapp Lane
Cheltenham
Gloucs GL50 3QJ
Tel: 01242 539494
Website: www.ship-ltd.co.uk

Advice on buying a freehold or extending a lease

Leasehold Advisory Service
4th floor
70-74 City Road
London EC1Y 2BJ
Tel: 020 7490 9580
Website: www.lease-advice.org.uk

Where to find a financial adviser

IFA Promotion
17-19 Emery Road
Brislington
Bristol BS4 5PF
Tel: 0117 971 1177
Website: www.ifap.org.uk

National Directory of Fee-based Advisers
c/o Matrix Data Services
Freepost
Gossard House
7-8 Savile Row
London W1X 1AF
Tel: 0870 013 1925
Website: details available on www.iii.co.uk

Association of Private Client Investment Managers
and Stockbrokers (APCIMS)
112 Middlesex Street
London E1 7HY
Tel: 020 7247 7080
Website: www.apcims.co.uk

Society of Financial Advisers (Sofa)
20 Aldermanbury
London EC2V 7HY
Tel: 020 7417 4419
Website: www.sofa.org

Association of Solicitor Investment Managers (ASIM)
Chiddingstone Causeway
Tonbridge
Kent TN11 8JX
Tel: 01892 870065

Solicitors for Independent Financial Advice
10 East Street
Epsom
Surrey KT17 1HH
Tel: 01372 721172

Association of Pension Lawyers
c/o Eversheds
Senator House
65 Queen Victoria Street
London EC4V 4JA
Tel: 020 7919 4500

Ethical Investment Research Service (EIRS)
80-84 Bondway
London SW8 1SF
Tel: 0845 606 0324

Where to find an accountant

The Institute of Chartered Accountants in England & Wales
Moorgate Place
London EC2P 2BJ
Tel: 020 7920 8100

The Institute of Chartered Accountants in Scotland
21 Haymarket Yards
Edinburgh EH12 5BH
Tel: 0131 347 0100

The Association of Chartered Certified Accountants
29 Lincoln's Inn Fields
London WC2A 3EE
Tel: 020 7242 6855
Website: www.acca.org.uk

The Chartered Institute of Taxation and the Association of Tax Technicians
12 Upper Belgrave Street
London SW1X 8BB
Tel: 020 7235 9381
Website: www.tax.org.uk

Where to find an actuary

Association of Consulting Actuaries
1 Wardrobe Place
London EC4V 5AG
Tel: 020 7248 3163
Website: www.aca.org.uk
Email: acahelp@aca.org.uk

Legal matters

The Law Society
113 Chancery Lane
London WC2A 1PL
Tel: 020 7242 1222
Websites: www.lawsociety.org.uk
www.make-a-will.org.uk

The Law Society of Northern Ireland
Law Society House
98 Victoria Street
Belfast BT1 3JZ
Tel: 01232 231614

The Law Society of Scotland
26 Drumsheugh Gardens
Edinburgh EH3 7YR
Tel: 0131 226 7411
Dial-a-Law information line and referral service: 0870 545554
Website: www.lawscot.org.uk

Specialist magazines

Money Management
3rd floor
Maple House
149 Tottenham Court Road
London W1P 9LL
Tel: 020 7896 2525
Subscriptions: 01444 445520

Planned Savings
69-77 Paul Street
London EC2A 4LQ
Tel: 020 7553 1000
Subscriptions: 01206 772113
Money Management and *Planned Savings* are aimed at professional advisers, with performance statistics and articles on aspects of financial planning.

Moneyfacts
Moneyfacts House
66-70 Thorpe Road
Norwich
Norfolk NR1 1BJ
Tel: 01603 476476
Subscriptions: 01603 476100
Website: www.moneyfacts.co.uk
The magazine publishes a monthly round-up of all savings account rates. For
more up-to-date listings, see its website.

Trade bodies

Association of Investment Trust Companies
Durrant House
8-13 Chiswell Street
London EC1Y 4YY
Brochure line: 0870 707707
Websites: www.itsonline.co.uk
         www.aitc.co.uk
Provides information on aspects of investing in investment trust companies.

Association of Unit Trusts and Investment Funds
65 Kingsway
London WC2B 6TD
Tel: 020 8207 1361
Website: www.investmentfunds.org.uk
Provides information on investing in unit trusts and Oeics.

Proshare
Centurion House
24 Monument Street
London EC3R 8AQ
Tel: 020 7394 5200
Website: www.proshare.org.uk
Advises on setting up investment clubs and runs education programme for
schools on share ownership.

Association of British Insurers
51 Gresham Street
London EC2V 7HQ
Tel: 020 7600 3333
Website: www.abi.org.uk
Publishes information sheets on all aspects of insurance.

The British Insurance Brokers Association
14 Bevis Marks
London EC3A 7NT
Tel: 020 7623 9043
Website: www.biba.org.uk

Building Societies Association
3 Savile Row
London W1X 1AF
Tel: 020 7437 0655

Council of Mortgage Lenders
3 Savile Row
London W1X 1AF
Tel: 020 7440 2255
Website: www.cml.org.uk

National Association of Estate Agents
Arbon House
21 Jury Street
Warwick CV34 4EH
Tel: 01926 496800
Website: www.naea.co.uk

Royal Institution of Chartered Surveyors
12 Great George Street
London SW1P 3AD
Tel: 020 7222 7000
website: www.rics.org

Association of Residential Letting Agents
Maple House
53-55 Woodside Road
Amersham
Bucks HP6 6AA
Tel: 01923 896555
Websites: www.buytolet.co.uk
          www. arla.co.uk

Association of Policy Market Makers
Holywell Centre
1 Phipp Street
London EC2A 4PS
Tel: 020 7739 3949
Trade body for dealers in second-hand endowments – has directory of members.

Charities

Age Concern England
Astral House
1268 London Road
London SW16 4ER
Tel: 020 8765 7200
Website: www.ace.org.uk

Age Concern Cymru
4th floor
1 Cathedral Road
Cardiff CF1 9SD
Tel: 01222 371566

Age Concern Scotland
113 Rose Street
Edinburgh EH2 3DT
Tel: 0131 220 3345

Age Concern Northern Ireland
3 Lower Crescent
Belfast BT7 1NR
Tel: 01232 245729

Help the Aged
St James's Walk
Clerkenwell Green
London EC1R 0BE
Tel: 0800 800 6565
Website: www.helptheaged.org.uk

Age Concern and Help The Aged can provide advice and information on many
financial matters for retired people.

Borrowing

National Debtline
Tel: 0808 808 4000

Association of British Credit Unions
Holyoake House
Hanover Street
Manchester M60 0AS
Tel: 0161 832 3694
Website: www.abcul.org

Credit information agencies

CCN Group
Consumer Help Service
PO Box 40
Nottingham NG7 2SS

Equifax Europe (UK)
Consumer Affairs Department
Spectrum House
1a North Avenue
Clydebank
Glasgow G81 2DR

Websites

There are a huge number of websites offering information aimed at savers, investors and borrowers. The following are, necessarily, only a small selection of those available in February 2001. For further information, consult *The Sunday Times Guide to Money Online*.

Buying a home

The following websites have details of property for sale:
www.assertahome.com
www.fish4homes.co.uk
www.huntahome.com
www.propertyfile.co.uk

For buying and selling direct:
www.propwatch.com
www.easier.co.uk
www.houseweb.com

For house swaps:
www.webswappers.com

Investment information and advice
www.investment-gateway.com
www.new-online-investor.co.uk
www.find.co.uk

Offers of free financial newsletters and guides
www.financial-freebies.com

Online bookstore for investment books
www.global-investor.com

Books on investment

Beginners Guide to Investment, Bernard Gray, Random House
The Wealth Guide, Financial Times, Penguin
The New Online Investor, Peter Temple, J Wiley
The Motley Fool Investment Workbook, T Gardner, Simon & Schuster
One up on Wall Street, Peter Lynch, Penguin

Index